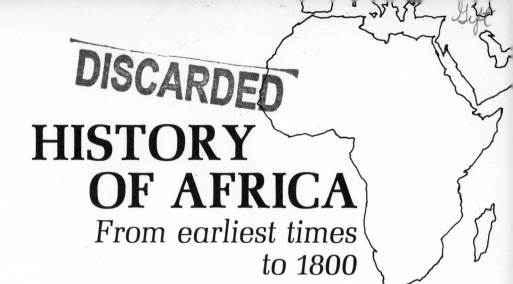

HISTORY OF AFRICA

From earliest times to 1800

HARRY A. GAILEY, JR.
San Jose State College

HOLT, RINEHART and WINSTON, INC.
New York, Chicago, San Francisco, Atlanta, Dallas,
Montreal, Toronto, London, Sydney

Copyright © 1970 by Holt, Rinehart and Winston, Inc.

All rights reserved

Library of Congress Catalog Card Number: 70–103462

SBN: 03–077630–9

Printed in the United States of America

1 2 3 4 5 6 7 8 9

Preface

Two decades ago African history was considered
a minor adjunct to European studies. Africans
were believed to have undergone a series of experiences which
had never been recorded and thus their past could not be recovered. This myth has been largely exploded today. A few
pioneers in African studies provided the initial clues for the
historical reconstruction of nonliterate people. The intrusion
of Africa upon the world scene in the 1950s focused attention
upon the continent and resulted in the creation of a number of
African studies centers, the teaching of special African courses
in dozens of universities and colleges, and foundations supporting research projects for Africa.

The upsurge of interest and concern for Africa has provided a mass of scholarly information in all disciplines of African
studies. As more researchers are trained, the body of knowledge
becomes increasingly more difficult to master, and it has become
necessary for Africanists to specialize. African history as a recognized specialization is new and most African historians devote
their time to detailed investigations of specialized subjects. Thus,
there are few general studies adequate to their level of prepara-
tion. Teachers of basic courses in Africa have had to rely upon a
series of assignments from different books, totally inadequate
histories, or excellent works which are far too complex for the
student. This book was conceived because the lack of good supporting materials frustrated me as a teacher.

From the outset I was aware of the difficulties of writing
a text on African history. The continent is so large and the
people and cultures so diverse that no one can be equally
familiar with all its facets. Despite the growing amount of

linguistic, anthropological, political, and historical evidence available, there are certain important areas of the past where almost nothing is known. And the volume of information which is now available on certain subjects is so great that a writer of a general history is foredoomed to mistakes, or at least to controversy. Every attempt has been made to minimize outright error, to guard against overspeculation. In relating information for which there is inadequate information, I have attempted to qualify my statements in such a manner as to indicate the tentative nature of the conclusion.

The book is an outgrowth of my experiences as a teacher and tends to follow the format I use in presenting the first semester of the basic African history course. The African experience is, for the convenience of the student, arbitrarily divided into geographic sections. The history of people within those areas is pursued from the earliest periods to approximately the year 1800. This allows the student to follow the history of an area without having to skip throughout the text. This type of organization should also be helpful for the beginning teacher who has to give form to a basic African course. The closing date for the history was selected because it represents one of the most logical places to end the first semester of a one year survey course. A conscious effort was made to keep detail to a minimum, to stress instead generalized movements and developments, and to avoid overwhelming the student or the general reader with an awesome array of facts.

A list of acknowledgements for a textbook which truly reflects one's debt would be almost impossible to construct and would exhaust the reader. I wish, therefore, to thank only three of the people who were very important in determining the final form of this work. Dr. G. Wesley Johnson of Stanford University read the manuscript in its entirety and criticized it most thoroughly and fairly. Miss Barbara Dubins of San Jose State College read and commented at length on the East African section. My wife, Rosalie, in addition to encouragement, contributed her skills of proofreading and tried to correct my awkward phraseology. She was also indispensible as the chief typist for the many drafts of the manuscript.

Harry A. Gailey

Los Gatos, California
December 1969

Contents

List of Maps

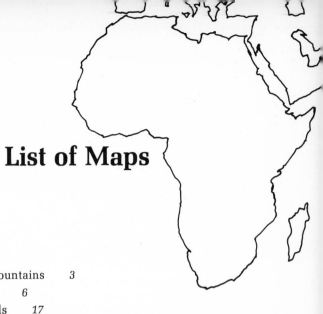

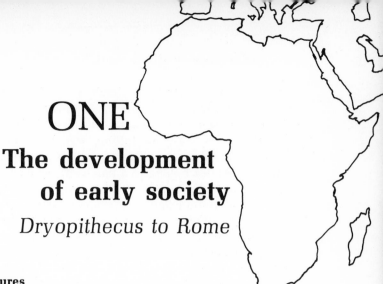

ONE
The development of early society
Dryopithecus to Rome

Geographic features

The first salient feature of Africa, often not noted by any but geographers, is the size of the continent. Africa encompasses an area of approximately 11,-600,000 square miles. The extreme north-south and east-west distances are almost 5,000 miles, and at its narrowest point the continent is over 2,000 miles wide. These figures have more relevance when one considers them in relation to more familiar territories. The Sahara Desert alone is over one and a half times larger than continental United States. Ghana, one of the smaller African states, is approximately twice the area of Great Britain, and Kenya is almost exactly the area of France. Where communications are poor distance, even without other contributing factors, creates a diversity of peoples and cultures and tends to limit the size and stability of political units. If this single geographic fact is so important, it is necessary to isolate and discuss briefly other features in the physical environment that have affected the history of Africa. Such concern with geographic factors does not imply determinism but rather the recognition that geography sets bounds to cultural and economic development which may be difficult to overcome.

The structure and relief of Africa by comparison with other continents is relatively simple. The greater part of Africa is a stable uplifted plateau resting upon a base of Precambrian rock. These ancient rocks are actually exposed over approximately one third of the plateau area. Little mountain building has taken place in Africa in the last 200 million years except for the activity that resulted in the series of mountains in the Atlas chain of North Africa. This chain was formed in the mid-Tertiary period at the same time that extreme folding across the Mediterranean created the European mountains. The mountains of eastern and southern Africa belong to a much earlier period. Elsewhere the major physical features of Africa are the results of elevation, late sedimentation, and weathering by wind and water.

By the Miocene age the ancient earth block of Africa had been reduced to an almost level plane. Since then this surface has been raised, in some places thousands of feet above sea level. The process of uplift caused the block to crack in a number of places. The most notable of these fractures is the Great Rift of East Africa. The area within this fracture later collapsed, forming valleys and canyons thousands of feet deep. The great lakes of East Africa resulted from this same geologic activity. Volcanic activity accompanied the process of uplift and cracking, with the areas adjacent to the rift line undergoing the most extreme volcanic eruptions. A combination of uplift and lava flow formed the Ethiopian highlands and the Ruwenzori and Aberdare ranges. The highest peaks in Africa — Elgon, Ruwenzori, Kenya, and Kilimanjaro — are all extinct volcanoes.

The rift in Africa begins in the Sinai Peninsula and runs southeastward parallel to the Red Sea until it enters Ethiopia in the Danikil plains. From these lowlands (380 feet below sea level) the floor of the rift rises to above 6,000 feet near Addis Ababa and from there descends to only 2,000 feet in southern Ethiopia. The highlands of Ethiopia are adjacent to the rift, where most of the country is covered by two different basaltic massifs ranging in elevation up to 9,000 feet.

In East Africa there are two different branches of the rift, the eastern and western. The floor of the eastern segment is 1,300 feet above sea level at Lake Rudolf, rises to 7,000 feet in central Kenya, and falls to less than 2,000 feet at Lake Natron near the Tanzanian border. The rift is most apparent in Kenya and northern Tanzania, where it is over fifty miles wide in places. The southern portion of the eastern rift, with the exception of the Shire Valley, is less spectacular and ends near the coast in Mozambique. The western rift area is shared by Uganda, Rwanda, Burundi, and the Congo.

The main periods of uplift in Africa were followed by periods of quiescence, so that at least three distinct erosion

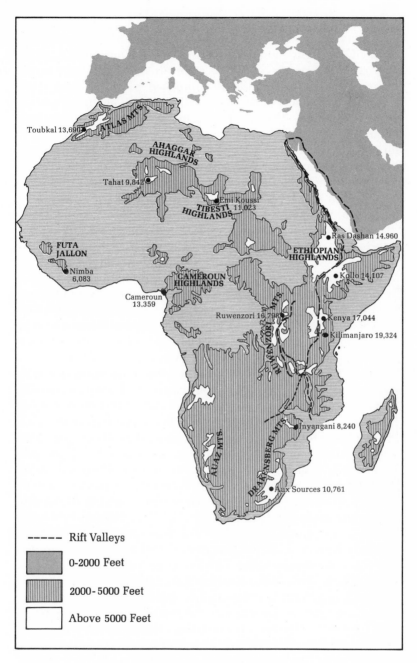

Toubkal 13,690
ATLAS MTS.
AHAGGAR HIGHLANDS
Tahat 9,842
Emi Koussi
TIBESTI HIGHLANDS 11,023
Ras Dashan 14,960
FUTA JALLON
ETHIOPIAN HIGHLANDS
Nimba 6,083
CAMEROUN HIGHLANDS
Kollo 14,107
Cameroun 13,359
Ruwenzori 16,798
RUWENZORI MTS.
Kenya 17,044
Kilimanjaro 19,324
Inyangani 8,240
AUAZ MTS.
DRAKENSBERG MTS.
Aux Sources 10,761

----- Rift Valleys

0-2000 Feet

2000-5000 Feet

Above 5000 Feet

Highlands and Mountains

3

cycles ran their course, resulting in a series of plains of different elevations. Weathering produced a number of scattered remnants of the older mountain or plateau surfaces. Perhaps the best examples of the effect of such erosion are found in the Sahara Desert. The Sahara is composed of rocky land intermixed with fixed and shifting sand planes at an elevation usually below 1,000 feet. The most prominent feature of the central Sahara is the high ridge that runs diagonally from southeast to northwest. The broad Ahaggar and the more ridgelike Tibesti highlands anchor this high plateau with peaks over 9,000 feet high. These two highlands are joined by a narrow saddle over 3,000 feet in elevation. All of these formations are survivals of the ancient mountain system.

There are only two major highlands in West Africa, the Futa Jallon and the Cameroun highlands. The Futa Jallon, located mainly in Guinea, have rather moderate elevation. They are the source of the Niger, Senegal, and Gambia rivers. The Cameroun highlands extend inland from the coast, blending into the Adamoua massif, which covers the northern part of the Cameroun at an elevation of between 2,500 and 4,500 feet. The coastal range of mountains are volcanic in origin, as is Mount Cameroun, the highest peak in West Africa.

The dominating physical characteristic of Central Africa is the great basin of the Congo. The height of the basin varies from 1,000 feet at the center to over 3,000 feet at its rim. From the southern rim of the basin the land runs relatively flat near this elevation to the Drakensberg chain in the extreme southern portion of the continent. This range separates the high veld and semiarid regions of the north from the fertile coastal plain. The Drakensbergs are old, deeply folded mountains beginning near the southern Mozambique border and running parallel to the coast approximately to the middle of Cape Colony.

Although many geographic factors help to isolate the people of Africa, the most obvious one is the Sahara Desert. In the strictest topographic sense only a small portion of this vast area is true desert. In the western Sahara the ergs, which cover approximately 20,000 square miles, are composed almost entirely of shifting, blowing sand. The same is true of that portion of the Sahara called the Libyan Desert which borders Egypt on the west and southwest. Elsewhere the land is rocky with a vegetation cover of thorn scrub. In the central Sahara are the extensive Ahaggar and Tibesti highlands. Crisscrossing the desert, particularly near the highlands, are many dried-out river beds, some of which are subject to heavy flooding during rains. Climatic changes, particularly after 2500 B.C., possibly combined with overgrazing, converted the then grassy, timbered area into the arid territory of today. The only other major desert in Africa is the Kalahari and its coastal extension, the Namib, in the far south.

Immediately below the Sahara is the beginning of the pastureland called the savannah or the Sudan. It is defined by rainfall (between ten and twenty inches a year) and the type of vegetation that the land will support. There is a well-defined wet-dry season in savannah areas. The land cover is normally prairie grass merging into mixed grass and trees where rainfall is more abundant. The savannah covers nearly the full width of the continent, including the Niger and Chad basins. It also extends southward, bordering the Congo basin on the east, and makes up the bulk of the area of central and southern Africa.

The tropical rain forest covers only about eighteen percent of Africa and is confined to the coastal areas of western Africa and the territory from the Cameroun to the edge of the great lakes region of East Africa. It is most apparent in the northern segment of the Congo basin. There is no marked dry season and rain falls from ten to twelve months in the year. The vegetation is always lush and in the dense high forest of the Congo trees sometimes grow to over 150 feet tall.

The soils of tropical Africa, however different they may be, normally have one common feature. They are marginal in fertility. The bulk of land in the northern savannah and the tropical rain forest is laterite, composed to a varying degree of iron and aluminum hydroxides. In its pure form laterite does not decompose and contains nothing that plants can absorb. In areas where the laterite content is not the major element the land can be cultivated, but it is nevertheless poor. Savannah soils are light and susceptible to erosion by both wind and water. As long as the natural ground cover is not disturbed erosion is minimal. The European agricultural methodology improperly applied, and slash and burn techniques without a proper fallow period, can be disastrous for such land.

Because of the lush tropical growth the land in the rain forest is often believed to be extremely fertile. This is far from true. Most tropical plants need very little nourishment from the soil. In the heavy forest tons of foliage fall on an acre of

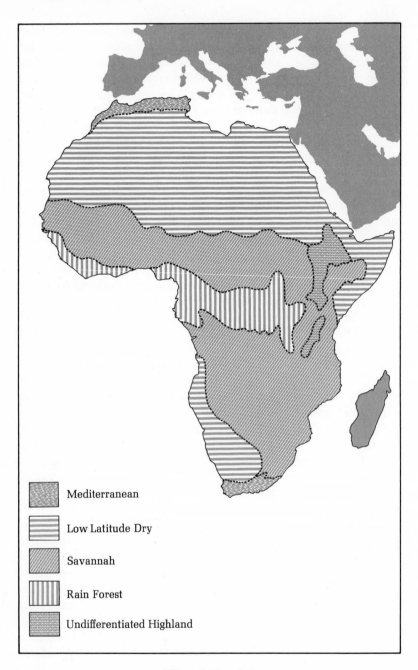

Climatic Regions

Mediterranean

Low Latitude Dry

Savannah

Rain Forest

Undifferentiated Highland

land every year. Under the climatic conditions of the rain forest the debris is quickly converted into the food that trees and other plants need. The humus and salts thus produced, if not used immediately, are leached out by rains and thus there is little chance for plant food to be stored. Any significant clearing of the trees upsets the delicate balance between humus production and use, and not even the application of modern chemicals will make the cleared land fertile.

Desert soils are low in humus and unleached. They contain a high percentage of carbonates and are potentially very fertile if water is available. The productive capacity of desert areas is evidenced by the oases of the Sahara. Some of the oases have been sustained by natural artesian wells. Elsewhere the Arab-Berber ruling classes, using Negro slaves, constructed and maintained elaborate foggaras, or underground galleries, sometimes more than fifty feet below ground which draw moisture from the subsoil. During the great period of Arab hegemony in the western desert hundreds of miles of foggaras were dug. The results were great yields of agricultural products, particularly dates, from the sandy and normally unproductive soils. This agricultural wealth as much as the caravan trade made the rulers of the oases rich.

The only soils in tropical Africa that are naturally very fertile are new ones which have not yet had time to become poor. The bulk of the highlands along the East African rift are relatively new and are composed of nonacid volcanic ash. Other excellent soils are those recent alluvial deposits along the banks and at the mouths of rivers. The most obvious such area in historic times was the lower valley of the Nile.

Africa south of the Sahara is interlaced with rivers which have their sources in various highlands. The most fruitful water-producing areas of Africa are the plateaus and mountains of eastern and northeastern Africa. The sources of the Nile, the Shire, and the major contributing streams to the Congo are located here. In West Africa the low-lying Futa Jallon and its associated hill systems give rise to a number of rivers. The most important are the Senegal, the Gambia, and the Niger. In Central Africa the southern edge of the Congo rim is the origin of a series of such large rivers as the Kwango, Kwilu, Kasai, Lomami, and Lulua, which flow northward into the mainstream of the Congo. It is also the starting point for the Zambesi, which flows in a generally eastward direction 1,600 miles to the Indian

Ocean. In the extreme south the Drakensberg mountains are the source of the Orange, Limpopo, and Vaal rivers.

Of the five major rivers of Africa the longest and historically the most important is the Nile. The Nile system is composed of two main and a number of minor tributary streams. The White Nile begins at Lake Victoria at an elevation of approximately 3,700 feet. It joins the stream issuing from Lake Albert and then flows northward over 1,600 miles until its confluence with the Blue Nile north of Khartoum. The source of the Blue Nile is Lake Tana in the Ethiopian highlands. Beginning at an elevation of over 6,000 feet, it descends rapidly to its juncture with the White Nile and contributes over fifty percent of the water to the lower reaches of the combined river.

The largest river system in Africa is the Congo complex. Actually a composite of a number of rivers, the Congo drains an area of over 1,600,000 square miles. It begins in East Africa as the Chambezi and emerges from Lake Bangweulu as the Luapula, which changes its name at Lake Mweru to the Luvua. This river flows into the Lualaba, which is joined by the Ubangi below Mbandaka (Coquilhatville) and the Kasai above Kinshasa (Leopoldville). The major portion of the course of the Congo and most of its tributaries is through dense equatorial forest.

The third longest river in Africa is the Niger, with a length of over 2,600 miles. It rises in Guinea near the present border of Sierra Leone, close to the source of the Senegal River. The river flows northeastward for almost 800 miles to the vicinity of Timbuktu, where it begins a great bend extending for approximately 200 miles. It then flows southeast across the savannah lands until it is joined by the Benue River just north of Lokoja in Nigeria. The Benue, with a length of 800 miles, delivers a volume of water almost the equivalent of the Niger. The united stream flowing southward loses itself in mangrove swamps which cover over 14,000 square miles. At its delta the main river is broken into hundreds of smaller rivers and creeks before flowing into the Gulf of Guinea.

The Zambesi River has its source in Angola at an elevation of approximately 5,000 feet. It is soon joined on the north by the large Cuando River. After Victoria Falls the Zambesi is sluggish and in places becomes a sand flat up to six miles wide. Joined by the Mazoe and Shire, the river becomes better defined and enters the Indian Ocean by several mouths. The last long river of Africa is the Orange, which has its source in the Drakensberg mountains approximately 100 miles west of the coast-line of Natal. It flows westward over 1,300 miles and is joined by a series of smaller streams, the most important of which are the Vaal and Caledon rivers. The volume of the Orange varies more than that of any other major river, being greatly influenced by the very arid conditions of much of the territory through which it flows.

In addition to these giants Africa has dozens of rivers that in most other settings would be considered huge. The coastal area of West Africa is a melange of rivers, streams, and man-grove swamps. Rivers such as the Senegal, Gambia, Rokel, Bandama, Volta, and Mono extend hundreds of miles into the interior. The eastern coastline of Africa has fewer but still a significant number of large rivers such as the Juba, Tana, Shire, Sabi, and Limpopo.

Despite the multiplicity of waterways, few African rivers can serve today as good highways for trade and communica-tion. The mouths of most West African rivers are blocked by sandbars and the interior reaches clogged by mangrove. The southern rivers are greatly affected by the lack of rainfall and the dry lands through which they flow. In addition, almost all African rivers are interdicted by falls, rapids, swamps, and sandbars. A closer examination of the navigability of the Nile, the longest of the African rivers and in many ways the best, illustrates certain problems common to most of the rivers. From Aswan to the delta the lower Nile is navigable over its entire length. South of the first cataract at Aswan to the sixth cataract just above Khartoum the river can be used only between the cataracts, and its use there in some places is restricted to the flood season. The Nile can be navigated freely southward to the swampy area of the Sudd and from there to Gondokoro where rapids impede its use. South of this barrier the river becomes broad and deep once again as far as Lake Victoria. The Blue Nile can be used only in the lowland areas just before its confluence with the White Nile above Khartoum.

It is apparent that man in Africa has been confronted with a series of difficult environmental problems. Immense distance in combination with mountains, rivers, forests, and deserts has acted as a barrier to swift movement and easy communication. These factors in turn favored isolation of peoples and played an important role in the evolvement of the hundreds of different languages and political systems of pre-European Africa. Poor soils, in some places too much water, and in other areas the lack of water presented different challenges to different peoples and in most cases restricted the development of rich, diversified economic systems.

The people of Africa have overcome the challenges presented by geography with a variety of solutions. The horse and camel made possible the conquest of the great land-sea of the Sahara. Water in the desert was trapped in a number of ingenious ways, creating the oases so necessary for the desert crossings. The use of iron implements and experimentation with crops and agricultural techniques enabled men to cope with the laterite soils of the savannah lands. Shifting agriculture ensured that a reasonably large population could live harmoniously in areas where erosion was an ever-present threat. New plants such as yams and bananas, which were first introduced in East Africa and then spread to Central and West Africa, enabled people to live and prosper in the heretofore hostile tropical forests.

In most areas of Africa people sought to achieve an equilibrium with their environment. Once this had been satisfactorily accomplished, the African resisted change. He had learned that too often a change in technique or even emphasis meant disaster. With few exceptions, therefore, traditional African economic systems, whatever their emphasis, were very conservative. The economic system was reinforced by political and religious sanctions designed to maintain the status quo. It was not that the African was by nature uninspired or noninventive — he was merely reluctant to experiment with the system he knew offered security.

Early man in Africa

Ancestors of the gibbons, chimpanzees, and gorillas first appeared during the Miocene epoch. All such great apes were classified in 1945 by George Simpson into one subfamily, the Dryopithecinae, and all their living descendants into another called the Pongidae. This practice has since been followed by most anthropologists. In Africa all of the dryopithecines belong to a single genus earlier called Proconsul but now generally referred to by scientists as simply *Dryopithecus*. There are three identifiable species of African *Dryopithecus*. The smallest, *africanus*, was gibbon-sized, *nyanzae*, the size of a chimpanzee, and *major*, almost as large as a gorilla.

Remains of all three species have been found in East Africa, but those of *africanus,* the smallest, are the most complete. The first such discovery was made at Koru near the Kavirondo Gulf in Kenya and was dated to the middle Miocene epoch, or fifteen to twenty million years ago. In 1942 an almost complete jaw was found, and in 1948 Dr. L. S. B. Leakey, on fossil-rich Rusinga Island in Lake Victoria, recovered an almost complete skull and some of the arm and leg bones of *africanus.* After lengthy study of these remains Dr. Wilfred Le Gros Clark of Oxford reported that *africanus* exhibited many non-apelike features. The dental arch was horseshoe-shaped, there was no simian shelf, and the candyles joining the jaws were small. All of these features were similar to man. However, the thumb was not opposable, indicating the animal had not yet been completely liberated from the trees, and its large canine teeth were more similar to the apes than to man. It seems, nevertheless, that the three species of *Dryopithecus* not only provide us with very likely candidates for the ancestors of the modern chimpanzees and gorillas but possibly also for those of man.

In March 1962 Leakey announced the discovery the previous year of two fragments of the upper jaw of a new primate at Fort Ternan on Kavirondo Gulf. He called it *Kenyapithecus wickeri,* and it has been dated by the carbon 14 system to fourteen million years ago. The teeth of the creature are quite small, being within the human range in size, with the canines short and not apelike. Many consider *Kenyapithecus* to be the same genus as *Ramapithecus,* discovered in India, which was dated to approximately six million years ago. Until more specimens are unearthed the position of *Kenyapithecus* in the descent of man remains speculative, but it does appear that the branching off of man from the other primates might have occurred far earlier than previously believed.

So far there are no recognizable discoveries of ape-man (or man-ape) in Africa for the very long Pliocene epoch (twelve million years). In the past generation, however, there have been a number of important finds dating from the Pleistocene period. Some of these discoveries, which have been dated by means of new radioactive procedures, have made a shambles of previous time scales for the Pleistocene. Since the first discoveries of early man had been in Europe, dating of events in the Pleistocene had been tied to the periods of glaciation there. It is now believed that even if there is a correlation of African pluvials with the northern glaciers the beginnings of the first or Günz

glaciation was set too low. Certainly since the discovery of
Zinjanthropus bosei many anthropologists believe that the Pleistocene, instead of being only three quarters of a million years
old, probably began three million years ago.

This reinterpretation began with the discovery in 1924 at
a limestone cave at Taung in South Africa of the brain case and
facial skeleton of an infant. Dr. Raymond Dart of Witwatersrand
University named the primate *Australopithecus africanus*
(southern ape) and startled his northern colleagues by boldly
reconstructing from the evidence a manlike creature who existed approximately one million years ago. According to Dart,
the full-sized *africanus* had been about four feet tall, erect, and
bipedal, and weighed approximately ninety pounds. Most European anthropologists were either neutral or definitely hostile
to such a hypothesis. Even with the later discovery of thousands of fragments of this primate there was no general agreement with Dart. Some of his further postulations were disrupted
even more vehemently. Dart maintained that *Australopithecus
africanus* was carnivorous and a very efficient hunter. The
presence of the humerus bone of a small antelope found in the
caves taken with matching indentations in the skulls of large
numbers of baboons indicated that *Australopithecus* used this
bone as a weapon — a primary tool.

In 1936 Robert Broom discovered in a cave at Sterkfontein
near Johannesburg part of the skull of an adult australopithecine. Despite the great services rendered by Broom, the naming
of this find continued the taxonomical confusion already apparent in anthropology. He named it *Plesianthropus transvaalensis,*
although it was most probably a mature example of the type
discovered at Taung. Dart found at another site at Makapan a
different type of australopithecine which he believed used fire.
He called this ape-man *Australopithecus promethius.* Recent
evaluations, particularly those by Professor K. P. Oakley of the
British Museum, indicate that there is no need for all of these
separate categories, since all of these finds belong to the same
genus and species, *Australopithecus africanus.*

While working at Sterkfontein in 1938 Broom learned of a
schoolboy who had discovered some large teeth. Acting on this
information, Broom found the major portion of a new man-ape
which he called *Paranthropus.* From this and later discoveries
Broom concluded that this specimen was not as old and not of
the same type as the other cave discoveries. The most startling

difference was in the teeth. While the incisors and canines were small, the premolars and molars were very large by contrast with the presumed meat-eating *africanus*. In 1949–1950 Broom and his associates made a series of further finds at Swartkrans, near Sterkfontein. These were divided into two groups, *Paranthropus crassidens* and *Telanthropus capensis*. Despite the needless proliferation of names, the Swartkrans discoveries were most important in confirming the presence in southern Africa of another type of australopithecine.

Oakley considered that the Sterkfontein and Swartkrans finds belonged to *Australopithecus robustus* and were different from *Australopithecus africanus*. *Robustus* was as tall as many modern men and weighed as much as 150 pounds. The specimen was heavily muscled and had a thick, crested skull. In comparison also with its smaller cousin *robustus* was probably a vegetarian. An analysis of the faunal evidence indicated that in southern Africa *robustus* lived approximately 200,000 years later than *africanus*. Until 1960 it was believed that in some fashion *robustus* had evolved from the smaller australopithecine.

In July 1959 Mrs. Leakey chanced upon a partially exposed fossil skull in the oldest geologic bed of Olduvai Gorge in Tanganyika. The 400 fragments of the skull were painstakingly reconstructed. The restored skull in conjunction with the many pebble tools found there caused Dr. Leakey to announce the discovery of the oldest true man. Leakey named this discovery *Zinjanthropus bosei* and believed it to be perhaps one million years old. This early date was later confirmed by argon dating, which gave a date of 1.3 million years. However, Leakey's claim for a separate genus-species for the find was immediately questioned. The skull, although differing in some respects, is generally similar to those of Broom's specimens from Sterkfontein and Swartkrans. The teeth of *Zinjanthropus* were very large — so large that it was early named Nutcracker man. There seems little doubt that the Leakeys' discovery was that of an omnivorous East African variety of *Australopithecus robustus* which predates those found in southern Africa.

In February 1961 the Leakeys found a mandible and two parietal bones of a child in bed I of Olduvai Gorge. These matched foot and hand bones that had been previously uncovered. Leakey believed that these remnants belonged to a distinct type of hominid that had existed before *Zinjanthropus*, and he named it *Homo habilis* for its presumed tool-making abilities. From later classifications of the Olduvai fossils it appears that *Homo habilis* and *Zinjanthropus* lived in the same locale throughout the period of bed I and the lower levels of bed II. *Habilis* in all probability continued to live through the period covered by bed II. Le Gros Clark believes that much of the difficulty would be resolved by considering the new find an australopithecine. On the basis of the immature specimen he concluded that its relation to later man was questionable while its link with the australopithecines was apparent. Others also consider *habilis* to be only a more highly developed type of *Australopithecus africanus*.

The current state of our knowledge of these ape-men is largely conjecture. It is suspected that two different kinds of ape-men lived in Africa a million years ago. One was a small savannah-roving killer while the other was larger, slower, and basically a vegetarian type which lived in the wetter forest lands. Both types of primates had abandoned their tree life for the dangerous and presumably more rewarding life on the ground. *Africanus* was a tool-maker only in the sense that bone weapons are considered tools. *Robustus* in all probability was the creator of pebble tools. If he did not construct these rudimentary tools, it is necessary to postulate a third creature as yet unfound that lived in close conjunction with him. Of the specimens so far discovered of both types the brain cases indicate a human form but with cranial capacities within the upper range of modern apes (325–685 cubic centimeters).

It is not yet known how widespread were these man-apes. Their modes of life and their distance in time from us make it difficult to find further specimens. A 1961 discovery of presumably one of the oldest australopithecines in Chad, however, indicates that they were not confined to eastern and southern Africa. A final, most important, conclusion can be predicated. One of the australopithecines, probably *robustus*, was the ancestor of man. The closest juxtaposition of the australopithecines to man yet discovered is at Olduvai Gorge, where the remains were found just below those of *Homo erectus*.

The next stage of man's development in Africa was *Homo erectus* (earlier called *Pithecanthropus*). There is substantial agreement among experts on the dating and meaning of the specimens so far discovered. *Homo erectus* was in many ways not much different from modern man (*Homo sapiens*), although it is still convenient to refer to him as if he belonged to a different species. The oldest specimen of *erectus* in Africa was discovered in bed II at Olduvai Gorge and has been dated to approximately 490,000 years. Dr. Leakey called this specimen Chellean man. The dating fits in well with that of European example of *Homo erectus,* the Heidelberg mandible, and the Asian samples formerly known as *Pithecanthropus erectus* and *Sinanthropus pekinensis.* Chellean man had a larger cranial capacity (approximately 1,200 cubic centimeters) than any previous example, although in many ways its skull appears more primitive than even the australopithecines. Another early example of *Homo erectus* was found in the quarries of Sidi Abderrahman in Algeria and has been tentatively dated to 350,000 years. This northern find has been called by some *Atlanthropus mauritanicus.* One can expect relatively few specimens to be found in sub-Saharan Africa, since in this climate there was no need for men to live in caves and the bones of the thousands of men who lived in the open at this early stage would have been destroyed by scavengers.

Homo erectus in Africa was the maker of the culture associated with the Chelles-Acheul hand axes. Although few specimens of men have been found, stone artifacts have turned up in all parts of Africa. The most important single source is Olduvai, where examples have been identified in eleven different stages from the middle to the end of the Pleistocene epoch. Other important sites for tools in East Africa are at Olorgesailie and Lewi in Kenya, Paraa Lodge and Mweya Lodge in Uganda, and Isimila in southern Tanzania. In the Sudan the important locations are Khar Abu Anga and Wadi Afu and in Ethiopia Melka Kontoure.

Despite the richness of the stone tools covering this entire period, there are no remains of *erectus* until almost 300,000 years after *Atlanthropus.* The first discovery from after this very early period was also made by Dr. Leakey near the Kavirondo Gulf. Called the Kanjera skull and dating from 65,000 years ago, the specimen was recovered in fragments and is so far from complete that it is not known whether it is that of an adult or child. The facial skeleton is small, and some experts believe that it represents a *Homo sapiens,* possibly proto-Bushmanoid, but this is only conjecture. Discounting this example, one finds that the earliest definitely dated skull of *Homo sapiens* is Florisbad man, discovered in the Orange Free State, whose date is no earlier than 35,000 years.

The connections between *Homo erectus* and his successors who lived toward the end of the Pleistocene epoch are speculative. Neanderthal man, so common in Europe, has been found only in North Africa. It appears that Neanderthal man in Africa is the result of the separate line of evolution from *Homo erectus* in Asia. The North African specimens would, therefore, be the result of migrations from Asia similar to those that populated Europe. However, there were men in Africa contemporary with the Neanderthals which represent the African evolution of *Homo erectus*. These are the Rhodesioids of southern Africa.

The first and still the most complete of the Rhodesioid discoveries was made at Broken Hill, Zambia, in 1921. This amazing skull was very thick-walled and narrower than that of a Neanderthal but with a smaller cranial capacity (1,280–1,400 cubic centimeters). The most noticeable features of the skull were the huge brow ridges, which were much larger than those of the Neanderthals. Broken Hill man was probably between sixty-seven and seventy inches tall. He walked very upright and his weight was approximately that of an average modern man. On the basis of faunal dating, Broken Hill man lived approximately 25,000 years ago. Other skeletal fragments of Rhodesioid man found at Saldanha Bay in South Africa, Lake Eyasi in Tanzania, Singa in the Sudan, and Dire Dawa in Ethiopia indicate how widespread was this type. Earlier some anthropologists believed that Rhodesioid man was Negro, but all that can definitely be said about this speculation is that both negroid and caucasoid characteristics are present in the Broken Hill skull.

Although little is known of the men of Africa in late Acheulean times, their culture is more definitely known. African men had finally discovered how to make fire approximately 200,000 years after the skill was known in Asia. One site in East Africa at Kalambo Falls south of Lake Tanganyika indicates the use of fire perhaps as early as 60,000 B.C. Also for the first time man began to live regularly in caves and rock shelters. Presumably with a lowering of temperatures connected with the last glaciation in Europe, Mediterranean flora extended across what is now the Sahara, enabling man to spread and prosper in most areas of Africa. In this later period the older hand axes and cleavers disappeared and new and better chopping and cutting tools were developed. The new culture, called the

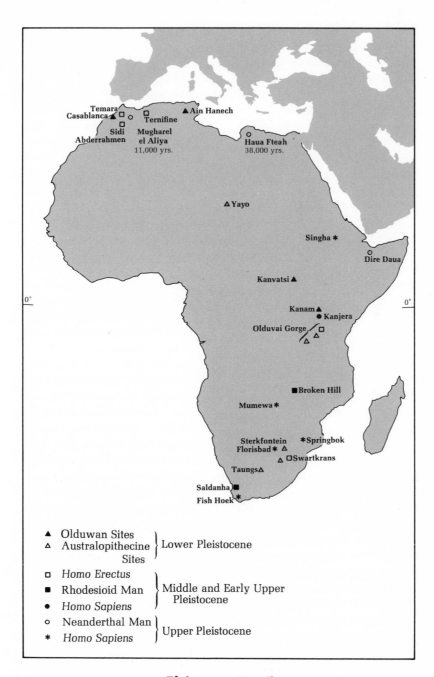

Temara
Casablanca ▲ ◻ ○ ◻ Ternifine ▲ Ain Hanech
      Sidi   ◻
Abderrahmen Mugharel
          el Aliya   ○
          11,000 yrs.   Haua Fteah
                         38,000 yrs.

△ Yayo

Singha ✳

○
Dire Daua

Kanvatsi ▲

Kanam ▲
        ● Kanjera
Olduvai Gorge ◻
           △
          △

■ Broken Hill

Mumewa ✳

Sterkfontein
Florisbad ✳ △ ✳ Springbok
        △ ◻ Swartkrans
Taungs △

Saldanha ■
Fish Hoek ✳

▲ Olduwan Sites
△ Australopithecine } Lower Pleistocene
        Sites
◻ *Homo Erectus*
■ Rhodesioid Man } Middle and Early Upper
● *Homo Sapiens*   Pleistocene
○ Neanderthal Man }
✳ *Homo Sapiens*   } Upper Pleistocene

Pleistocene Fossils

17

Sangoan, became typical of man throughout West, Central, and parts of East Africa. Different types of stone implements are evidence that man in this period engaged in a variety of activities. There are few noticeable differences in the details of the instruments found in different areas.

On the southern and East African grasslands the older stone-making tradition of the Acheulean period persisted and is called the Fauresmith. In North Africa the Acheulean gave way to a more sophisticated culture known as the Levallois-Mousterian (or Aterian), which is normally associated with Neanderthal man. From such sites as Haua Fteah it is known that the Neanderthals were cave dwellers, fire users, and very competent flake tool-makers. Their culture is contemporary with the Sangoan and Fauresmith of the Rhodesioids to the south.

The Mesolithic period began in approximately 30,000 B.C. and ended about 8000 B.C. In this period the Rhodesioid type throughout most of Africa was replaced by Homo sapiens. However, the stoneworking techniques practiced by earlier types lingered on throughout this middle Stone Age. There are recognizable variations of this culture in different parts of Africa. In the savannah and eastern and southern grasslands of Africa the Stillbay was developed which concentrated on lighter cutting and piercing instruments. The Lupemban culture of the Congo area specialized in heavier chopping and cutting instruments while the Aterian of the north used the tanged point.

By the end of the Pleistocene the four main ethnic types of modern Africans were already present. There are differing theories concerning their creation. All are speculative, since they are based almost entirely upon skeletal evidence and comparison of artifacts with those of places where a racial type had been more positively identified. One type of man considered to be the ancestor of the modern-day Bushman and perhaps the Negro has been called Capoid by Professor Carleton Coon. Despite the present small size of modern Bushmen and Hottentots, it is generally agreed that the Capoids were full sized. In all probability at one time they occupied most of the drier parts of Africa from the Sahara to southern areas. The Singha skull found 200 miles south of Khartoum in 1924 suggests for the Capoid a line of descent from the Rhodesioid type. Presumably the reduction in the Bushman's size did not take place until his arrival in southern Africa. All indications place the Bushmen in their present locations late. Excavations at Fish Hoek

and at Matjes River in South Africa exposed twenty-three skeletons and showed that both full-sized and shrunken individuals
were present. There is no satisfactory hypothesis that explains
the partial dwarfing of some Bushmen, since full-sized Capoid
skeletons have been found in the northern Transvaal dated as
late as A.D. 1400.

The pattern of Caucasian development does not appear to
be as complex as that of the Capoid. However, the relation
between the Neanderthal-like inhabitants of North Africa represented by the Haua Fteah relic (34,000–38,000 B.C.) in Cyrenaica
and the later *Homo sapiens* is not clear. Shortly before 10,000
B.C. an invasion of presumably Near Eastern Caucasians called
the Mouillians entered the area, bringing a different microlith
culture. Physically these people were stocky, muscular, and
broad faced. Presumably they intermarried with some of the
local Aterian peoples while forcing the bulk of that population
southward into the Sahara. A second wave of Caucasians called
the Capsians followed the Mouillians in the early post-
Pleistocene epoch. The earliest carbon 14 date for this culture
is 6450 B.C. Remains of the Capsians indicate a near-modern
man, perhaps of the Cro-Magnon type, whose artifacts resemble
those of the Natufian culture of Palestine. The intermarriage of
the Capsians and Mouillians created in time the Berber population of North Africa.

A separate Capsian population occupied a limited area in
East Africa. Remains of these people, whose origin is not known,
have been discovered at Olduvai and Gambles Cave in Kenya.
It was once believed that they migrated from North Africa.
However, new dating techniques indicate that some of the
Capsian remains are earlier than those to the north, suggesting
a separate development, possibly also derived from Palestine.
The small East African Caucasian population seems to have
been absorbed by later invaders of East Africa.

Despite his present dominance of Africa, the origin of the
Negro is shrouded in mystery. The oldest skeleton identifiable
by most anthropologists as Negro is definitely post-Pleistocene.
This, the so-called Asselar man, was discovered in 1927 by
Besnard and Monod 400 miles north of Timbuktu. The specimen,
a tall (five feet, seven inches) adult male, was found associated
with the remains of fish, mollusks, and small game no longer
living in the Sahara. Other presumably Negro discoveries have
not been completely evaluated. One specimen located near

Khartoum seems to have lived in the very late Paleolithic period. Because of the scarcity of early Negro skeletons and the discoveries of Capoids scattered throughout the continent at this same time, it is tempting to view the latter as ancestral to the Negro. Perhaps by isolation and mutation a separate racial type did develop from the Capoids. However, there is no good evidence for this or, for that matter, any other theory. All that can be said with reasonable certainty is that the Negro evolved very late, probably after 10,000 B.C.

Another mystery group is the Pygmies, who in the Neolithic period inhabited a large portion of the northern forest area from the great lakes to West Africa. One speculation concerning the origin of the Pygmies is that they were driven into the forest environment from the grasslands. Once there genetic factors for dwarfing, aided by isolation, took on a survival value, and within time this condition became dominant. Another theory, based upon blood typing, states that the ancestors of the Pygmies were also ancestors of the Negro. According to this thinking the Proto-Pygmy–Negro people were full sized and perhaps the decendants of the Rhodesioids. However interesting these speculations are, they remain only that. All that is definitely known is that the Pygmies were present in Africa in significant numbers at the close of the Pleistocene.

Beginning in approximately 5500 B.C. and lasting for almost 3,000 years was the Makalian wet phase in Africa. The climate and vegetation during this phase allowed easy movement and continual contact between the peoples of North Africa and those of the Saharan and sub-Saharan regions. This was a time of specialization and distinctive cultures. In all probability there occurred population increases and a subsequent reduction in the amount of territory covered by a single hunting group. At the same time more efficient weapons — the bow and arrow, harpoons, and perhaps even poisons — were developed and their use spread rapidly. Man also began to exploit the seas, rivers, and lakes for fish and shellfish. Bone harpoons, attesting to the importance of these activities, have been found throughout the southern Sahara, the Nile, and Central African regions.

The Neolithic in Africa

Even with new and better weapons a Mesolithic hunting and fishing culture could support only a very limited population. Further innovations were necessary before there could be a significant population increase and the development of town life with its specialization of labor and resultant leisure time. These advances resulted from the Neolithic Revolution, which was caused by two probably unrelated discoveries. The first was the domestication of animals and the second was the planting of seeds and the development of regular farming techniques. The beginnings of this revolution are first noticeable in western Asia. Sites in the foothills of Kurdistan in Iraq and at Mount Carmel and Jericho in Palestine indicate a Neolithic culture that predates the earliest African site by approximately 3,000 years. Contrary to previous theories concerning settlements in river valleys, it now appears that the earliest Neolithic developments occurred in the foothills adjacent to river valleys. Wheat and barley and varieties of sheep and goats flourished in a wild state in the hills. In a manner not clearly understood the hunters in daily contact with animals in time learned to domesticate them; at the same time man began to harvest grain. Modern experiments have demonstrated that in times of drought animals congregate near human settlements. These animals, particularly the young, can then be tamed by giving them food. The reproduction of grain from seeds was probably observed long before man began to plant crops. Once man started to sow grain he could control both the location and size of his crops.

The Natufian culture at Jericho, represented by the bottom layer of a continuous succession of villages at the same site, dates from at least the eighth millennium B.C. Here Neolithic farmers using stone implements harvested grain and kept animals. At Jarmo and Tepe Sarah in Kurdistan, Neolithic village life was well developed after 7000 B.C. Compared to these early settlements in Asia the first Neolithic sites in Africa are quite late, dating to the fifth millennium B.C. Their locations, however, follow the same pattern as the Near Eastern villages. Such Egyptian sites as Deir Tasa, Badari, and al Omari are all located on the high terraces at the edges of what was then dry steppe land along the banks of the Nile's tributary streams.

Some time before the early Egyptian settlements the land along the Nile began to emerge from the water as the tributaries that had previously been filled throughout most of the year began to dry up. By the fifth millennium B.C. the Nile by its periodic deposits of good soil over a gravel base had created the alluvium necessary for the future development of Egypt. The climate became drier and the desert steadily encroached on settled communities of the higher land. The Tasians, Badarians, and other Egyptian villagers, drawn by the better land in the river valley and pressured by drift sand, moved down from the hills. Following these beginnings of agriculture in the fertile valley the population increased at a phenomenal rate. Some experts place the maximum number of people that the Nile Valley could have supported at the beginning of the Mesolithic at 20,000 people. By the time of the Old Kingdom the population of Egypt had grown to an estimated three million persons. By 3500 B.C. the Egyptians had formed sophisticated competitive states, which within 300 years were combined into one great kingdom by the unification of Upper and Lower Egypt. All of the essentials for the future greatness of pharaonic Egypt were present by the third millennium B.C.

It appears from present evidence that the Nile Valley was the source for the Neolithic in Africa. Some archeologists, however, argue for a separate development of the Neolithic to the west, pointing to similarities between the tools and weapons of the Khartoum Neolithic and those of the southern Saharan region. Evidence which would indicate that northern and Sudanic areas were influenced by such a separate development and diffusion is now only suggestive. The presence at such an early date of a series of Neolithic villages, extending from central Egypt to Fayoum in the north, leads most experts to conclude that the Neolithic discoveries were transmitted from Egypt to the rest of Africa. If this hypothesis is correct, the westward movement of these new methods was rapid. Neolithic techniques were in use in the highlands of Cyrenaica by 5000 B.C. and at a slightly later period at the present-day location of the oases of Kharga and Siwa. The implements found in both areas are the highly polished stone farming tools representative of the Fayoum settlements. Further to the west in Algeria and Morocco the people remained primarily hunters until after 3000 B.C. On the basis of current information it is not possible to date the changeover to farming in this area.

Very early Neolithic communities were also located in the middle Nile region of the Sudan in what was probably by then Negro Africa. At Shaheinab carbon dating indicates that the Negro people there had reached the Neolithic stage by the fourth millennium B.C. A. J. Arkell, an expert on the ancient Sudan, believes that the people there did not practice sedentary agricul-

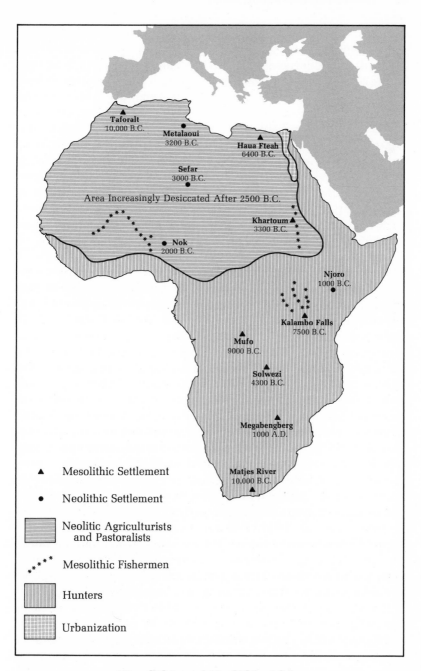

Taforalt
10,000 B.C.

Metalaoui
3200 B.C.

Haua Fteah
6400 B.C.

Sefar
3000 B.C.

Area Increasingly Desiccated After 2500 B.C.

Khartoum
3300 B.C.

Nok
2000 B.C.

Njoro
1000 B.C.

Kalambo Falls
7500 B.C.

Mufo
9000 B.C.

Solwezi
4300 B.C.

Megabengberg
1000 A.D.

Matjes River
10,000 B.C.

▲ Mesolithic Settlement

● Neolithic Settlement

Neolitic Agriculturists
and Pastoralists

✳✳✳✳✳ Mesolithic Fishermen

Hunters

Urbanization

Mesolithic and Neolithic Africa

ture but that they did keep domesticated goats. Examination of the various implements found at Shaheinab suggests that they were probably derived from the contemporary Egyptian culture to the north. This is further evidence that the domestication of animals and probably the planting of crops proceeded up the Nile to the Sudan and beyond.

The earliest reliable date for a fully Neolithic site in the central Sahara is 3450 B.C. Most of the other Saharan sites investigated date from some 500 years later. Much of the Sahara at this time was fertile and could have supported a very large population. In the highlands of Tibesti and Ahaggar different peoples left an indelible, if confusing, record of their times in rock paintings and etchings. The work of Henri Lhote in these highlands in the period from 1930 to 1957 has been particularly valuable in transcribing the thousands of carvings and paintings. The works have been grouped according to similarity of theme into four classifications — hunters, herdsmen, horses, and camels. Only a few scenes from the many belonging to the herdsman period (3500–1000 B.C.) indicate sedentary agriculture. The earlier carvings are of stags, hippopotamuses, and crocodiles, with only a few figures of men. The probably religious depiction of individual animals gave way in part in the herdsman period to representations of herds of oxen, goats, and sheep. Still interspersed with these pictures, however, are scenes of hunting. These rock drawings indicate the slow change from an existence based solely upon the hunt to a society that was primarily pastoral, with perhaps some sedentary agriculture but with hunting remaining an important element.

Beginning before 2500 B.C. rainfall in the Sahara seems to have lessened. This factor probably in conjunction with the overgrazing of herds of animals, particularly goats, slowly transformed the arable land to desert, forcing people into the more favorable lands of the desert fringes. Those who migrated north blended with the indigenous Caucasian inhabitants. There emerged in northern Africa after 2000 B.C. a group of hybrid people, speaking kindred languages, called Berbers. Berber agriculturists and pastoralists who controlled the North African coastal region as well as territory south of the Atlas range eventually made contact with their Bronze Age neighbors in Spain and Egypt and developed a distinct Bronze Age culture. Some of the Berber kingdoms became so powerful that, armed with bronze weapons and war chariots, they threatened Egypt a number of times from the fourteenth through the twelfth centuries B.C. Eventually in the middle of the tenth century B.C., perhaps driven by the growing barrenness of their lands, the Libyan Berbers conquered and imposed their rule on Upper Egypt for almost 200 years.

Responding to the same pressures of population and growing infertility of the Sahara, some Neolithic men migrated southward into what is now the savannah belt. The migrations created important new problems which had to be solved before the area could become productive. A prime necessity was new grain crops. The barleys and wheats of the north were winter rainfall crops that could be grown successfully in the tropics only by irrigation. Experimentation eventually allowed the populations of the savannah regions to develop several indigenous foods as replacements. In Guinea and near the bend of the Niger native rice was planted. More important were the varieties of millet such as *Sorghum* (Guinea corn), *Pennisetum* (bulrush), and *Eleusine corocana* exploited by the early farmers.

Knowledge of the Neolithic in tropical Africa in the very early period has been obtained largely by inferences drawn from scanty archaeological, agricultural, and linguistic evidence. Neolithic cultivators, the Nok people, were in Nigeria after 2000 B.C., and Capsian pastoralists were in Kenya and Ethiopia even before that date. The only other places in Africa where Neolithic industries are well known are in the Congo basin and these belong to a much later period. One problem concerned with identifying early Neolithic societies in other areas of Africa comes from the presumed connection between stone farming implements and Neolithic cultivation and the fact that few such tools have been found. It is possible that settled agriculture was practiced without sophisticated tools but rather with wooden digging sticks. The example of early Jericho in Palestine indicates that such primitive methods of agriculture could support a large population.

However debatable are the origins of agriculture in tropical Africa, there is no question that animal husbandry was not developed in the sub-Saharan regions but was introduced from elsewhere. The ancestors of cattle, sheep, and goats are not native to Africa. The technique of domestication was developed in western Asia and the skill was probably brought first to Egypt and then transmitted to other regions by way of the Nile Valley. Evidence of early herders dates from the fourth millennium in the vicinity of Khartoum and in Kenya. The cattle-herding scenes depicted in the Saharan highlands indicate how widespread pastoralism had become by 2000 B.C. Nomadic herders, therefore, were present throughout the savannah belt during the post-Makalian dry phase. The diffusion of new techniques and products in Africa did not necessarily mean their immediate acceptance by all the people who had access to them. Various cultures viewed the new objects and ideas in different ways. The permeability of a society depends upon a number of factors. The coming of the skills necessary for the Neolithic Revolution and later Iron Age technology did not mean the end of the older hunting and fishing or even collecting societies. Thus in certain areas it was possible to find Neolithic agriculturists, pastoralists, and collectors existing in close proximity. Geographic, historic, and religious factors could operate either to slow down or halt entirely the assimilation of foreign ideas.

The Iron Age and Bantu migrations

There was no duplication of the Bronze Age of the north in most of the areas south of the Sahara. Instead, most sub-Saharan societies went directly from the Stone Age to the Iron Age. Iron technology in Africa appears to have originated with the Egyptians, who learned it from the Assyrians in the seventh century B.C. Soon the rulers of Kush had iron, and the most advanced ironworking techniques in Africa were developed at their capital city of Meroë. From Kush iron probably spread quickly along well-established trading routes to West, Central, and East Africa. This would explain why the peoples immediately south of Kush, protected by the swamps of the Bahr-al-Ghazal, did not receive the advantages of the new technology while Negro groups such as the Nok people were using iron by 250 B.C. The diffusion of iron to Central and East Africa shortly after the opening of the Christian era is closely related to the migration of the Bantu.

Lack of definite information on tropical Africa at this crucial period of the late Neolithic and early Iron Age has led to a number of conflicting theories to explain the complex interconnections between the Bantu, iron, and new tropical foodstuffs. One of the boldest of these, proposed by the American anthropologist George Murdock, deals primarily with the introduction of new plants and by extension with the migration of the Bantu. Murdock suggests that agriculture was begun by Mande Negroes in the upper Niger region in about 5000 B.C. independently of its development in Egypt. As proof for his idea Murdock points to the difference between the millet and Guinea yam found in West Africa and crops elsewhere. Although this part of Murdock's thesis is provocative, there is no real evidence for separate development. These new products could simply have been added to the stock of materials that had come from the east.

Murdock developed an even more elaborate and debatable theory concerning the introduction of certain tropical foodstuffs to Africa. He suggests that species of yams, bananas, cocoyams, and sugarcane that are found today as staple crops in the forest areas of Central and West Africa probably originated in Indonesia. Murdock hypothesized, probably correctly, that these had been brought by the Indonesian invaders of Madagascar. Briefly stated, Murdock believes that the new Indonesian plants were adopted by the Cushitic peoples of Kenya and Uganda. From there they were transmitted northward to the central and of West friendly om their the long, ew plants to

tain questionable were introduced to East Africa from Madagascar, why did they take such a round-about route to the immediate interior? More logical than the route stated by Murdock would be an east to west route into Central Africa. Murdock also assumes that the Proto-Bantu in West Africa could not have cultivated such items as Guinea yams, which would have allowed them to live in a forest environment before the arrival of the East Indian crops. Finally, Murdock accepts without modification the conclusions of the linguist Joseph Greenberg concerning Bantu migrations.

The spread of relatively advanced agricultural and iron technology throughout the central and southern parts of the continent seems to have depended upon Bantu movements. Archaeological and historical evidence for the 1,500-year diaspora is scant, and in many cases that which is available is ambivalent. Therefore linguistics is important in attempting a reconstruction

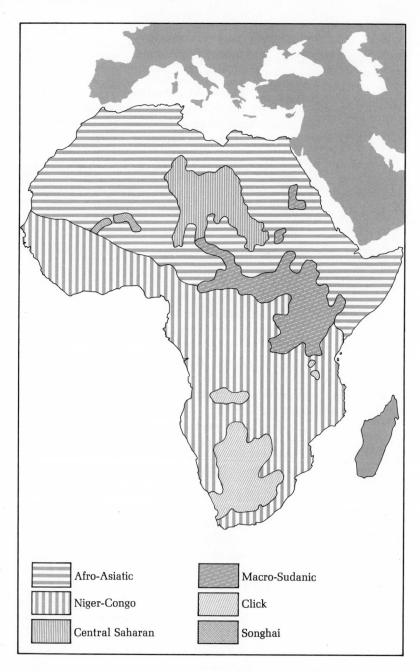

Language Families According to Greenberg

of the relation of the Bantu to other Negro peoples and the pattern of their early migration. Greenberg compared the equivalents for approximately fifty ordinary words spoken by many present Western Sudanic Negro groups and also by Bantu speakers. He concluded that the various Bantu dialects as well as the Western Sudanic all belong to the Niger-Kordofanian language family. Aside from clarifying previous confusion in language classification, Greenberg's analysis, if correct, had tremendous historical significance. It meant that when the Negro population began to move into the forest belt some groups from the vicinity of eastern Nigeria proceeded southward and eastward to eventually occupy most of central, eastern, and southern Africa.

The British linguist Malcolm Guthrie disputed Greenberg's conclusions after analyzing over 20,000 related words in approximately 200 Bantu languages. He found 2,300 common words and over 500 general root words distributed over the entire Bantu area. Guthrie then reduced the number of general roots that appeared in each language to percentages. The tribes with the highest percentages are presumably nearest the area of the original point of diffusion of the language. The zone of highest percentages is an ellipse in the central Congo, with its center in the Luba districts of the Katanga. The logic of Guthrie's investigations indicates that this was the original homeland of the Bantu.

The seeming incompatibility of the Greenberg, Guthrie, and Murdock theories has recently been bridged by a perceptive composite analysis by the British historian Roland Oliver, who views the early Bantu migrations as belonging to two separate stages. In the first stage a small number of pre-Bantu speakers migrated to the areas immediately south of the Congo forests. This movement would account for the similarities in Bantu and Western Sudanic languages observed by Greenberg. The recent arrivals found the new land, which was lightly wooded with a rainfall of between twenty and thirty inches a year, surprisingly like much of the territory they had left. Thus the millets and sorghums that the early Bantu already possessed could be cultivated satisfactorily. It was also a land of streams with good fishing potential. In addition, these early Bantu, who Oliver presumes possessed a metalworking technology, found both copper and iron ore in their new environment. Thus it was in this area, coterminus with Guthrie's ellipse of high-frequency usage, that the Bantu developed their language and culture. The

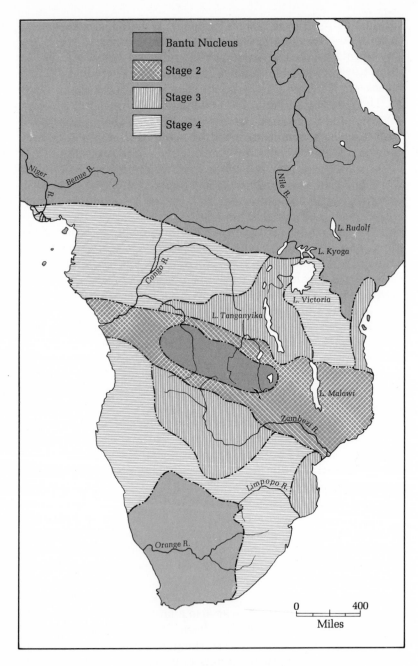

Patterns of Bantu Expansion

pressure of an increasing population and probably encounters with the southeast Asian food plants some time in the first five centuries A.D. gave the Bantu both the excuse and, with their iron implements, the means to expand further both south and north.

The second stage, the actual period of dispersion, is discussed more thoroughly in the chapters concerned with central, eastern, and southern Africa. It is sufficient to note here only a few general observations. Oliver's theory at present appears to reconcile most of the known evidences drawn from linguistic and agricultural evidence. Final proof for it cannot be produced now, and perhaps the questions concerning the early Bantu migrations will never be conclusively answered. Of the same order are questions having to do with iron and the Bantu. Without doubt the Bantu carried with them the knowledge of iron-working. On the basis of current data, however, it seems that the knowledge of iron smelting preceded the Bantu invasions. Skeletal evidence from much later Iron Age sites indicated that Bushmanoid types were mining ore and fabricating iron equipment. What is probable is that the Bantu brought the technology with them from the west and that this knowledge was diffused to certain areas before the Bantu drove out the indigenous inhabitants.

Before closing this brief, generalized discussion of the Bantu another group of important and debatable questions should be mentioned. These concern placement and dating. Oliver's thesis indicates that the early Bantu in East Africa were of a later date than those along the Zambesi. In this theory Oliver is at variance with such archeologists as Desmond Clark and Brian Fagan, who believe that the Bantu of Central Africa migrated from the vicinity of the great lakes. Existing carbon dating, however, tends to support Oliver. In the Zambesi area there are sites dating to the first century A.D. while at present the earliest dates for Bantu settlements in southern Tanzania are the sixth century and in Uganda the eleventh century. Despite lack of information and conflicting theories, this later period of Bantu dispersions is better documented than the movement from West Africa. From numerous Iron Age sites, oral tradition, and much later from Arabic and European accounts it is possible to reconstruct with some accuracy the Bantu societies and their effect on the previous inhabitants of those territories where the Bantu are now dominant.

Egypt, Kush, and Meroë

Although Egyptian hieroglyphics dating to 3100 B.C. have been discovered, little is known of this very early period. The "rulers of the two lands" are shadowy, mythical figures and the details of their cultural and political development are lacking. Nevertheless, reasonable inferences can be made based on the more abundant materials of the early Old Kingdom. This archaic age was one of experimentation in politics, religion, and art. The need to maintain control over a large territory dictated a centralized political organization controlled by a warrior-king. The need to overcome the complicated challenge of controlling the Nile flooding was another reason for centralization. Beginnings of pyramidal funeral structures indicate the early unity of religion and politics, and long before the construction of the huge step pyramid at Saqqara the warrior-kings must have been considered deities.

Egypt in the period of the Old Kingdom (3200–2250 B.C.), with its capital at Memphis at the apex of the Nile delta, was already one of the richest agricultural areas in the world. It has been estimated that the peasants, aided by the new control of Nile flooding, could produce three times their own needs. Political, economic, and religious institutions became fixed in the early years of this period. Egypt became isolated from outside influences both by the choice of its rulers and by geography. The northern approaches to Egypt were protected by the Mediterranean. Not until the rise of the maritime power of the Minoans over one thousand years later would there be a threat of a seaborne invasion. The Sinai Desert and the Red Sea to the east and the sand sea of the Libyan Desert to the west blocked any easy penetration of foreign armies or ideas. The cataracts of the Nile above Aswan and the bareness of the southern approaches also provided adequate protection from invasion. Isolated and secure, with nature itself seeming to mirror the orderliness and stability of their government, the Egyptians created a culture that satisfied them for centuries.

The keystone of Egyptian institutions was the pharaoh, who was not merely a king but was divine. At his coronation he became the god Horus, and at his death he was transformed into the more powerful Osiris. He alone had direct access to ma'at, which is roughly translatable into truth, beauty, justice,

and goodness, and his well-being was necessary for the continued prosperity of the land. The building of the pyramids of
Giza represent not only a great technical and administrative
achievement but also the reverent attitude of the masses who
were concerned for the pharaoh's welfare in the afterlife. The
bulk of the work on the great tombs was done voluntarily by
the people, who were paid by the state, with a minimum of slave
labor being used.

From the earliest Old Kingdom times Egypt was a special
type of theocracy. The pharaoh in his dual role linked both the
secular and the religious. The gods of Egypt were many, with
overlapping functions and responsibilities. Such illogic did not
seem to disturb either the priests or the worshippers. Some of
the most important deities of Egypt were Amon, the sun god;
Osiris, who controlled the Nile; Set, his brother, represented by
the desert; Isis, the wife of Osiris; and Horus, the god of new
life. Even in the Old Kingdom the priesthood had great power.
Priests were responsible for the dates, means, and format of the
ceremonies designed to please all the gods and cause them to
continue to favor Egypt. There were two divisions of the priesthood, the prophets and the ordinary servants of the temples.
Each of the many temples was staffed by a large number of the
latter. In addition to controlling religious practices, the priests
were responsible for all religious and secular education.

The high respect for the deified person of the pharaoh
explains the favored position of his mother. The queen mother
was treated with great reverence and honor and was normally
a very powerful influence in state affairs. The need to maintain
the spiritual potency of the royal line explains why despite
polygamy the pharaoh usually wed a queen sister. Many of the
important positions in the pharaoh's highly centralized and
efficient bureaucracy were held by royal relatives. The pharaoh's
chief adviser and next to him the most powerful man in the
state was the vizier, who dealt with most of the everyday problems of government. Also present near the person of the
pharaoh were the chief priests, the royal treasurer, and the chief
architect. In the field the pharaoh's power was represented by
over forty nomarchs, or governors of provinces. Although these
were appointive positions, in time they became hereditary.
During the Old Kingdom there were few professional soldiers.
Many of the rank and file of the armies were slaves. In Upper

Egypt near the borders of Nubia the nomarchs with their large, experienced military forces were soon a formidable factor in limiting the practical autocracy of the pharaoh.

The growing independence of many of the nomarchs, particularly those of Upper Egypt, led eventually to a complete breakdown of central authority. The long ninety-year reign of the weak pharaoh Pepi II marked the end of the Old Kingdom and ushered in the First Intermediate Period (about 2250–2050 B.C.). A series of weak monarchs followed who could not control their powerful nobles and they became pharaohs in name only. Factional quarrels rent Egypt for almost 200 years. Nubia was lost to Egypt by the invasion of the mysterious "C" people, who were perhaps the ancestors of the modern Beja, nomads of the Sudan.

The disorders were brought to an end by the princes of Thebes, probably with the aid of Nubian troops. The reunification of the two lands had been completed by 2065 B.C. under Menthuhotop II, the first great pharaoh of the Middle Kingdom period. The goal of the Theban pharaohs, the restoration of the pre-Intermediate autocratic system, proved impossible to attain, however. To complete their conquest and to insure against future revolts a large standing army became necessary. Even more fundamental were the religious changes that took place during this period. The pharaohs of the Middle Kingdom were still regarded as god-kings, but they found it more necessary than their Old Kingdom counterparts to rule by talent. They had to be accessible to their supporters and were forced to depend more on the priesthood as a sanction for their rule. Religion became more formalized and ritualistic and turned to an almost morbid concern with the world of the dead.

The Middle Kingdom was a time of great affluence, with the rich pharaohs and nobles demanding more luxury items such as ivory, gold, fine stones, and exotic woods. New mines were opened in Sinai and Nubia and trade with Syria and the Middle East expanded. The Sudan trade and the Red Sea routes to the land of Punt became more important than ever before. This was also a boom time for the construction of dams, canals, temples, and forts in all sections of the restored empire. Such opulence, however, did not hide the weaknesses of the Middle Kingdom. The nobles still retained great power and the influence of the priesthood had been greatly expanded. The pharaoh and his central administration had to remain strong. A combination of a weak pharaoh and an outside threat would be disastrous. This possibility became actuality after the reign of Amenembet III (about 1800 B.C.) with the Hyksos invasion.

The Hyksos, who had been a part of the Indo-European migrations toward the west from central Asia, possessed weapons far superior to those of the Egyptians. Despite the availability of metal, the Egyptians still used stone for their arrows although their other weapons were made of copper. Shields and body armor were usually of leather. Only a few nobles could afford armor or weapons of bronze. The Hyksos had bronze weapons and composite bows; more important, they utilized the horse and war chariot. The Egyptians fell to the Hyksos onslaught, and the new rulers completely dominated Lower Egypt for over 150 years. They left relatively undisturbed the political system of Upper Egypt, satisfied with the tribute they exacted from the nobles there. Hyksos rule affected the culture of Egypt even less, although in time the Egyptians adopted the weapons and military tactics of their conquerors. Under the leadership of the princes of Thebes, particularly Ahmose I, the Hyksos domination was ended in the early sixteenth century B.C. The new military dynasty and their priestly supporters then tried to expunge from Egypt all records of the long, infamous period of foreign domination. In the war of liberation Ahmose I liquidated the separate power of the nomarchs and created the most centralized and despotic government that Egypt had yet seen, although its organizational pattern was modeled on that of the Old and Middle Kingdom periods.

Armed with new weapons and aware of the vulnerability of Egypt, the pharaohs of the New Kingdom launched a program of imperialism. The large professional army created to expel the Hyksos was utilized to establish more secure frontiers. The zenith of this expansion came under Thutmose III (about 1479 B.C.) with the establishment of Egyptian power over western Asia as far as the Euphrates and southward into the Sudan. The pharaohs Amonhotep II and III carried on the same expansionist policy in Asia and Africa. Military power rather than national unity had become the basis of the pharaoh's power. There was a concomitant increase in the powers of centralized bureaucracy and the priesthood. The wealth not only of the Nile but also of the most developed part of the world flowed to Egypt and was concentrated in the hands of a few.

Egyptian religion became dominated by formulas and

rituals. The attempt by Amenhotep IV (Ikhnaton) (1375–1358 B.C.) to reform the corrupt religious practices by establishing a national monotheistic religion proved disastrous. The end of his reign was marked by civil disorder and revolts in the provinces and threats of foreign invasion. The pharaohs who followed Ikhnaton allowed the priesthood to widen its political influence. This factor combined with luxurious-living, weak pharaohs, and selfish nobles sapped the ability of the state to withstand outside pressures. The greatness of some of the late pharaohs, notably Ramses II (1298–1232 B.C.), masked the weaknesses of the state. Libyans and Kushites reduced first the empire and later, after 950 B.C., conquered Egypt itself.

EGYPT IN THE SUDAN

Rich in ivory, ebony, and cattle, Nubia was often raided in the early days of the Old Kingdom. By the time of Mernera (about 2300 B.C.), who had cleared a channel through the rocks at the first cataract, the trade relation with Nubia had been formalized. From Elephantine on the Nile Egypt controlled the territory and trade south of the first cataract. The duties of the nomarch of Elephantine were to defend southern Egypt and to foster and protect trade into the Sudan. Trade routes included one to the southwest from Elephantine to El Fasher in Darfur by way of the oases of Selima and Bir Natrum. From this point another route led west toward Lake Chad. Several others were also beginning near the first cataract leading south to Abu Hamed.

Soldiers accompanied the Egyptian donkey caravans to protect them from attack by the Sudanese. In addition, the lords of Upper Egypt maintained permanent military forces for punitive expeditions. Many of these Egyptian soldiers were Sudanese Negroes. The Egyptians left behind records of at least two major early invasions of Nubia, one under Mernera and the second under his son Pepi II. The need to maintain relatively large military forces in the south gave the lords of Upper Egypt great power, a factor that hastened the downfall of the Old Kingdom. Egypt lost control of Nubia in the disorders of the First Intermediate Period. Probably because of their interests elsewhere, the Elephantine rulers could do nothing to stop the invasion of Nubia by the "C" people. These Caucasian invaders were both pastoralists and agriculturists. They were probably responsible for helping to revive the prosperity of Nubia, which had been so disturbed by the Egyptian raids of the Old Kingdom.

The restoration of the authority of the pharaoh during the Middle Kingdom period brought Egyptian power once more to Nubia. The affluent Egyptian society demanded more luxury items, cattle, and metals, which could be obtained in the southern trade. Nubia was incorporated into Egypt and the frontier was moved from Elephantine up the Nile past the second cataract. Elaborate mud forts were built as far south as Semna to secure the Nubian trade. Egyptian trading influence also extended further up the Nile into Kush as far as the third cataract. At Kerma, six days' journey beyond Semna, Egyptian traders, scribes, and soldiers lived in harmony with the local African populace.

The greatest of the Middle Kingdom pharaohs, Senwasret III (1887–1850 B.C.), improved the forts and operated from them to pacify territory as far west as the Saharan oases and southward into Kush. To improve the river link northward he caused a new deep channel to be cut at the first cataract and opened new gold mines in Nubia. The rule of Senwasret's son Amenemhet III was the apex of Egyptian influence in Nubia and Kush in this period. The weakness of his successors as well as the Hyksos invasions allowed individual nobles to fight among themselves and to dispute central authority. The Nubian fortresses were allowed to decay and the Egyptian enclave at Kerma was destroyed.

Ahmose I, the conqueror of the Hyksos, rebuilt the Nubian forts and cleared the canal at the first cataract. With new and better weapons and the use of the horse his successors found it easier to control Nubia. The New Kingdom monarchs, however, were also concerned with Kush, the land beyond Nubia. The area above the third cataract was fertile and supported a large population, and possibly the chiefs in this region were a threat to Egyptian control of Nubia. Thutmose I (about 1530 B.C.) led a major force by land and water into Kush almost as far as Napata, conquered the Sudanese chiefs, and appointed a viceroy to govern the area. His successor was forced to send an army to Kush which ruthlessly crushed a revolt against Egyptian authority. After this the viceroys of Kush had little difficulty in ruling the region until the abortive revolt against Amonhotep III (1405–1375 B.C.).

By this time Nubia seems to have been almost completely Egyptianized, but the process obviously took longer in Kush.

It was, however, the practice for important men in Kush to send their sons to Thebes to learn Egyptian customs. A growing trade with areas further to the south acted as a perpetual lure for Egyptians in Nubia, and Kerma and Napata became flourishing centers for trade and Egyptian culture. Evidence of the value of Nubia and Kush can be seen in innumerable temples of the New Kingdom period. Perhaps the most notable examples of the degree of Egyptianization of these areas are the great temples built in Nubia by Ramses II, the ruins of which have been largely covered by the waters of the Aswan Dam.

The collapse of the New Kingdom, followed by the Libyan conquest of Egypt, left the nobles of upper Nubia and Kush relatively free from outside control. The city of Napata, near the fourth cataract, soon became the leading city of Kush. It was the northern terminus of a well-traveled overland trade route from Meroë and was located in one of the most fertile areas of the Sudan. It appears that the rulers of Napata were able very quickly to establish their hegemony over the other areas of Kush. The effective range of their control included the grasslands south of the fifth cataract, which gave them an additional source of wealth in cattle. Meroë served as the second capital of the kingdom of Kush.

The disorganization of Egypt offered the rulers of Kush an opportunity to expand northward. In the eighth century B.C. Upper Egypt was taken by Kush from the Libyan dynasty of Egyptian rulers. King Piankhy (751–716 B.C.) of Kush invaded the delta, eliminated all opposition, and united under Kushite control all the lands from the fifth cataract north to the Mediterranean. His successor moved the capital from Napata to Thebes, and King Taharqa of the seventh century B.C. ruled from the old capital of Memphis. These alien pharaohs strove hard to restore not only the unity of Egypt but also its traditions and customs.

Reunification was hindered by the conflict of interest in Syria between Egypt and the greatest Asian power, Assyria. Angered over the aid the Kushites had given to his enemies, the Assyrian king Esarhaddon, using camels for transport, moved his armies quickly across Sinai and into Egypt. Esarhaddon's troops were armed with iron weapons while the Egyptians, despite the fact that they had been confronted with the iron weapons of the Hittites six centuries earlier, persisted in using bronze armaments. Kushitic kings who had access to iron ore had followed the conservative Egyptian practices. The Kushite and Egyptian forces were defeated, Memphis was lost, and Tarharqa fled to Upper Egypt. Within one year he rallied his forces, invaded the delta, and reestablished his rule. The Assyrians, however, responded with a larger expeditionary force and reconquered Lower Egypt. In the subsequent war in 666 B.C. the Kushite ruler Tanutemun was decisively beaten. Thebes was taken and sacked, and probably only distance saved the kingdom of Kush from being incorporated into the Assyrian empire. This series of defeats ended Kushitic control of Egypt. During the Saite dynasty in Egypt the rulers of Kush launched one more invasion of Egypt in 591 B.C. but were driven back. The victorious mercenaries of Egypt then invaded Kush and looted Napata. Afterwards the delta monarchs withdrew, leaving troops behind at the second cataract to guard the frontier, and the Kushitic kings turned their ambitions toward extending and consolidating their rule in the Sudan.

Despite its continuing symbolic significance, Napata became secondary to Meroë, and the northern area gradually became less important. Contact with Nubia and Persian-controlled Egypt after the sixth century B.C. seems to have been minimal. The capital of Kush was moved to Meroë, probably because the northern grasslands had been overgrazed and because both iron ore and fuel were present in southern Kush. The Kushites had learned from the Assyrians not only the effectiveness of iron but obviously also the technique of ironworking. The slag heaps found in the vicinity of Meroë are evidence of how important the iron industry later became. One anthropologist was so impressed by these that he called Meroë the Birmingham of Central Africa. The possession of iron weapons and tools enabled the Kushites to establish their trade even more securely than before.

The great period of Meroë extended from the third century B.C. until just before the Christian era. In addition to iron weapons and agricultural implements, Kush exported slaves, ebony, gold, ostrich feathers, and other products drawn from the interior of Africa. On the import side goods and ideas possibly came from as far away as India. The prosperity of Meroë was perhaps tied to the revival of Egypt under the Ptolemaic dynasty. Despite these evidences of an extensive foreign trade, Kush was more isolated from the main currents of Mediterranean-Asian civilization than before. The furnishings of the pyramidal burial

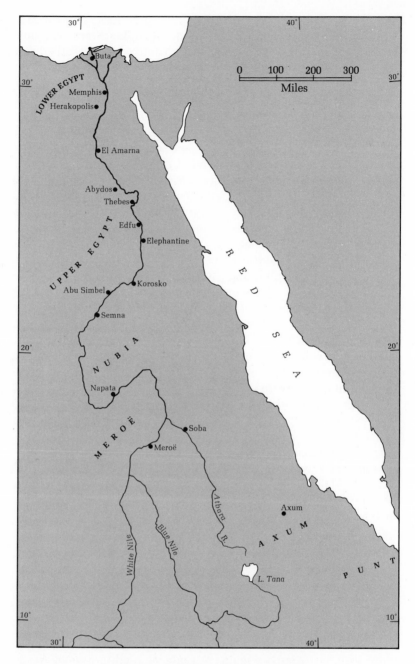

Ancient Egypt, Nubia, and Kush

chambers, derived from the Old Kingdom, indicate a departure from the Egyptian form, and in the second century B.C. the still undeciphered cursive of Meroë was introduced.

The Kushite systems of administration and justice were still based on Egyptian models. The kings referred to themselves as the lords of the two lands and played the priestly roles of a pharaoh of Egypt. They married a queen sister and the queen mother was held in the same high regard as in Egypt. Amon was the chief deity of basically an Egyptian pantheon of gods. The power of the ruler of Kush derived not only from his control of the bureaucracy and the military but also from his position as a god-king whose well-being was necessary for the general prosperity of all the people.

In the two centuries before the Christian era southern Nubia was an area of conflict between Kush and the Ptolemys. After their conquest of Egypt in the first century B.C. the Romans inherited this border problem. A major raid against Elephantine and the sacking of Philae by the Kushites caused the Romans in 23 B.C. to dispatch an army to Nubia. The Romans occupied all of Nubia, destroyed Napata, and ravaged as far south as the fourth cataract. They then retired to Nubia and established their southern frontier at Elephantine. Meroë, which emerged unscathed, continued to control a large kingdom. Because the Romans obtained African materials from their bases elsewhere in North Africa, trade between Egypt and Kush decreased in importance, and the wealth of the Kushites rapidly declined. The Beja, desert nomads from the east, and a new people, the Nobatae, invaded and settled in Nubia and northern Kush. The kingdom of Axum cut off contacts with the Red Sea area and eventually gained political control over eastern territories previously ruled by the rulers of Kush. In the fourth century A.D. Axum took and destroyed the impotent Meroë. The rulers of Kush may have led the refugees westward along the savannah routes toward Lake Chad, and in the process the Kushitic culture, including the technology of iron, was possibly diffused to the peoples of Africa.

Carthage and Rome in North Africa

After the collapse of the Minoan empire the most affluent traders of the Mediterranean were the Semitic Phoenicians, whose control of land areas adjacent to their ports or colonies was always minimal. The Hebrews who captured the Palestinian interior from the Phoenicians called them Canaanites and constrained them to a thin strip of the Levantine coast. From the cities of Sidon, Bibylus, and particularly Tyre along this coast the Phoenicians for almost a thousand years dominated the trade of the Mediterranean. To facilitate trade with new areas of the central and western Mediterranean the Phoenicians established small colonies, usually composed of only a few hundred people. The function of the colonists was to collect the goods of the interior and retain them until Phoenician ships picked them up.

The most important Phoenician colony was Carthage (Karthadasht), or the New City, which was probably founded in the eighth century B.C. as a staging post for long journeys. Its favorable strategic location, the richness of the agricultural and trading hinterland, and the growing importance of the Mediterranean all combined to spur the growth of this city to the point where it surpassed Tyre in economic importance. At its height in the third century B.C. Carthage had a heterogeneous population of Phoenicians, Berbers, Greeks, and Jews in excess of one quarter million. The city had two large artificial harbors, one for merchant ships and the other for the navy. A citadel dedicated to the gods, the Byrsa, overlooked the harbor. Not until centuries after Carthage was founded did the Carthaginians erect strong walls to surround the city on three sides. Even then they considered their navy their major defense against attack. Although they later expanded their control of the immediate hinterland, the Carthaginians remained primarily a commercial and maritime people. Economic ties with their mother city, Tyre, remained close until the latter was occupied by the Persians in 538 B.C. Until then the people of Carthage sent a large yearly gift of money to Tyre for their ancestral gods. Politically all permanent Phoenician colonies were independent, although their political forms tended to follow the same patterns.

Considering their great importance for such a long period in Mediterranean history, very little is known of Phoenicia and Carthage. The savage nature of the final Roman conquest of Carthage in 146 B.C. partially explains the lack of detailed information. One can, however, sketch a general outline of Carthaginian history. The city was ruled by an oligarchy, which was dominated by the older nobility, who traced their ancestry to the original Tyrian settlers and who tended to be tradition bound and religious. A senate controlled by these nobles and the merchant aristocracy was the chief legislative body. After the fourth century B.C. power was further concentrated in the hands of a thirty-member council. A larger assembly of perhaps 500 members existed which, while the exact nature of its powers is unknown, appears to have had little authority. The Carthaginian executive was appointed. Two sufets, roughly the equivalent of Roman consuls, were chosen for one-year terms. Although the nature of the connection is not certain, there was a close interrelation among traders, the nobility, and the military. The most successful generals and admirals were not necessarily members of the inner ruling circle, and it appears that the council was suspicious and probably afraid of such men. Indeed, many Carthaginian field commanders were chosen on the basis of their mediocrity. Although such a policy protected the state from military despotism, it had a disastrous effect upon Carthage during the first two wars with Rome in the third century B.C.

After the fall of Tyre Carthage assumed the dominant role over the Phoenician colonies of the western Mediterranean. The growing commercial power of Greece was contained in North Africa in Cyrenaica at Arae Philoenorum. West of this point Carthage controlled the coast. Eastward the Greek colonists dominated the Libyans. There were few colonies along the Tripolitanian coast from Lepcis to the eastern frontier. Lepcis was an important center for trade with the interior, although not to the same degree as later under the Romans. Other major Carthaginian colonies were Utica and Magador in western Morocco. These, combined with their stations on Sardinia, Corsica, Sicily, and the Iberian peninsula, gave Carthage a near-monopoly of western trade until challenged by Rome in the third century B.C.

The Carthaginians affected Africa in a number of ways. They ruled directly over a large number of Libyan Berbers who were converted to their culture. Although their prime source of wealth was from trade, the Carthaginians controlled much productive land, particularly in the Tunisian plain. Many Libyans in this area became agricultural laborers utilizing advanced techniques. The bulk of the Carthaginian army in the third century B.C. was composed of Libyan and Numidian recruits. These mercenaries obviously were greatly affected by their association with more advanced weapons and techniques of war. By the beginning of the second century B.C. Berber chieftains in Numidia had begun to base the economy of their states on agriculture and their political organization on Carthaginian models.

Carthaginian ideas and techniques spread primarily as a result of trading. There is no direct evidence concerning the methods and scope of the overland trade between Carthage and the peoples in the Western Sudan. It is highly improbable that the Carthaginians, with their concern with trade, did not tap the interior for carbuncles, chalcedony, slaves, and ivory. The maintenance of such trade would have depended upon the goodwill of such interior peoples as the Garamantes, since it is doubtful that the Carthaginians would have been more successful than the later Romans in directly controlling the trans-Saharan trade. Magador, a colony on the coast of western Morocco, is evidence that the Carthaginians utilized the seas in their trade with the African interior.

One of the most tantalizing but disputed stories relating to Carthaginian exploits in Africa has to do with the voyage of Hanno. According to a Greek translation of a Phoenician stele at the temple of Baal at Carthage, Hanno, a sufet, led an expedition of sixty ships beyond the Pillars of Hercules some time after 500 B.C. If the account is true, Hanno's expedition, sailing along the west coast, could have reached as far south as Sierra Leone. According to the text, Hanno established a colony called Cerne on a small island at the head of a gulf. The exact location of the area described is not known, although it could have been a few days' sail north of the mouth of the Senegal River. Later Hanno explored the river he called the Chretas, which was probably the Senegal. Hanno investigated this stream and sailed south to another river, possibly the Gambia, and reported seeing the banks aflame with brush fires. After many other adventures which could have taken the Carthaginians offshore from Mount Kakulinia in Sierra Leone Hanno ostensibly returned to Carthage. Later Roman historians mentioned Cerne and reported it to be an important trading center. If it was, the colony could have been a most important entry point for Mediterranean ideas and practices into sub-Saharan Africa.

The long hegemony of Carthage over North Africa was ended by three wars with Rome. The first, which began as a result of trading conflicts over Sicily, was not decisive, although the Carthaginians lost their key bases in Sicily, Sardinia, and Corsica. The second conflict, which ended in 202 B.C., was the

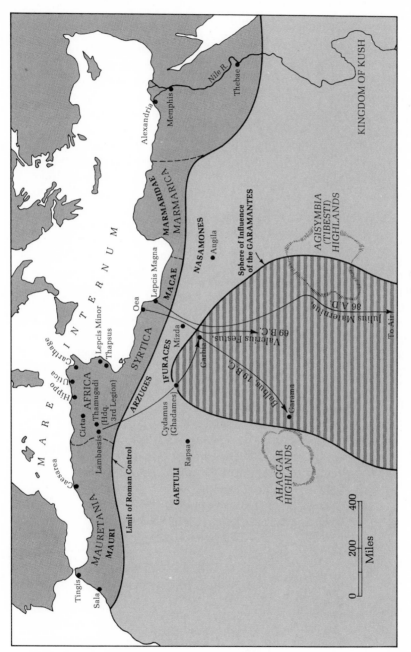

Roman North Africa, about A.D. 117

45

crucial one. After winning some initial victories on mainland Italy the Carthaginians found their home territories being invaded. Part of the success of the Romans was due to the fact that they had gained the support of Berber leaders. Even before 146 B.C. when Carthage was ruthlessly destroyed such states as Numidia had seized power over many of the areas that had previously been Carthaginian spheres of influence.

Roman interest in northern Africa had an economic basis only in the sense that the Romans sought to free the western Mediterranean from competition by Carthage. Rome took over the direct administration of the small province of Africa, which comprised about 5,000 square miles. The rest of the territory was left to Punic cities and the coastal Berber kingdoms that had supported Rome in the last war. The agricultural riches of the territory, particularly in wheat, barley, oil, and wine, soon drew the interest of the food-poor Romans. In 122 B.C. Gaius Gracchus sent 6,000 colonists to the area of Carthage. Thereafter Marius, Julius Caesar, and Augustus all resettled discharged soldiers in North Africa. Gradually Rome asserted its authority along the coast and into the interior toward the mountains. In 46 B.C. the client kingdom of Numidia became a Roman province. Mauretania was converted into a client state in 33 B.C. and became a province during the reign of Caligula in A.D. 40. Under Roman rule such cities as Caesarea, Utica, Sabratha, and Lepcis Magna became major trading centers, and Latin culture replaced the thin overlay of Punic civilization along the coast.

The slow expansion of investment and administration brought the Romans into contact with the nomadic pastoralists of the interior. The wandering Nasamones and Gaetuli habitually moved their animals northward for better grazing during the summer. The Romans attempted to restrict this movement in the southern part of their newly conquered territory and eventually garrisoned the northern oases. The nomadic tribes, particularly the Gaetuli, resented any control and continued to cause Rome and its allies great trouble. In 22 B.C. and again in A.D. 6 major Roman military expeditions were sent against these people. In A.D. 17 the Libyan Tacfarinas led a combination of disaffected Berber groups, particularly those who lived near the desert places, against the Romans. For seven years Tacfarinas kept the border areas of Africa and Numidia in turmoil until he was defeated and killed.

Early in the first century B.C. the Romans probably made their first contacts with the Berber kingdom of the Garamantes. Roman historians have left few records concerning the political, social, or economic structure of this state. What evidence there is, however, points to their military power and economic wealth. The center of their state was Garama (modern Germa), and their control extended into the Sahara as far east as the Fezzan. Herodotus in the fifth century B.C. mentioned the Garamantes as powerful raiders into the interior lands of the Negro. Much of the influence of these people was based on their possession of horses and war chariots. The main trading route from Lepcis Magna in Syrtica to the Fezzan passed through territory controlled by them. Given the unrest among all the Libyans in the first century B.C., it was logical that Garama should become the focal point of anti-Roman activity. This position, in turn, brought Roman reprisals, the first of which was a major force under Lucius Balbus sent in 20 B.C. to destroy the Garamantes. This expedition, the first Roman venture into the Sahara, captured Cydamus (modern Ghadames), and Garama, and penetrated into the Fezzan. Balbus' army was not sufficient to garrison a hostile territory so far from its supply base and he did not attempt to hold his conquests. Within a few years the Garamantes had restored their state.

The Garamantes continued to plague the Romans. For example, one major reason for Tacfarinas' success against the Romans was the support he received from the Garamantes. Border clashes between the Garamantes and the Romans continued almost yearly, and in A.D. 69 the Roman general Valerius Festus led another invasion of the Sahara. Festus discovered for the Romans a shorter interior road and again defeated the Garamantes. Once more the Romans did not attempt to hold the conquered territory. Shortly after this war a truce was agreed upon between the protagonists which lasted for centuries. The friendly atmosphere produced two Roman explorations of the deep interior. One expedition led by Julius Maternius reached beyond the Tibesti highlands, perhaps as far as Air, probably the deepest Roman penetration into the Sahara.

After the first century A.D. Rome was satisfied with holding the fertile areas of North Africa and allowing Berber peoples such as the Garamantes to conduct the trade with the Negro areas beyond the desert. The size and richness of Lixis at the head of one major cart track in Mauretania and Lepcis Magna, the northern terminus of one from the Fezzan, seem adequate evidence that such trade was large and profitable. The items of trade from the interior were ivory, gems, ostrich feathers, wild animals, and gold, which Berber merchants exchanged with the Negro traders for various manufactured goods. Salt was probably the most important item, since it was readily available in the Sahara and almost nonexistent throughout much of the Negro savannah lands.

Roman North Africa reached its peak of prosperity under the rule of the African-born Septimus Severus early in the third century. Thereafter its decline paralleled that of Rome itself. The introduction of the camel as the major means of desert transportation in the later years of Roman rule had major political as well as economic ramifications. It gave a new mobility to nomadic peoples just at the time when the power of the sedentary coastal peoples to retaliate was decreasing. The camel enabled the nomadic Sanhaja and Zenata Berbers to reverse the centuries-old dominance of agriculturists over pastoralists. The Berber Tuaregs, living a predatory life, converted vast areas of the Sahara and also fertile northern territories into their spheres of influence. Differences between Berber groups became intensified. For example, the Sanhaja of the western Sahara were related to the sedentary Berbers of the Kabyles. The new free life of the nomad soon obscured this relation as the Sanhaja created an entirely different culture.

The coming of Christianity to northern Africa also aided the nomadic peoples. The schismatic doctrine of Donatism divided the coastal population into warring camps. It has been speculated that many of the Berbers accepted Donatism less for religious reasons than as a means of opposing the Romans. In the fifth century the urban areas of northern Africa were conquered by the wandering Germanic tribe of Vandals. The dislocations of this invasion were compounded by the religious persecutions of both Orthodox and Donatist Christians by the new Arian conquerors. This period of semianarchy, which worked to the benefit of the nomads, lasted until the Byzantine conquest of North Africa in the sixth century.

TWO
Islam and the Western Sudan to 1800

The expansion of Islam in North Africa

In the city of Mecca in southern Arabia, Muhammed, a trader who had made a fortunate marriage with a rich, older widow, claimed to be the recipient of revelations from God. Although the full body of revelation was not collected until after his death, he was able to persuade a large number of persons in Mecca that he was the prophet. Internecine quarrels between factions in Arabia at first blocked his ambitions. He and a few followers were forced to flee Mecca for the city of Yathrib in A.D. 622 (year 1 of the Arabic calendar). Here by a combination of persuasiveness and shrewd politics Muhammed converted the city and changed its name to al-Medina, the city. From this base the new faith spread to the neighboring desert tribes. Islam (meaning submission) grew powerful enough to recapture Mecca two years before the prophet's death in A.D. 632. By then the new religion claimed the loyalty of perhaps one third of the peoples of Arabia.

Islam, although a composite of Muhammed's revelations, Judaism, Christianity, and older primitive Arabian religions, was a direct, uncomplicated faith. Its monotheism was not modified by Muhammed's position. He had claimed only to be the prophet of Allah, who had chosen him to be merely the medium of divine revelations. The rituals of worship were simple and did not demand a separate priesthood or complex theology. This was one of the major reasons for the quick acceptance of Islam by unsophisticated

49

people. Another factor that helped the rapid spread of Islam was that it was a religion born in the desert. Many allusions in the Koran were couched in terms that desert peoples anywhere could understand and appreciate.

Muhammed established both the theory and practice of intervention into political affairs. In order for a polity to operate properly it should do so in accordance with the precepts of the Koran. In practice there was often a great gulf between the actual and the ideal, but Islam stressed the responsibility of rulers to do justice. There were also sanctions for pursuing the jihad, or holy war, against those who had not been converted. Those who died in battle against the infidel would die in a holy cause.

The expansion of Islam out of Arabia was only partially caused by religious zeal. Overpopulation of the sparse land was a major factor. The unification of previously feuding Bedouin tribes under one banner provided the means of easing the problem. Open conflict with the two mighty neighbors, Byzantium and Sassanid Persia, provided further motivation. The relatively easy early victories of the Arabs over their powerful foes opened the riches of the Middle East to the warriors of Islam. Expansion, therefore, became an excuse for further conquest.

Syria was occupied by 636, and at the same time Muslim armies were conquering Mesopotamia and Persia. With these conquests the Arabs had at their disposal wealth beyond their earlier dreams and permanent occupation of very fertile lands. Egypt, because of its wealth, attracted the Arab leaders very early. The first invasion occurred in 637, and two years later Amr ibn al-'As with a few thousand men set out to conquer Egypt. His task was relatively simple because the Byzantine rulers could command little support from the native Christians. The Muslim leaders early gained the support of these Coptic Christians by guaranteeing their right to continue to practice their religion. In return the Egyptians agreed to recognize the Arabs as governors and to pay the taxes levied by them. The final defeat of Byzantium in Egypt came when Alexandria was evacuated in 642.

The Arabs quickly consolidated their position in Egypt and their armies moved south and west. They occupied Aswan and fortified it against raiders from the south. A military expedition penetrated into Nubia as far as Dongola in 651, laying siege to the city and forcing the king to sign a treaty of friendship with the Arabs. This treaty, which guaranteed the independence of the kingdom of Dongola in return for a yearly tribute of 360 slaves, remained in force for almost six centuries.

Cyrenaica was quickly occupied, but the desert areas to the west, combined with Byzantine control of the sea lanes, temporarily halted the Muslim conquests. In 670, after constructing a navy, the Arabs launched an attack upon the Maghrib. They established a new city, Kairwan, which acted as their main military as well as administrative headquarters. Byzantine control of the cities was gradually ended and their main bastion, Carthage, fell in 695. The Arab conquerors had no trouble in overawing the sedentary Berber population. The Berber pastoralists were more formidable foes, however. One legend of the Kahina, the Jewish queen of the Aures mountains, relates how Berbers under her control drove the Arabs out of many of their coastal strong points in the late seventh century. Mythical as the Kahina might be, the story indicates how fierce the opposition to Arab control was. Ultimate Arab victory over the Berber pastoralists was achieved more by the religion of Islam than by force of arms. The Berbers had been prepared for monotheism by long association with Jewish merchants and Christian overlords, and many were still Donatist Christians. There is no way of accurately ascertaining how quickly Berbers accepted Islam. One indication of the rapidity is that the Arabs began the conquest of the Iberian peninsula in 711 with substantial Berber help.

The religiopolitical schisms within Islam played an important role in the history of Muslim Africa. In 659 the governor of Syria, Mu'awiya, seized the power of caliph from Muhammed's son-in-law Ali and established the administrative capital for the united empire at Damascus. The dynasty founded by Mu'awiya was called the Umayyad and was supported by the mass of Muslims until its overthrow in 750. These orthodox supporters of the new dynasty were called Sunnis.

The overthrow of Ali resulted in the creation of two major opposition factions within Islam. Those who viewed the deposition as illegal developed a contrary religious interpretation of Islam. Called Shi'ites, the leaders of this movement in time developed mystical concepts such as the return of the Mahdi, the great leader. Another deviationist group was the Kharijites, who tended to stress purity. Their doctrine was accepted by many

Berber groups in the Maghrib, particularly near Sijilmasa and in the Tripolitanian hinterland. It has been suggested that Berber nomads adopted this belief as a form of protest against authority, much as they had earlier embraced Donatist Christianity.

The Arabs in the Mideast absorbed the culture and habits of the more advanced peoples such as the Syrians and Persians whom they had conquered. As early as the eighth century the united Arab empire began to lose its vitality. This decline was first noticeable on the periphery of the empire. After 756 Spain had its own government all but independent of central control. In the middle of the eighth century the Umayyad caliphs were replaced by another dynasty, the Abbasids. The capital was moved from Damascus to Baghdad, thus shifting the center of the empire to the east. The nature of the empire changed under the Abbasids, and the distinct Arab character of Islamic culture was lost, particularly in the Mideast.

In Ifriqiyah (the old Roman province of Africa), the local dynasty had become practically independent from the caliphs by 800. The position of governor became hereditary, and this Aghlabid dynasty consolidated its position in Tunisia, restored its agricultural productivity, and reopened the trade routes to the interior. In Egypt the rulers were Turkish favorites of the Abbasid caliphs. By the close of the ninth century these Turkish governors broke with Baghdad and formed their own mercenary armies to resist the Abbasid attempts at reconquest. Egypt was to be controlled in future centuries by foreigners who were more concerned with maintaining their power than with providing good government.

The Shi'ites, persecuted by the Abbasids, worked everywhere to undermine Abbasid rule. At the close of the ninth century they were successful in converting the Berbers of Kabyles. They overthrew the Aghlabid rulers of the Ifriqiyah and established their own dynasty, the Fatamid, which aimed at the conquest of all Islam. The Fatamids compelled the obedience of most of the Berber tribes of the Maghrib and in 969 conquered Egypt. The conquest of Syria and the Hejaz soon followed, and the Fatamids moved their capital eastward to a new city, Al Kahira (Cairo), in 973. The Berbers thus reversed the direction of the previous conquests. The move of the Fatamid caliphs away from the Maghrib, however, was the signal for an uprising by the Sanhaja Berbers of the Kabyles. In order to crush this movement the Fatamids eventually shifted a num-

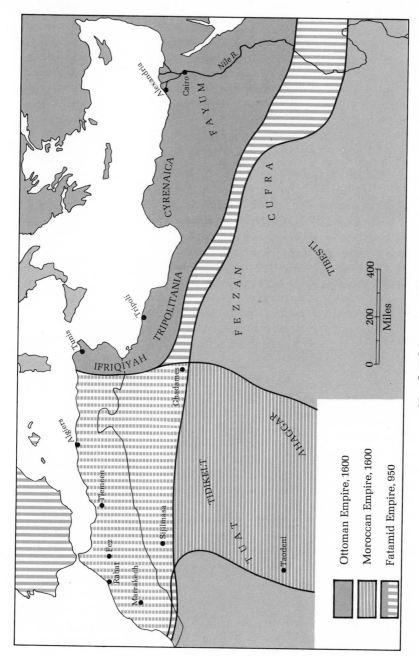

North African Empires

Ottoman Empire, 1600

Moroccan Empire, 1600

Fatamid Empire, 950

Miles

0   200   400

Alexandria
Cairo
Nile R.
FAYUM
CYRENAICA
Tripoli
TRIPOLITANIA
IFRIQIYAH
Tunis
CUFRA
FEZZAN
TIBESTI
Ghadames
Algiers
Tlemcen
Fez
Rabat
Sijilmasa
Marrakech
TIDIKELT
TUAT
AHAGGAR
Taodeni

ber of Arab Bedouin tribes from upper Egypt to the Maghrib. These Bedouin, particularly the Beni Hilal, were extremely primitive and had caused much trouble in Syria and Egypt. The arrival of the Bedouin in large numbers in the Maghrib broke the power of the Sanhaja in the eleventh century and eventually of the Zenata Berbers of the immediate hinterland. The Berbers absorbed the Arab culture and their societies began to disintegrate, although they retained their customs in a parochial form in part of the Atlas ranges. Their political system became fragmented into competitive tribal groups.

Fatamid caliphs retained power in Egypt until 1171, although in a greatly reduced form. Their possessions in the Maghrib had been lost, and the invasions of the Seljuk Turks wrested Syria away from them. Turkish generals in Syria were directly involved in containing the European crusaders. As a part of this defense against Christianity one of the generals, Saladin, overthrew Fatamid rule and established another short-lived foreign dynasty, the Ayyubids, in Egypt. This dynasty gave way in the middle of the thirteenth century to the military oligarchy of the Mamluks, which ruled behind the facade of an Abbasid caliph until the conquest of Egypt by the Ottoman Turks in 1517. Thereafter the Mamluks continued to govern Egypt under Turkish suzerainty. Their continued struggles for power, however, allowed the agricultural potential of Egypt to decay, and their commercial policies irreparably damaged the Egyptian economic system.

There emerged in North Africa no large, permanent political unit but rather a series of competitive polities created because of ethnic, religious, and personal differences. The triumph of Islam was cultural and religious. However different were the political systems, there existed a unitary culture with a common literary language. Christianity almost disappeared, particularly in the Maghrib. In northern Africa its strength had been sapped by the Donatist heresy, the Vandal conquest, and later the Byzantine occupation. The fact that Muslims were given preference for state offices in northern Africa also played an important role in the defeat of Christianity. In Egypt Coptic Christianity proved more viable, and throughout the early period of Arab conquest most of the population belonged to this native church. In time, however, with foreign settlers, mercenaries, and rulers more Egyptians became Muslim and began to merge with their conquerors to create the present Arabic-speaking Egyptian population.

In the western Maghrib divisions within Islam enabled Idris ibn 'Abd Allah in the latter part of the eighth century to create a large kingdom. Here he established the city of Fez, which became a major nothern terminal point for the trans-Saharan trade. This centralization imposed on the Berber peoples of the west was disturbed by the expansion of the Fatamids and intervention by the rival Umayyad dynasty of Spain. Such struggles for power allowed the Berber nomad tribes to regain control. The Sanhaja dominated the areas of southern Morocco, but they were being pressed in the tenth century by the eastern Berber nomads, the Zenata and the Tuareg. By the eleventh century southern Morocco and the western desert became an area of considerable conflict between hostile nomadic tribes.

Negro people of the Western Sudan

Little is known of the Negro people of West Africa before the rise of the kingdom of Ghana. Their lack of a written language and of any substantial architectural remains have forced the historian to depend for information upon observations made by later Mediterranean visitors. The Carthaginians and Romans, as already noted, had little direct contact with the peoples below the Sahara, since their economic interests among the Negro population were usually handled by Garmantian traders. In the time of troubles following the collapse of the Roman Empire even this type of trade was probably minimal. Good reports on the-peoples of the Western Sudan exist only from a period long after the kingdom of Ghana was established. These are accounts of the political, social, and economic situation of these people as seen through the eyes of an Islamic reporter. The earlier period is left largely to conjecture.

It is reasonable to assume that the present divisions of the Negro, as defined linguistically today, were apparent very early in the western savannah lands. In the extreme west in Futa were the ancestors of the Wolof and Serer. In a central location from the upper Senegal in the west to the great bend of the Niger in the east and extending to the forest areas to the south were Mande speakers. The northern group of the Mande have been called Soninke and Serakole and were located on the very fringes of the Sahara Desert. Along the Niger, downriver from present-day Gao, were located groups of Songhai fishermen and agriculturists. South and east of the Mande lived the Gur-speaking Negroes. Almost nothing is known of the groups living on the coastal forest fringes from the Gambia to the Niger delta. Movement into the forests was late, and one can only assume that the ancestors of the major forest Negro groups were settled somewhere in the savannah zone.

Observations of economic, political, and social organization among present West African peoples gives some basis for generalizing as to the probable way of life of the early savannah Negro. The economic basis for all of these people was a composite of agriculture, animal husbandry, hunting, and in some special areas fishing. Presumably the cultivation of various grains was the most important element for the majority of the people until the later introduction of East Indian plants. Slash and burn techniques were used to clear the land, and by allowing much of the available land to remain fallow agriculturists reached a compromise with the marginal soil. Iron implements made tasks easier and enabled people to increase their productivity to meet the needs of the growing population. In a few areas iron and gold were mined and worked. Village-based economies tended to be self-sufficient, with their own craftsmen providing the tools, utensils, and clothing needed by the village. In a very restricted way trading was carried on between the small political units. Mande and Serer groups living near the desert fringes were involved from a very early date in the trans-Saharan trade. Salt was one item in great demand among the savannah peoples. Except for the villages located near the sea the only way of obtaining this important commodity was by exchange with desert merchants.

Although the political structures of the Negro peoples varied, the majority were probably organized on the basis of descent groups. Under this arrangement the leader of the group was the eldest male. As the descent group became larger segments split from the original parent group. In some cases expansion incorporated other peoples into the political system. Thus many small villages in time developed around the original settlement. When this situation had come about one lineage was recognized as superior, and the political leader of all the villages would be chosen from it. The head of each satellite village was chosen in a manner similar to that used for selecting the chief.

It is important to realize that these political units were very small and functioned in a manner similar to the system, familiar to us, used by many of the Bantu clans as late as the nineteenth century. Further territorial expansion of these units and the complex, sophisticated bureaucracies needed to control them probably depended upon the arrival of new concepts brought by northern invaders.

Each political unit was also a modified theocracy, with chiefs and village heads having religious as well as secular duties. The religious system varied from area to area, but a few common characteristics can be hypothesized. A supreme deity was recognized along with a pantheon of lesser gods, most of whom were anthropomorphic. The deities were of two general types, those who directly controlled or were represented by natural forces and those who had once been men and who were responsible for the founding of the descent group or larger unit. The gods as spirits were always present, and there was no neat dividing line between the living and the dead. Concepts of the afterlife were expressed in the familiar terms of everyday existence. Spirits, both good and evil, were believed to have great power over the living. Therefore the chiefs and the people were concerned to keep away the bad and to propitiate the friendly spirits. Later this concern led to the development of special groups, priests, or secret societies which created and were responsible for the rituals of worship. Relatively sophisticated religious and secular attitudes and practices upon which more advanced ideas could build were present very early in these village societies. Later practices that were even more complex were brought from the north and changed unalterably the mode of life of the Negro people. In time the amalgam of the old and new political and religious concepts created institutions with common features throughout the savannah regions. Roland Oliver called this type of theocratic polity the Sudanic state.

Trans-Saharan trade routes

Early Islamic merchants, most of them from Syria, followed the soldiers and administrators into northern Africa. Later, as stability was assured and wealth increased, traders were drawn to North Africa from all parts of the empire. The Maghrib, with its well-established agriculture and flourishing cities, was well located to profit from the seaborne trade that linked the Muslim world. Interior trade routes were reopened, and the camel, which had been in general use in North Africa since before the third century, provided the means for conquering the desert.

Among the most important items of trade from the Maghrib to the east were slaves. In the years of conquest the pastoral Berber people had provided the bulk of these slaves. As the larger part of the population north of the Atlas mountains became converts to Islam and therefore could not legally be enslaved Arab traders turned to the trans-Saharan route to provide black pagans for the market. These routes had been utilized for trade at least as early as Carthaginian times. By the eighth century, however, many trading caravans were regularly making the dangerous desert crossing to trade with the Bilad-es-Sudan (the land of the blacks).

Before the desert could be traversed with maximum safety the water sources of the Sahara had to be tapped. Presumably many of the oases, particularly in the north, had been in use for centuries before the Arabs began to push south. These oases were located where water could be obtained by a minimum amount of work. There is considerable underground water in the Sahara. Rivers flow radially away from the Ahaggar and Tibesti highlands, and the Savornins Sea in the central and northern deserts covers an area of over one quarter of a million square miles. This sea is in reality an underground stratum of sand, in places a mile thick, which acts like a giant sponge to trap water. Further east there are two long, parallel fault lines extending south from the Gulf of Sirda. In some places in the low-lying areas created by the fault, called the Fezzan, there are permanent lakes, and water is found only a few feet below the surface.

Arab entrepreneurs began to develop the oases at the same time the caravan trade became important. In some locales the task of reaching water was easy, while in others, such as the Souf, one of the hottest, most arid parts of the Sahara, it was necessary to construct elaborate underground foggaras to intersect the water table and draw moisture from the subsoil. Some foggaras were as much as fifty feet below ground. The Arabs used great numbers of slaves to build and maintain the irrigation systems and to work the extensive date groves which were planted at all the oases. The slaves of the oases were initially Negro, but in time another type of slave, called Haratin, of mixed Arab-Berber-Negro antecedents, emerged.

Many oases, for example, Sijilmasa in the north and Walata in the south, became not only stopping places for caravans but also flourishing trade and manufacturing centers. Thousands of Arabs, Berbers, and Jews took up permanent residence in the Saharan towns. Agriculturists, businessmen, craftsmen, and bankers were all drawn by the opportunities offered at the oases. Perhaps as important as the advance of trade was the concomitant movement of Islam across the desert. At every oasis there would be a mosque, teachers, and perhaps holy men. In time large numbers of Islamic missionaries from these permanent desert bases followed the traders into the land of the blacks.

By the tenth century a number of major trans-Saharan routes had been developed. In the west one track began near the great bend of the Niger and proceeded north through the Taodeni oasis to Tindouf and Sijilmasa. From Sijilmasa routes branched to different North African cities. Another route began further west at Walata and went north to Taodeni, Taut, and then to the coast. The Fezzan route originated in the vicinity of Lake Chad and passed through Bilma, Kawar, and the Fezzan oases to Tripolitania. There were also east-west routes which linked far western towns such as Audaghost to the Niger bend, Lake Chad, and eventually to Dongola and Sennar on the Nile. Many secondary routes were also used to connect the trading cities of the north, and later there developed similar feeder routes linking the towns of Bornu to the Hausa cities and those of the Niger bend.

The relatively self-sufficient Negro societies of the savannah and fringe forest areas prized one product above all others — salt. Except for villages located near the sea there was no way to obtain this valuable commodity except by trade. Presumably salt had been the major item brought by the Garamantes in their trading ventures in the Sudan before the Christian era. Salt was easy to obtain in the Sahara, with large salt mines at Taotek, Taodeni, and Taghaza. At Taghaza, Ibn Battuta, a fourteenth-century traveler, reported that the people built their houses of salt blocks. This report confirmed the strange account of such a town by the Greek historian Herodotus 1800 years earlier. Some of the Negro peoples had gold, another commodity besides slaves that was in great demand throughout the Mediterranean world. There was no gold in the areas where the great trading cities on the Niger developed, but, further south there was much alluvial gold along West African streams. The southern watershed area of the Futa Jallon was particularly productive. Other forest products such as kola nuts later became important trade items. Besides salt the Arab traders brought with them manufactured products, dates, cowrie shells, and the curious blue and multicolored "aggrey beads" so prized by Negro traders.

The lands immediately to the north of the great Niger bend were in a most strategic location. Although neither gold nor salt was found there, they were a natural stopping place for traders. North African merchants had to prepare for a desert crossing as carefully as for a long ocean voyage. Ibn Battuta reported his crossing of the Sahara in detail. His caravan took twenty-five days to travel from Sijilmasa to Taghaza, and the entire journey to Walata lasted two full months. The distance, Tuareg marauders, and the possibility of losing the route and dying of thirst were ever-present dangers. The territory adjacent to the Niger provided such caravans the opportunity for a much needed rest and refitting. Arab traders probably had discovered very early that they could not safely penetrate to the sources of the gold. In this strategically located middle area there developed the first of the great western Sudanic kingdoms, the kingdom of Ghana.

The kingdom of Ghana

The first of the great states of the Western Sudan was Ghana, whose chief city was located approximately 200 miles north of present-day Bamako. It is not known when or how the kingdom was formed. Maurice Delafosse in 1912 hypothesized that the great changes in the traditional mode of living of the Negro people was caused by Judaicized Berbers who early established themselves as masters of the Soninke. In part this interpretation was based upon seventeenth-century collections of documents in the Western Sudan which referred to the earliest kings of Ghana as white men. With some modification this theory of foreign invaders has been repeated by the historians Roland Oliver and J. D. Fage, who point to the many similarities in patterns of ritual and organization in Ghana and the Mediterranean and Egyptian worlds. The presence of large numbers of Jewish merchants, craftsmen, and pastoralists in the Sahara at this period is well established. Large, prosperous Jewish populations were reported later to have lived at Tuat and Walata. The presence of pastoral Berbers on the fringes of the desert in the fourth century is also beyond question. The fact that a large number of persons were living in the Sahara who had knowledge of more advanced political, military, and economic systems lends support to the theory of northern origins for the people of Ghana.

There need not have been the type of master and servant relation implied by these explanations. It is possible that because of the need to establish better controls over the north-south trade some opportunistic Soninke Negroes in the Awkar area developed a larger state. If this occurred as tradition suggests in the fourth century, the region could have evolved into a major empire with a complex bureaucratic system by the time Arab visitors first wrote of it. Such an explanation would not rule out the incorporation of practices learned from Berber or Jewish traders.

By the time Islamic writers first mentioned Ghana the area had already developed far beyond a petty kingdom linking together a few village groups. Even if the original rulers had been foreigners, they had been absorbed into the local population. The kings of Ghana were Soninke, and they had established a far-flung territorial empire based on trade and village agriculture. Kingship in Ghana contained many elements of what has been called the Sudanic state. The king, who was held to be semidivine and whose well-being was considered necessary for the good of the state, was the fountainhead of justice and the intermediary between the people and the gods. His rule had divine sanction, but it was maintained by a centralized bureaucracy and an efficient army. Although the chief officers of the state were given economic prerogatives, Ghana did not operate from a feudal structure. These officials were appointed by the king and held their positions not by hereditary right but at the pleasure of the king. This efficient, centralized system contrasts sharply with the loosely organized, kinship-based village government observable among other West African Negro peoples.

The administrative center of the kingdom was a town called Al Ghaba by Arab geographers. Al Bakri, the eleventh-century geographer of Cordoba, described Al Ghaba as a big town com-

posed mainly of mud and thatch buildings. The king's compound, encircled by a wall, was very large and comprised a
number of dome-covered service buildings and a palace. Located
a few miles from the Soninke site was Kumbeh Saleh, the town
reserved for Muslim traders and businessmen. Originally a
small makeshift place where foreign traders were sent to live
until they had completed their trading, the town in time became
a permanent one. Many stone buildings were erected here, including the mosque. To this second town came not only men
interested in business but diplomatic representatives, wandering scholars, and perhaps most important, imams, muezzins, and
reciters of a still-dynamic Islamic faith. It is impossible to ascer-
tain how successful Islam had been in converting the pagan
peoples of Ghana by the eleventh century, but the existence of
the two towns indicates that the king and his bureaucracy still
remained aloof from the new religion. It is therefore doubtful
that many of the people of Ghana, except for those on the
fringes of the desert, had given up their old religions.

The continuing greatness of Ghana was based upon its control of the territory between the desert and the highland areas
of West Africa. Ghana did not itself produce anything valuable
either for the North Africans or for the village traders of the
south. However, Ghanaian power effectively stopped the northern merchants and forced them to accept the good offices of the
king if they wished to obtain gold and slaves. After the establishment of titular control over its rival, Audaghost, in 990
Ghana controlled the supplies that made the great oases towns
wealthy. Gold was the most sought-after commodity by the
Arab merchants, and the gold trade was a near-monopoly of
the king of Ghana. Much of the gold came from the Wangara
district just beyond the southern frontier of Ghana, a frontier
that presumably had been established by economic necessity
and the failure of Ghana to conquer the gold-producing lands.

Gold was obtained from the southern areas by means of
the silent trade. The Arab georgrapher Al Ma'sudi, who visited
Ghana in the tenth century, described in detail this method of
business. At the border of Wangara, presumably at well-known
trading places, merchants from Ghana would leave their wares.
These goods varied, but they included manufactured items such
as knives and cloth, and always salt. The merchants then went
away and the forest traders came and left what they believed
to be the equivalent in gold and then retired. If the Ghanaian

traders were satisfied, they took the gold and left. The southern traders could then take the other barter goods. If one party was not satisfied, the procedure would continue by subtraction until a bargain agreeable to both sides had been reached.

There is no way of ascertaining the value of the gold trade. A tenth-century traveler, Ibn Hawqal, reported that all trading cities such as Audaghost and Sijilmasa depended for their prosperity upon Ghana, whose king was the richest prince in the world. He told of seeing one draft by a merchant at Audaghost for the equivalent of one quarter of a million dollars. Other commentators related details of the tolls imposed by the king upon traders. These included all nuggets of gold found or purchased and a share of the gold dust. The king also collected heavy duties on every load of salt entering the country and twice the amount for each load leaving. Presumably there were also tolls imposed on all other trade items.

Ghana's domination of the economy of the Western Sudan was contested by the Sanhaja Berbers, who in turn were being pressed on the north by the Zenata Berbers. The city of Audaghost was the major trading center controlled by the Sanhaja. Ghana conquered Audaghost in 990, but this victory did not end the threat of the Sanhaja. Trade competition against powerful Ghana helped create the environment that made possible the Almoravid conquests.

The Almoravids

The Sanhaja Berbers, who controlled the territory around Audaghost and the city itself until the conquest by Ghana in 990, were not unified but were divided into three rival branches — the Lemtuna, Masufa, and Godala. Until 1054 the Berber population was ruled by a governor appointed by the king of Ghana. This was a period of intermixing between Berber and Negro, and the territory around Audaghost became a battleground between Islam and the older religion of Ghana. The conflict was resolved in favor of Islam by the activities of the leaders of a new puritanical sect, the Almoravids.

The traditional story of the beginnings of the Almoravids is that Yahia ibn Ibrahim, a devout leader of a Godala group of the Sanhaja, made a pilgrimage to Mecca. Visiting the holy places, he became aware of the deficiencies of the practice of Islam in the Sudan. On his return journey he discovered at

Sijilmasa a puritanical Marabout, Ibn Yacin, whom he per-
suaded to accompany him to Audaghost. The preaching of Ibn
Yacin, however, irritated most of the Berbers of the Sudan, and
after the death of his protector Yahia he was forced to retire
with his followers to an island in the Senegal River. There at
his monastery, or ribat, the devotees followed an extremely puritanical regime. Gradually the influence of the Almoravids (the
people of the ribat) spread among the Berbers. Legend says that
Yacin and his newly formed army united the three segments
of the Sanhaja by 1042. Later Yacin proclaimed a jihad, and
in 1054 Audaghost fell to the Almoravids. Ibn Yacin died in
1057, but the united Berbers under Yasuf ibn Tashfin swept
north, conquering Morocco by 1069. Within twenty years the
Almoravid tide had moved into the Iberian peninsula.

A schismatic movement within the Almoravid leadership
was of more importance to the Western Sudan than was the
main northern effort. The leader of this smaller group was Abu
Bakr, who directed the attention of his followers toward seizing
complete control of the southern end of the trans-Saharan trade
routes. The campaign against Ghana began in 1062 and was
completed in 1076. Abu Bakr was killed while suppressing a
revolt in 1087, and Almoravid central power in the Sudan soon
disappeared. The influence of its leaders was then concentrated
in smaller, weaker city-states such as Walata. Ghana regained
its independence in a much reduced form, with its power effective only in Aukar and Bassikunu.

The major political contributions of the Almoravids were
disruptive. They had conquered Ghana but were not strong
enough to dominate the entire region, which previously had
owed allegiance to the rulers of Ghana. The vacuum of power
this formed was filled by a number of competitive political units,
each under its own ambitious leaders. The most lasting result of the Almoravid interlude was the speeding up of the
rate of conversion of animistic peoples to Islam. In this connection it should be noted how easy it was for people to accept
Islam. A recitation of the statement, "There is no God but Allah
and Muhammed is his Prophet" was the first step. The new
convert was not required to change his old patterns of living
to any great extent. He accepted the necessity of saying five
prayers a day in a prescribed fashion, renounced alcohol, and
put on a cloak to conceal his nakedness. The social and familial
structure remained relatively untouched after acceptance of the

new religion. This permissiveness, although making possible quick conversions of large areas, was responsible for the absorption into Islam of concepts and beliefs that were foreign to the purer form of the religion as practiced in the Middle East.

Mali

The destruction of Ghana's power over the southern trading sphere led to the consolidation of power on the local level, which in turn led to wars between these smaller political units to decide which was to control the riches of the trans-Saharan trade. In addition to Ghana and the Muslim state of Walata, the most important of these successor states were Kaniaga and Kangaba. Fulani, who had moved eastward from the Tekrur area, seem to have provided the rulers for the mixed population of Kaniaga. Because of the importance of the So clan in this process, the short-lived empire was called the Sosso. The Sosso king, Sumanguru, incorporated the neighboring area of Duara into his empire and in 1203 conquered Ghana. In the south the Mande rulers of Kangaba began to expand their authority, at first away from the territories of the Sosso. Inevitably, however, the two states came into conflict. The struggle was motivated not only by competition for economic and political influence but also by religious differences. Most of the Sosso had not been converted to Islam, while this process had been completed among the Mande rulers in the twelfth century.

In 1230 a new king, Sundiata (Mari Djata), came to the throne of Kangaba. He revised the bureaucracy of the state and created a standing army. With these reforms completed he challenged the Sosso for mastery of the Western Sudan. In 1235 at the battle of Karina Sundiata decisively defeated and dispersed the Sosso army. Five years later all of Ghana was incorporated into his domains, and he destroyed the old capital of Kumbeh. Sundiata shifted his place of residence from Jeriba in Kangaba to a new city, Niani, further down the Niger, which was more centrally located within his empire. The term Mali, meaning where the king lives, came to be applied to the new Mande state created by Sundiata. By the time of Sundiata's death (about 1260) all of the Sudan from Tekrur in the west to the borders of Songhai in the east was under Malian rule.

With the reimposition of centralized authority in the Western Sudan trade with the north, which had fallen off during the period of wars, began to flourish once again. Niani became the richest and most important city in the Sudan. Like Kumbeh, its importance was based on the control exercised by its rulers over the north-south trade. Uli, Sundiata's son and successor, attempted the conquest of Songhai and probably brought the gold-producing areas of Wangara under Malian rule.

Throughout its history Mali, not unlike European states of the same period, is a study of both strength and instability. The comparison can be extended further because the institutional problems in feudal Europe were of the same type as in Mali. Large states with a heterogeneous population are difficult to rule, particularly when communication between various parts of the polity are slow. In Mali there was early developed a bureaucracy of able administrators appointed by the king to deal with such problems as finance, defense, and foreign affairs. Conquered areas were administered in the name of the emperor by appointed governors and their aides. In time the higher positions came to be regarded by the officers as hereditary, and certain powerful factions operated openly at the courts of the Malian rulers. Strong emperors could keep these divisive forces in check either by playing one against the other or by overawing them by force. Weak rulers or men whose claim to the throne was questionable found it difficult to control the factions.

There were three main periods of disorder in Mali created by disputed claims to the throne. The first followed soon after the creation of the empire. Sundiata was succeeded by three sons, Uli, Wati, and Khalifa. The last of these seems to have been weak-minded and cruel and was probably overthrown by the adherents of Abu Bakr, the son of one of Sundiata's daughters. Abu Bakr's reign was quite brief and subsequently the throne was seized by Sakura, a freed slave of the royal family. Thus Mali in the thirty years following the death of Sundiata had five rulers, only two of which, Uli and Sakura, possessed the ability necessary to rule the newly formed empire.

After Sakura the throne reverted to the royal line. The third emperor of the fourteenth century, a descendant of a brother of Sundiata, was Musa, the greatest of the Malian rulers. After his death, probably in 1337, a brief struggle for power ensued before Sulayman, Musa's brother, came to the throne in 1341. Sulayman's death in 1360 was a signal for civil war between his descendants and those of Musa and a consequent weakening of the position of the emperor. Mansa Magha II, who took

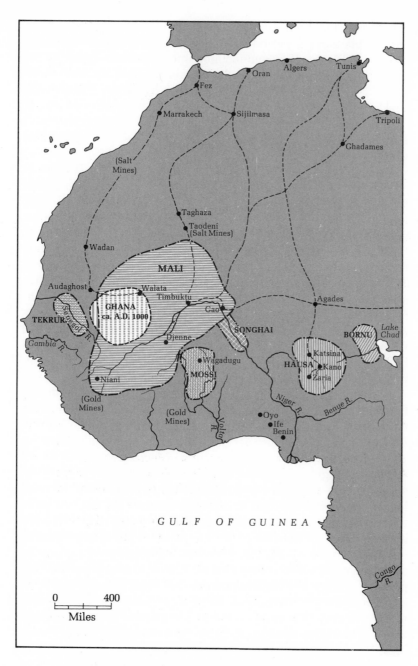

Major States of the Western Sudan, about 1332

the throne in about 1390, and his chief adviser, Mari Djata, ended this second period of near-anarchy in Niani. Since the power of Magha II depended not upon his own capacity but upon that of his counselor, the period of stability was short-lived. The decline of Mali in the fifteenth century can in large part be attributed to the weakness of the successors of Magha II. This third period of decentralization was not arrested by a strong man, and Mali gradually ceased to be the major state of the Western Sudan.

The intrigues at court first affected the empire on its periphery. Tekrur, Wangara, and later Songhai and some of the desert areas pursued independent policies whenever the situation allowed. Despite the political struggles at the capital, Malian domination of the Western Sudan was not really shaken until the fifteenth century. There were enough strong rulers before then not only to hold the empire together but also to expand it. The usurper Sakura in the latter thirteenth century put down a revolt in Tekrur and pushed the Malian border north to the copper-producing areas of the Sahara. Musa was so successful as a ruler that before his death only the rising trade city of Djenne and the Mossi states lay beyond his domination. Songhai had been conquered, and even though it soon regained a large part of its freedom its rulers paid tribute to Niani.

Malian civilization and power were at their peak during the reigns of Musa and his brother Sulayman. Ibn Khaldun, the Arab historian of the Western Sudan, and the Egyptian observer Al Umari have both left detailed accounts of Musa's reign. In 1324 Musa undertook a pilgrimage to Mecca by way of North Africa and Egypt. The reports, although probably exaggerated, state that the emperor was accompanied by 500 slaves carrying heavy gold staffs and that in his caravan were 100 camels laden with gold dust. These riches Musa used for alms, dispensing the gold so lavishly that even the Egyptians were impressed. On his return to the Sudan Musa brought with him an entourage of scholars, many of whom settled at Timbuktu and with the support of the emperor began the work that made the city the most influential seat of learning in the Sudan. Musa's reign was also a great period of building. One of his architects was probably the first to utilize fired brick in the construction of major buildings. Musa, too, was responsible for the erection of at least two great mosques, one at Timbuktu and the other at Gao.

Another major source of information concerning Mali is

Ibn Battuta, who was a visitor to Mali from February 1352 until December of the following year. He was deeply impressed by the administrative structure, the system of justice, the piety of the people, and the wealth of the emperor and country. He described in detail the panopoly of the court of Sulayman. Everywhere there were signs of the wealth and splendor of the master of the trans-Saharan trade whom other commentators noted was more careful with his expenditures than had been Musa.

Many interrelated factors were responsible for the decline and eventual eclipse of the great Mande kingdom. For one thing, the kingdom never really recovered from the civil strife in the period after 1360. In addition, the weakness of successive rulers was paralleled by dangers to the state from outside threats. The Berbers became more active in the fifteenth century, and the Mossi, who had never been conquered, grew bolder in their raids on Malian territory. By 1450 Walata, Timbuktu, and Macina were all independent of the emperor. In the 1470s Mossi armies plundered the central area of Mali and soon afterward the Wolof in Tekrur declared themselves independent. Aside from the ineptness of the late Malian rulers the major reason for the decline in the fortunes of Mali can be attributed to the growing power of the competitive Niger River state of Songhai.

Songhai

Before the seventh century the Songhai were located along the banks of the Middle Niger, upriver from Bussa. They were divided into two groups — the Sorko, who were fishermen, and the Gabibi, who were agriculturists. In the seventh and eighth centuries some Lemtuna Berbers from the desert invaded this territory and established the first large Songhai kingdom centered on the town of Kukya. Many of the Sorko resisted the new alien dynasty and moved upstream to found a new town, Gao, located near the southern terminus of an old trans-Saharan trade route which could have been used as early as Garamantian times. Gao and Kukya were in continuous conflict until the Sorko were overcome in the ninth century. By the middle of the eleventh century the Songhai kingdom had become second only to Ghana in wealth in the Western Sudan. The Dia ruling dynasty was converted to Islam some time in the eleventh century. The masses of the Songhai seem to have resisted the new religion of their rulers — many, in fact, still held their traditional beliefs at the time of Sunni Ali three centuries later.

Songhai was conquered by Mali in the early part of the reign of Musa but regained most of its independence shortly afterward (about 1335). The Songhai kings continued to pay tribute to Mali throughout the fourteenth century and to acknowledge the Malian emperors as overlords. Mali's growing weakness, however, enabled Songhai to expand its territories and its economic influence. As with Mali, the basis for the strength of the kingdom was as much support from the semi-pagan agricultural villages as from the Islamic merchants. By this time any Berber characteristics within the ruling families had long before been absorbed and the rulers of Songhai were Negro.

Although Songhai was a large, rich kingdom before the fifteenth century, the establishment of a great empire fell to Sunni Ali Ber (1464–1492). Perhaps because he was not a devout Muslim, Arabic records, without exception, picture him as a talented but remorseless and tyrannical ruler. Sunni Ali rejected the earlier practice of obtaining a fighting force by methods that were roughly equivalent to those used in Europe under feudalism. Instead, he created a professional army, which except in special cases would do all the fighting. The first major military triumph achieved by this force was the capture of Timbuktu, which had been a Songhai town before it was incorporated into Mali. Its location made it an important trade center, and the Malian kings had made it the most important center of learning in the Sudan. Internal problems within Mali, however, had enabled the Tuareg to conquer Timbuktu in the third decade of the fifteenth century. The rule of these desert warriors had generally been supported by the educated elites of the city, who continued this support even after Sunni Ali had announced his intention to take Timbuktu. In 1468 the plans of the Songhai king became an actuality, and Sunni Ali took his revenge upon the educated Muslims who had supported his enemies. Later chroniclers of the Sudan never forgave Sunni Ali his treatment of fellow-Muslims.

The next important addition to the Songhai empire was the city of Djenne, located approximately 300 miles southwest of Timbuktu on the Bani River, a tributary of the Niger. The city, founded in the late twelfth or early thirteenth century by the Soninke, was so defensible, protected as it was by swamps and

waterways, that it had withstood all attempts by Mali to conquer it. A great commercial center, Djenne was probably more
important in the fifteenth century than Niani. Like Timbuktu,
Djenne was a haven for scholars and theologians because of its
university. Sunni Ali could not obtain this prize by the usual
military methods. According to traditional accounts, he be-
sieged the city for seven years, shifting his army and canoemen
with the season to block the entrance routes. The city fell in
1473, and Sunni Ali is reported to have sealed the union of
Songhai and Djenne by marrying the queen mother of the city.
Other Songhai acquisitions were Walata and the eastern areas
of Mali. In 1480 Songhai suffered an invasion by the redoubtable
Mossi kingdom of Yatenga, whose armies reached and sacked
Walata before Ali drove them out of the kingdom.

Sunni Ali was succeeded in 1492 by his son, who was no
more careful in his religious practices than his father. Dissatisfaction with the flaunting of Islam must have been widespread
among the Muslim intellectuals even before the death of Sunni
Ali. Within six months the new ruler faced a major revolt, which
was at first contained but which eventually drove him from the
kingdom. The leader of the revolt, a very devout Muslim, Askia
Muhammad Touré, thus founded a new ruling dynasty. Within
three years Muhammad's control of Songhai was so secure that
he could leave on a pilgrimage to Mecca. The journey, begun in
1495, lasted two years and was hardly less ostentatious than
that of Musa 170 years before. The vast sums of gold that he
took to distribute as alms caused great comment everywhere
he went and indicate the great wealth of the kingdom.

Upon his return Askia Muhammad undertook a series of
campaigns to extend the political and economic influence of
Songhai. In 1498 he revenged the earlier Mossi invasion by taking and plundering Yatenga. He annexed even more of Malian
territory in the west in the early sixteenth century, and in 1515
the oasis of Agades was taken and Songhai authority was established in the district of Air. The Songhai army penetrated into
Hausaland, where the rulers of Kano were defeated. Only the
smaller kingdom of Kebbi, north of the Hausa states, was able
to oppose the Songhai successfully.

Although responsible for greatly increasing the territory
of the empire, Askia Muhammad's greatest contribution was
the construction of the most efficient administrative system
ever seen in the Sudan. The social system that existed even

before the Askia dynasty was relatively simple. At the apex were the descendants of the original Songhai leaders of Kukya. Next in importance were the free men of the towns and cities. In the towns the traditional rulers were the most powerful, while in the cities the wealthy traders occupied a favored position. The officers of the professional army held an ambivalent status, depending upon their birth, but generally were the social equals of the merchants. At the bottom of society were the war captives and slaves, many of whom were formed into labor battalions by the Askias. The social structure, although rigid, did allow for upward mobility.

Sunni Ali had created a central bureaucracy and divided the empire into provinces, each controlled by an appointed governor. Askia Muhammad improved this central organization by establishing permanent offices at Gao to supervise different functions of the state. Each office was controlled by a minister appointed by the king and directly responsible to him. The most important ministry was the treasury, but almost equally influential were the ministries of the army and navy, agriculture, The king acted as the supreme court and also reserved to himself the appointment of governors and the conduct of foreign affairs.

Askia Muhammad, after thirty-six years of rule, old and probably blind, was confronted by a palace revolt led by his sons. He was forced to abdicate and died in exile ten years later in 1538. After his abdication there was a further struggle for power between factions loyal to each of the sons. Three of Muhammad's sons ruled in succession between 1528 and 1539, and the empire was in danger of being torn apart. The decline was halted by Ishaq (1539–1549), who executed all his rivals. The new Askia despatched Songhai forces to Dendi and reimposed Songhai control over the salt mines at Taghaza. His successor, Daud (1549–1582), continued the forward military and economic policy of Songhai. Yatenga was invaded, Macina was reconquered, and Mali once again was incorporated into the empire.

Control of the caravan routes by Songhai in the time of Daud was being disputed by a new formidable force, Morocco. The expansion of European traders into eastern markets and their growing dominance of the Mediterranean had created a minor economic crisis among all the states of northern Africa. The Portuguese as early as 1415 had begun what they hoped to be a continuation of their crusades by seizing Ceuta. From this base the Portuguese rulers contested with the sultans for control of northern Morocco. The Spanish, who were at war with the powerful Ottoman Empire, attempted to seize Tripoli in 1560 and seized and plundered Tunis in 1573. With the economy of their state thus threatened by a resurgent Europe, the sultans of Morocco became more concerned with controlling as much of the rich trans-Saharan trade as possible. In 1581 an army of Sultan al Mansur occupied the Tuat and Tigurarin oases. Three years later a large Moroccan army was lost when it attempted to cross the Sahara to attack Songhai. In the following year the Moroccans were successful in taking the rich salt mining area of Taghaza from the Songhai.

In 1590 al Mansur sent another army into the desert whose objective was the conquest of Songhai. This army was a small, highly efficient group of approximately 3,000 men, well trained and armed with the latest European firearms. Its leader, Judar Pasha, a Spanish eunuch, had been raised in Morocco and was recognized as an excellent general. The desert was crossed with a minimal loss of life and Judar's army confronted the numerically superior Songhai force north of Gao in early 1591. The guns of the Moroccans triumphed over the Songhai cavalry and bowmen. Gao was evacuated, and shortly afterward Timbuktu also fell to the invaders. The Songhai empire disintegrated after these defeats and the Songhai were able to hold only the territory of Dendi. Ostensibly al Mansur controlled the central trade routes to the Western Sudan.

Successor states of the Western Sudan

The Moroccans soon discovered that the main object of their conquest, control of the gold-producing areas, was not possible. Nor did they have the manpower to reconstruct totally the empire they had destroyed. They could not even crush the remnants of the Songhai who had retreated to the swampy areas of Dendi. The defeat of the Songhai had been a signal for dissident peoples such as the Fulani and Taureg to move at will throughout the Western Sudan. The Moroccan conquerors could only hold firmly the areas adjacent to the cities of Gao, Djenne, and Timbuktu. Profits accruing to the sultans of Morocco from their new conquest, although substantial, were much less than was expected, not only because of the inability of the Moroccans to dominate the trade and politics of the Sudan but also because the trans-Saharan trade was becoming less important. European traders on the fringes of the West African coast were diverting large amounts of materials that previously had found their way to the trade marts of the Western Sudan. The sultans of Morocco continued to send men and supplies from the north until 1618, when they concluded that the project was not worth the cost and it was abandoned.

Moroccan authority in the Sudan was in theory maintained by a pasha at Timbuktu, who until 1660 claimed to represent the sultan of Morocco. There were kaids located at Djenne and at Gao with a portion of the Moroccan army. Traditional rulers living under the rule of the new masters of these cities were generally left alone so long as they paid the tribute money demanded of them. In time the bulk of the army became Negro and the officers were the sons of Moroccans and local women. These mixed upper classes called themselves the Arma and chose their own leaders, including the pashas. The dependence of pashas and kaids upon the army led to extreme political instability, since a pasha could be unseated as easily as created. In the latter seventeenth century the weakness of the pashas was attested to by their payment of tribute to the Bambara rulers of Segu. The importance of the great trading centers declined at about the same rate. Long before the death of the last pasha in 1780 the economic importance of Timbuktu and Gao were minimal, and the reality of political power in the Western Sudan was divided between the desert Tuareg, the Mande kingdom of Macina, and the Bambara states of Segu and Kaarta.

The failure of the pashas of Timbuktu to reconstruct an empire comparable to the one they had destroyed resulted in the appearance of competitive states in the Western Sudan. The three most powerful successors of Songhai were the Bambara states of Segu and Kaarta and the kingdom of Macina. The Bambara were a branch of the Mande and formed at one time a part of the kingdom of Mali. With Songhai hegemony many Bambara began to concentrate near the Niger port city of Segu. By the seventeenth century the city was an important secondary trading center for the Western Sudan. The people of Segu resisted conversion to Islam, and its rulers maintained their independence from Songhai and later the pashas of Timbuktu. In the eighteenth century Segu dominated the Niger territory from Timbuktu west to Tekrur on the upper reaches of the

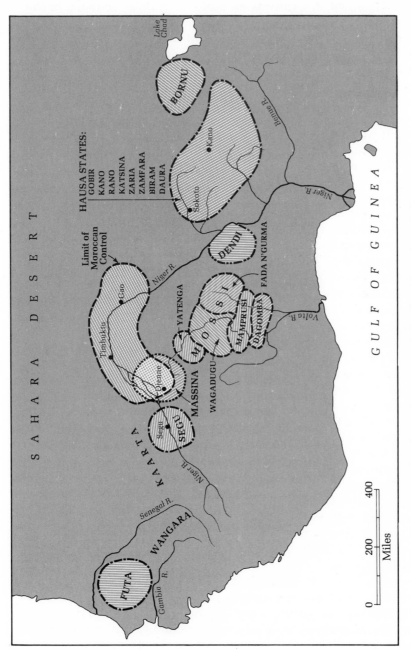

HAUSA STATES:
GOBIR
KANO
RANO
KATSINA
ZARIA
ZAMFARA
BIRAM
DAURA

Limit of
Moroccan
Control

Major West African States in the Seventeenth Century

Senegal River. Kaarta was an offshoot of Segu, founded in the seventeenth century. Located northwest of Segu, it was much weaker than the parent state but retained enough power throughout the eighteenth century to resist a series of attempts by the kings of Segu to conquer it.

Another political unit with localized power was the "pagan" kingdom of Macina, the center of which was a fertile island in the Niger River below Djenne. The kings of Macina were not really independent, since they paid tribute to the pashas of Timbuktu and later to the kings of Segu. Although the majority of the people were Mande agriculturists, a significant minority were Fulani pastoralists. These Fulani had a special position within the kingdom, having their own kings, the Diallo, who ruled alongside the Mande kings.

In the far west along the Senegal River was the kingdom of Futa, which had earlier been called Tekrur. As mentioned earlier, the Fulani (called also Peul, Fulbe, or Fula) appear to have originated there. The short-lived Sosso empire of Sumanguru was based upon Fulani migrants from Tekrur. After its defeat by Sundiata large numbers of Fulani retreated to the Senegal, where they reestablished a hegemony which lasted until the fourteenth century, when the Wolof broke away and formed their own states out of the western segment of Tekrur. A Fulani dynasty continued to rule in the remaining area eastward to the territory of Segu. The mass of people in Futa were not Fulani but a mixture of Bambara, Mandingo, Wolof, and Fulani, who were called Tucolors. Unlike their masters, they had a long tradition of adherence to Islam. In the eighteenth century Tucolor religious teachers launched a series of jihads which overthrew the Fulani overlords and reimposed Muslim law under Tucolor rulers. The opposition to the Fulani rulers of Futa was based as much upon protests against the Fulani political and social system as it was motivated by religious differences. The later jihad organized by the Fulani Usuman dan Fodio and directed against the Hausa states was part of this general protest begun in Futa.

By the eighteenth century the Fulani were located not only in Futa and Macina but small groups of them were scattered throughout the interior from the Senegal River to the Camerouns. Elements of the Fulani had reached Hausaland probably as early as the thirteenth century. They were originally ultraconservative cattle tenders. Although they reached some agreement with the dominant agriculturists among whom they lived, they held aloof from their culture. Because of this the Cow Fulani, the largest and most primitive group, retained their Caucasian characteristics even after hundreds of years of association with Negro peoples. In more developed areas such as Hausaland some of the Fulani moved into the towns, intermarried with other groups, took up trades, and became Muslim. These town Fulani (Fulanin Gidda) very soon lost their special characteristics and except for their language became indistinguishable from other townsmen. In the eighteenth century the town Fulani were very important in carrying forward reforms aimed at improving Muslim society and in converting the pagans. The jihad of Usuman dan Fodio was originally a protest movement of the Fulani against the excesses of the ostensibly Islamic Hausa states.

Other Sudanic states

Three major political areas which, although they intrude on the history of the Western Sudanic empires, actually belong to a separate line of historic development are the Mossi, Kanem-Bornu, and Hausa states. The Mossi resisted the later cultural, religious, and political influences from the north. Formed of a blending of pagan pastoralists and Gur and Mande farmers, the Mossi states retained their culture and independence long after their northern neighbors had been transformed by Mediterranean influences. Kanem-Bornu, located near Lake Chad, was perhaps initially influenced more by westward migrating ideas from the Nile region than from North Africa. Its location insured it from being incorporated into the great states of Ghana, Mali, and Songhai. Its development, although parallel in many ways to that of other Sudanic states, was accomplished within a more stable framework. Except for the Bulala wars, which drove them from Kanem, there were few outside forces that could challenge the dominance of the kings of Bornu. Finally, the Hausa city-states, partly due to their location but more because of the choice of their rulers, never became expansive in the same manner as the polities to the northwest. Even the greatest of the Hausa kingdoms such as Katsina and Zamfara politically affected only a small area. There was never in the period before the jihad of the nineteenth century even a meaningful political union of the city-states.

THE MOSSI STATES

The five Mossi kingdoms were located between the Volta River and the great bend of the Niger. The first of these states was Mamprussi, which was probably founded in the early thirteenth century. As more territory was conquered Mossi power created the states of Yatenga, Fada-N-Gurma, Wagadugu, and Dagomba. During the period of state building in Hausaland a group of pastoral people resident near Zamfara moved westward and invaded the areas of the Upper Volta region. Possessing cavalry and a better military organization, they imposed their will upon the indigenous Gur and Mande. These overlords intermarried with the Mande, but in time came to accept the language and religious beliefs of the Gur, thus creating at Mamprussi a composite culture.

The Mossi in the fourteenth and fifteenth centuries ranged far beyond the boundaries of their states. They ravaged Timbuktu in 1338 and thereafter acted as a block against further southward expansion of Mali and Songhai while continuing to threaten the rich trading cities to the north. An expedition from Yatenga in 1480 reached as far as Walata and even caused the great conqueror Sunni Ali considerable trouble. All of the Mossi states traded with the forest peoples and also with the trading cities of the Sudan. Major items from the south in this trade were gold, slaves, and kola nuts. The organization of each state was Sudanic in nature, with a quasidivine king, bureaucracy, and religion providing the means and sanction for rule. The rise of Ashanti in the eighteenth century blocked Mossi trade to the south, and in time Dagomba and Mamprussi almost became appendages to the Ashanti confederation. Nevertheless, the Mossi states maintained their religion, system of government, and a large area of stability in the open savannah lands south of the Niger until the coming of the French in the latter nineteenth century.

KANEM-BORNU

The stories of the founding of Kanem are tied to migrations of Zaghawa pastoralists in the seventh and eighth centuries. Earlier the Zaghawa were believed to be Berbers, but it now appears that they were probably Negro. They established he-

gemony over some of the Sao people who lived in the vicinity
of Lake Chad. The Sao had developed a relatively high material
culture, being excellent metal and pottery craftsmen. Their
political development, however, had not advanced beyond the
village-state level. The Zaghawa, who were certainly nomads,
established larger, more powerful political units based upon the
self-sufficient village societies. Practically nothing is known
about these societies, although one of them later grew into the
empire of Kanem, with its capital, Njimi, located somewhere
northeast of Lake Chad.

The kings or mais of Kanem before the coming of Islam
probably were considered semidivine. Their authority was
wielded through a bureaucracy and aristocracy, the most
important elements of which were royal relatives. Later when
the empire had grown the important governorships were always
held by members of the royal family. The queen mother held an
honored position in society and exercised great power over the
kings. The senior wife of the mai also had great influence. Much
of the wealth of ancient Kanem was gained from recruiting and
selling slaves to northern and eastern markets. According to
tradition, Mai Ume was converted to Islam in the latter part of
the eleventh century. In the next two centuries Kanem with its
highly organized army expanded not only north along the
Fezzan route but also southward into Bornu.

Quarrels between various factions of the ruling dynasty in
the thirteenth century ended the expansion of Kanem. The
system of appointing members of the royal family to be
governors of important provinces also aided in the breakdown
of central authority. This internecine conflict continued throughout the fourteenth century at the same time that the mais were
attempting to hold off the neighboring Bulala nomads. Finally,
in the 1380s or '90s Mai Umar ibn Idris abandoned Kanem to
the Bulala and moved his capital to Bornu. The seat of the mai's
authority was moved in 1470 to Birni N'gazargamo on the south
bank of the Yobe River, and this city remained the capital of
Bornu until its capture by the Fulani in 1812.

It took over a century after their defeat by the Bulala for
the mais to consolidate their power in Bornu. The Sao of Bornu
were eventually overcome, and a defensible frontier was established between the Bulala in Kanem. In the early sixteenth
century Mai Idris Katakarmabe (1507–1529) reincorporated
Kanem into the territories of Bornu and also became titular over-

lord of the Hausa states. Bornu became involved in the complicated struggle for power between the Songhai under Askia Muhammad and the ruler (kanta) of the small powerful kingdom of Kebbi. Until the defeat of the Songhai in 1591 the Hausa states were a battleground for contending empires.

Shortly before the fall of Songhai Mai Idris Aloma, the greatest of the Bornu emperors, came to the throne. In a long, brilliant reign Idris reformed the state, army, and religion. A devout Muslim, he reinstituted old punishments against idolatry, obscenity, and adultery. He subsidized charities, built a number of mosques, and most important instituted a strict observance of Islamic law in place of customary law. Judges utilizing the Koran and Sunna were given the responsibility of administering justice. Thus the expansion of Bornu during Idris Aloma's reign meant the expansion of Islam. The emperor continued the policy established by his predecessors of appointing men to positions of trust who owed everything to the ruler. Even slaves were given high office. Members of the royal house were given honors and kept close to the king's court. The lesson of the old empire of Kanem had been learned well. The army was similar to other Sudanese military forces. The cavalry of the nobility was the favored branch while the bulk of the villagers, armed with bows and spears, acted as infantry. Idris added a new element, a force of musketeers, handpicked from his household slaves and trained by Turkish instructors.

Most of the wars of Mai Idris were directed toward reimposing his control over tributary states. There were a number of campaigns against the Tuareg of Air, the Bulala of Kanem, and the Sao on the fringes of Bornu. At his death in 1617 Idris left Bornu in a position of supremacy in the central Sudan. Little is known of the detailed affairs of Bornu between this date and the Fulani jihad of the early nineteenth century. Soon after Idris the rise of the Jukun kingdom of Kororofa with its center on the Benue River posed a threat to Bornu. The Jukun were mainly raiders and did not attempt to hold their northern conquests. In the middle of the seventeenth century they attacked the Hausa states of Kano and Katsina and invaded Bornu in 1680. Nevertheless, the mais of Bornu held them in check and eventually a peace treaty, probably advantageous to Bornu, was arranged between the two empires. Continual pressure from the Tuareg on the northern boundaries of Bornu and the growing influence of the Hausa states of Katsina, Zamfara, and Gobir restricted the power of the mais to the area around Lake Chad. By the reign of Ali ibn Hamdun in the latter eighteenth century Bornu possessed only a shadow of its former influence. Even this position was challenged in the first decades of the nineteenth century by the Fulani-Hausa followers of Usuman dan Fodio.

THE HAUSA CITY-STATES

Many legends turn on the founding of the Hausa Bakwai, the seven original Hausa cities. Most tell of a man named Bayajidda who was forced to flee from Bornu after marrying the daughter of the king. He settled at Biram where his son became the first Hausa ruler of that village. Moving to Daura, Bayajidda married the queen. Their six grandsons later became the creators and first rulers of the Bakwai. According to tradition, the first seven Hausa cities were Biram, Daura, Kano, Zazzau (Zaria), Gobir, Rano, and Katsina. The Hausa consider seven other states to be Banza or "bastard" states which developed presumably after Hausa influence had spread. These secondary states were Zamfara, Kebbi, Nupe, Gwari, Yauri, Kororofa, and Ilorin. Despite the richness of such folklore and the existence of chronicles of the kings of Kano and Katsina dating to 1100, little is known of this shadowy early period.

Many Nigerian historians have speculated that the Hausa territory was originally occupied by Negro farmers who were much like the Sao people. Some time before the year 1000 invaders from the northeast, perhaps from Bornu, entered the area and established control over these villages. In time the fusion between these western-moving Afro-Asiatic speakers and the pre-existing Negro population created the Hausa culture. The distance of these growing cities from the empires of Ghana and Mali offered security in their formative years. Although all the city-states used the same language and had similar social and political institutions, their different geographic locations dictated different trading and military activities. Gobir on the edge of the desert was always troubled by desert nomads and did not become an important state until the eighteenth century. Kano and Katsina at the end of well-established trade routes early became the dominant trading cities. Zaria, the most southerly of the cities, based its prosperity upon slave raiding, and Daura for a long period was considered the spiritual home of the Hausa.

The political organization of all the states was similar. Kings, who were chosen from a particular dynasty, had great power over their subjects, but in theory they were not absolute. There was a well-ordered hierarchy of ministers, officials, and councils, all of whom exercised checks upon the autocratic powers of the king. Later, after the coming of Islam, the Koranic law, judges, and religious teachers all modified the authority of the rulers. Although the kings of the city-states attempted political domination of their neighbors, none ever proved strong enough to maintain such control. There was never any Hausa empire and the problems of administration were therefore fewer than in Bornu, Mali, or Songhai. The wealth of all the city-states depended upon thriving farming villages as well as trade and manufacturing. Kings appointed village heads whose major responsibility aside from the administration of the law was to collect taxes from the farmers. The rulers also received wealth by imposing taxes and customs duties upon traders and manufacturers.

Through the fifteenth century Kano was probably the most important of the Hausa states, although its rulers paid tribute to the mais of Bornu. In the sixteenth century Hausaland was a battleground among Bornu, Songhai, and the Junkun empire. Partially because of these events Kano lost its economic supremacy to the rival city of Katsina. Katsina benefited greatly from the decline of Kano and even more from the destruction of Songhai control over the trans-Saharan routes. For almost one hundred years Katsina was the leading cultural as well as commercial city in Hausaland.

In the early eighteenth century Zamfara, one of the oldest of the "bastard" states, began to challenge Katsina's dominance. In 1700 the Zamfara rulers conquered Kano, and from that time onward Katsina was forced to share power with Zamfara. Somewhat later Gobir, which was being threatened by desert peoples, began a southward expansion in the direction of the more fertile lands around Zamfara. In the latter eighteenth century the rulers of Gobir were constantly at war, and by 1800 Gobir was superficially the most powerful state in Hausaland. However, the continual warfare had weakened not only Zamfara, Katsina, and Kano but also Gobir and thus made the Fulani conquest easier.

Islam had been established in Hausaland as early as the fourteenth century. The ruling dynasties had been converted in this period largely as a result of contact with Bornu and the Malian empire. It is doubtful, however, whether the majority of the people had become anything except occasional conformists. There were many "pagan" elements present in the rituals of kingship in all of the city-states. Personal whims of the rulers added to geographic isolation made deviation from pure Islamic practices common. One group in Hausaland, the town Fulani, were more dedicated to Islam than was usual. Many of these people served as advisers to the Hausa kings. They had been greatly influenced by the jihads in the Futa Toro and Futa Jallon regions earlier in the century. Being a minority among the Hausa, the Fulani were also the first to feel misrule by their overlords. In the latter eighteenth century the general unrest of the town Fulani found an ardent spokesman in the person of the renowned scholar Usuman dan Fodio, a resident of Gobir. His preaching and the activities of his followers resulted in the creation of the first united empire in Hausaland in the early nineteenth century.

THREE

Forest states of the Guinea Coast

Forest States

The term forest state implies a uniformity of environmental conditions which in fact does not exist in West Africa. Either productive or swamp forest in most territories covers only a small portion of the land. The bulk of the heavy forest is concentrated near the coast. This belt extends at the maximum only a few hundred miles into the interior and in many cases there is little forest land even abutting on the coast. Thus it is a mistake to believe that in order for people to occupy most of the land of Guinea they had to wait for the arrival of the new crops or the new techniques of forest agriculture. Much of the land in this area is similar to the savannah of the north. The use of millets along with native rice and yams would have enabled the early peoples of the so-called forest areas to survive very well on land in many cases potentially more productive than that which they had abandoned. It is true that intensive settlement of the heavy forest area came very late and was caused by the pressure of population upon the land already occupied combined with the disturbances attendant upon kingdom building throughout West Africa. New crops such as yams and bananas enabled the savannah farmers to make the transition to the forest with relative ease.

Until quite recently many experts believed that the immediate hinterland of West Africa was practically unpopulated until just before the arrival of Europeans in the fifteenth century. Today, however, historians are certain that a large number of agriculturists lived in all the nonforested lands for hundreds of years before that time. This view has thus cast doubt on the older theory which linked the movement into this hinterland with iron technology. Use of primitive wood and stone implements might have allowed a significant number of agriculturists to move into the forest fringes long before the arrival of iron. Excavations undertaken by Professor Thurstan-Shaw in Nigeria indicate that the Nok settlements were not exceptions and that the middle belt area of modern Nigeria was well populated before the year 1000. If art is an indicator of the sophistication of society, the sculpture of Ile Ife shows that by the twelfth century there was present in the northern fringes of the forests of Nigeria a very complex, highly structured political and social organization that would have taken centuries to develop.

The great empires of the Sudan were never able to control for long even the village states of the broken southern savannah and forest. Therefore Islamic records, which are so valuable in tracing the development of Ghana, Mali, and Songhai, do not exist for the southern societies. After the fifteenth century there are some good, if diffused, accounts of the coastal African societies by European explorers and traders. Because of the nature of trade, however, few Europeans penetrated beyond the coast until the nineteenth century, and thus even these descriptions are of minimal value for the history of the hinterland. Most of the key questions related to the intermediate areas located south of the Sudan before the fifteenth century cannot be answered with any precision. There were village-oriented peoples occupying certain areas of West Africa before the Christian era, but their origin, the density of their population, and the nature of their political, religious, and social forms can only be inferred from scanty evidence and interpolations made from observation of later societies.

It appears that concepts and techniques reached Guinea from North Africa and the Nile Valley centuries before the establishment of the polities noted by European writers. The form of social and political organization called the Sudanic states was present throughout the subsavannah and forest area. It could be found in political units that claimed the allegiance of only a few thousand persons as well as in larger, more powerful entities such as the Ashanti and Yoruba states. The central figure in such a political organization was the divine king who had direct access to the deities and natural forces that controlled the destinies of the state. In many cases elaborate attempts were made to hide the king's humanity from the populace. No one, not even his closest advisers, was allowed to see the king eat or drink. He gave audience or handed down decisions from behind a screen or a full veil. The health of the divine king presumably was tied to the well-being of the state. Many divine kings were not allowed to die a natural death. Great celebrations were held at the funeral ceremonies of a monarch to assure his continuing support of the people and his successor. It was at such ceremonies that human sacrifices were offered to propitiate the spirit of the departed monarch.

Sudanic-type states, whether discovered in East, Central, or West Africa, had other features in common. The queen sister and queen mother had positions of great respect and potentially much authority. Each state, no matter how large, was operated not by an hereditary nobility but by an appointed bureaucracy responsible to the king. These features, combined with similar rituals and formulas in polities separated by thousands of miles, suggests a common origin. Very early, Africanists noted how closely these societal features resembled those of ancient Egypt. The first theories to explain this relation were relatively simplistic ones having to do with direct migrations of large numbers of people from Egypt into areas where the Sudanic state was prevalent. The answer to the diffusion of the Sudanic state from the Nile Valley is obviously much more complex. Direct movement of elements of the Hyksos, Nubian, and Kushitic empires provide only a part of the answer. Libyans and Garamantes influenced by the Egyptians ranged over a large part of northern Africa and were early involved in sub-Saharan trade. Long before the fall of Meroë there were well-established trade routes westward to the Sudan and south toward the Kenyan highlands. It seems obvious that Ghana, Songhai, and Kanem-Bornu, having adopted the practices common to a Sudanic state, were vital to the spread of such ideas.

With the scant evidence available it is not possible to deal accurately with the spread of common institutions and their assimilation in West Africa. However, almost all of the larger Guinea kingdoms had adopted the Sudanic organization in one form or another before the arrival of Europeans. A more detailed examination of five different West African peoples will illustrate not only the influence of the Sudanic state organization but also something of the patterns of early migration and later development of the states of Guinea. The five representative groups are the Wolof, the Ashanti, the Fon, the Yoruba, and the people of the Niger delta.

The Wolof of the Senegambia

The area between the Senegal and Gambia rivers had been at the westward extreme of some of the great Sudanic empires. The territory was certainly a sphere of influence of Mali and of Tekrur. By the thirteenth century there were probably already many different people living in uneasy juxtaposition with one another. Mande, Serer, and Fula (Peul) had been settled in the Senegambia region for some time before the Wolof arrived. The origins and early history of the Wolof are unknown, but it is probable that the first Wolof settlements were made in the late twelfth or early thirteenth century as a result of the upheavals in the Western Sudan following the Almoravid conquests.

The first Wolof kingdom was Jolof, located in the interior just south of the borders of the old kingdom of Tekrur. From there Wolof control had been extended by the fifteenth century to include most of the territory between the two rivers. In the sixteenth century there were six states dominated by the Wolof — Jolof, Cayor, Baol, Walo, Sine, and Saloum. The ruler of Jolof, called the burba Jolof, was overlord of the five other client kingdoms. The development and internal organization of the Wolof states are much better documented than those of most African polities. Aluise da Cadamosto, the first European explorer of the Senegambia region, in 1455 left an account of the Wolof political organization which was confirmed by later writers. Portuguese and after them French activities in Africa were at first concentrated in the Senegambia region. The accounts of Marmol, De la Courbe, Brue, Labat, Barbot, Jobson, and Moore written at different times give reasonably accurate descriptions of the Wolof from the sixteenth through the eighteenth centuries.

Wolof society was divided into three main segments of freeborn, low caste, and slaves, with further stratification within each of these divisions. The freeborn comprised royal lineages, nobility, and peasants. Rulers of the various states were chosen from members of a particular royal lineage. For example, the king of Jolof had to be of the patrilineage of N'Dyadyane N'Dyaye, the semimythical first ruler. Nobles not of royal blood had differential rights and privileges depending upon their families and their duties in the state. The nobility participated in the selection of the kings, although they were not eligible to be chosen themselves. In many cases they not only chose the ruler but also could legally depose him if he exceeded the limits of his authority. Peasants made up the bulk of the population in each of the agricultural Wolof states. Although freeborn, the peasants had no political power.

The low caste division included the smiths and leather-workers and the court musicians and praisers. Despite the fact that they were members of a lower order, smiths traditionally enjoyed considerable influence, particularly the blacksmiths, who made the knives and spears and repaired the guns so necessary in times of strife. The gewel or griots were the professional musicians, geneologists, historians, praise singers, and court jesters. Each lineage had its gewel who knew and sang of its history. Gewels could be irreverent to everyone, and in some cases because of a special relation with the kings a gewel would be very influential. While the lower castes enjoyed special privileges, there were also restrictions placed on them. Their right of marriage, for example, was circumscribed to members of their own caste. At death the gewels were not buried in the same manner as freeborn men but were placed in hollow baobab trees to keep their spirits from poisoning the crops.

The lowest members of Wolof society were the slaves, of which there were two types — those captured in war and those born into a free household. The former could be treated in any manner and resold at will. Household slaves were considered inferior members of the family and were assigned tasks similar to those performed by free men. Much of the heavy work of farming was done by the slaves. A household slave could not be sold unless he had committed a crime. As he grew older his master provided him with a wife and means of sustenance and in time, although his status had not changed, he acquired a great amount of freedom.

The Wolof were in contact with Islam for centuries, but the extent of Muslim influence in the early period of their history is questionable. European observers from the seventeenth century onward noted that many nobles professed Islam and that some chiefs kept Muslim teachers with them at court.

It appears that the conversion was not of the same order among Wolof notables as it was in the Western Sudan. Many chiefs were probably captivated by the magical aspects of Islam. The middle and lower classes were even less affected by the new religion. Indeed, they were not converted to Islam until the latter part of the nineteenth century and this was accomplished more by conquest than conviction. Even today when most of the Wolof are ostensibly Muslim they load themselves with magic amulets and believe in witches and good and evil spirits.

The political system of the Wolof states was, in theory, a balanced monarchy. In all of them the king was chosen by certain important nobles. Once chosen, the king's person was considered sacred. Petitioners were required to uncover the upper parts of their bodies and approach him on their knees while placing dust upon their heads. The ruler was always surrounded by large numbers of nobles, servants, men at arms, and gewels. There were also special rituals required of a king, and he was surrounded with prohibitions on certain activities which were designed to preserve his exclusiveness and mysterious power. Despite the respect and symbols of divine kingship, no Wolof king was really secure on the throne. The nobles who chose the rulers and other high officials could and did depose kings who tried to wield too much authority.

Although titles and specific functions differed from state to state, the most important central officials in all of the states were the treasurer, minister of lands, chief judges, and military leaders. Each ruler appointed lesser officials such as the chiefs in charge of groups of villages and the alkati, who were responsible for the trade centers. The king's income was derived from many different sources, including taxes on traders and fishermen, payments of grain and cattle by the peasants, tribute from conquered people, fines for various crimes, and part of the profits from the slave trade.

The history of the Wolof states during and after the sixteenth century is a complex of revolts and wars. The king of Jolof originally dominated the other five polities. In the late sixteenth century, however, Cayor rebelled against Jolof and its ruler took the title of damel. This leader invaded Baol, defeated the armies of Jolof, and killed the burba Jolof, beginning a long series of wars with the other Wolof states who refused to recognize the damel as overlord. Thereafter no Wolof ruler was able to dominate any of the other states for long, let alone restore the unity that had previously existed. The Wolof states were also under pressure from the Mauretanians who lived north of the Senegal River and the Tucolor people of Futa Toro. Intra-state rivalry was compounded by the firm establishment of European trading stations along the coast and on the Gambia River in the seventeenth century. As trade with Europeans became more of a factor in the economics of the Wolof states Jolof, located in the interior, was outdistanced in power and influence by the rival coastal kingdoms of Cayor and Baol. The continued political divisions among the Wolof made easier the dependence of coastal areas upon France and the piecemeal conquest of the separate polities in the nineteenth century.

The Akan states of the Gold Coast

Before the twelfth century there was a small scattered population living in what is now the modern state of Ghana. In all probability these people were the ancestors of the present-day Guan-speaking groups. Little more is known of these pre-Akan groups, largely because of the success of the later invaders in assimilating the indigenous population. Some time after the year 1000 relatively large numbers of Akan migrants reached the central Gold Coast. Contrary to the pattern discernible in Hausa-land, Bornu, and among the Yoruba, the Akan invasions were not those of a minority group that because of higher culture or military supremacy imposed itself upon the pre-existing society. The Akan moved in blocks and retained with only minor modifications their customs and language.

There are many explanations for the origin of the Akan. Perhaps the most reasonable is that of the Ghanese historian Professor A. Boahen, who believes that the Akan developed their linguistic and cultural characteristics in an area close to but northeast of the boundaries of modern Ghana. The clan was the basic sociopolitical unit. Migration, fragmentation, and later the development of more sophisticated states did not destroy the clans. Thus it was possible for an Ashanti to have a strong kinship tie with a person of another state which could even be a political rival. This recognition of clan obligations later helped the Ashanti to create their powerful union.

The Akan migrations were probably motivated by population pressure combined with disturbances attendant upon the wars in the Western Sudan in the eleventh and twelfth centuries. The earliest Akan states in the Gold Coast were Bono and Banda, both of which were located in the bush areas north of the forest zone. Until the fifteenth century further southward movement of the Akan tended to avoid the forests. In the fourteenth century large numbers of Akan moved southeastward through a gap in the Akwapim hills and crossed the forest at its narrowest point, settling not in the woodlands but upon the coastal grasslands of the Gold Coast. These invaders later created the states of Akim and Akwamu. Not until a century later did significant numbers move south from the area of Bono directly into the forest belt west of the Pra River. The Akan clans belonging to this later migration were responsible for the establishment of the kingdoms of Assini, Wassaw, Ahanta, and the Fante states.

Akan invaders from the north met other migrants expanding into the Gold Coast from the east onto the Accra plain. These were two linguistically related groups, the Ewe and the Ga. The Ewe moved into the area overland directly from the east in the thirteenth and fourteenth centuries, probably at the end of their own north-south migrations. The bulk of the Ga arrived near their present locations by sea from some place in southern Nigeria. Perhaps their exodus was caused by disorders attendant on the rise of Benin. There is some evidence to indicate that contact and trade was maintained by the Ga with Benin into the fourteenth century.

The early Akan polities, clan oriented and primarily agricultural, developed trade routes long before the arrival of Europeans. They traded with the Ga, Guan, and other Akan groups for fish and salt and by the beginning of the fifteenth century were deeply involved in the indirect trade with the Western Sudan. In what is now northern Ghana Hausa merchants traded finished wares and beads for kola nuts and salt. Gold dust and slaves were sent northward to the trading centers of Djenne and Timbuktu.

The arrival of Europeans in the fifteenth century had profound effects upon the development of the many competitive small Akan polities. The early Portuguese traders were mainly interested in acquiring gold, and with the construction of São Jorge da Mina there was created an alternate route for Akan goods. Some Akans were drawn early into the European orbit, being employed as carpenters, builders, and blacksmiths. In time coastal settlements such as Sekondi and Kormantin, which had been fishing villages, grew to be important trade centers with a sizable group of African merchants congregated there. The shift of European emphasis in the latter sixteenth century toward the slave trade further increased the importance of the coastal villages. Even with this change the Portuguese did not upset the traditional patterns of life of the interior peoples.

The capture of the São Jorge by the Dutch and the subsequent expulsion of the Portuguese in 1642 ushered in a new era for the Gold Coast. The Dutch opened almost a dozen forts along the coast. The British, who had a post at Kormantin in 1631, added seven major locations by the close of the century. Sweden and even Brandenburg also established trade forts. Competition among these European nations for slaves and gold introduced firearms in large numbers to the Akan clans of the interior. With more profits to be obtained by controlling larger areas, some clans began to use these new weapons to establish more powerful states.

The first of the larger Akan kingdoms were Denkyera and Akwamu. By the end of the seventeenth century Denkyera controlled most of the inland trade routes of the western Gold Coast and in addition had conquered much of the inland territory between the Pra and Ancorbra rivers. To the east Akwamu expanded to the Volta River and also exercised hegemony southward to the European settlements along the coast. Akwamu succeeded in its expansion partially because new administrative arrangements had been made that increased the centralized power of the king. The success of the Denkyera and Akwamu rulers was achieved at the expense of the economic and political liberty of the smaller Akan polities. A number of such fragmented groups were located in the vicinity of what later became the city of Kumasi. The Akan clans there had early realized the commercial value of the area, since they found both gold and kola nuts. The locale was made more valuable, since trade routes from Hausaland intersected near Kumasi those from the north. The Denkyera, who in the seventeenth century controlled this area, treated the smaller Akan states as conquered territory to be exploited for slaves and gold. This oppression ultimately caused a reaction that created a far greater military power than the Denkyera — that of the Ashanti Union.

In the seventeenth century the Oyolo clan moved into this strategic area and created a number of small states, each of which was independent, although they tended to cooperate with one another. One of these states was Kumasi, which had already by the 1670s substantially increased the area under the control of its chief. The ruler of Kumasi, Osei Tutu, at the beginning of his reign in the latter seventeenth century extended the kingdom even further and was responsible for the creation of the Ashanti Union. This ruler had earlier spent some time in Akwamu and had obviously learned from its rulers the advantages of a larger, more centralized state. With the aid of Anokye, his chief priest, Osei Tutu formed a military alliance with neighboring rulers to resist the migrations of the Domaa, another Akan group. By appealing to the common hatred of the Denkyera this military cooperation was continued and later expanded into a political alliance. At a general meeting of the leaders of the coalition Anokye contrived to have an ornate golden stool he had constructed appear as if by magic. The assembled rulers were informed that the stool contained the soul of all Ashanti and was the symbol of their unity. This gift of the gods was made to Osei Tutu and his descendants to keep in trust as the symbol of divine favor to the new nation.

The enterprising Osei Tutu and his religious adviser then created new rituals and a new administrative form for the Ashanti. The paramount ruler was called the asantahene and ruled with the advice of a council composed of the rulers of the previously independent states. Each of these subkings or omanhenes was to rule his territory on condition of faithful service and obedience to the asantahene. Failure to conform to these obligations could result in his loss of office by destoolment. Anokye designed a special festival called the odwira, which was held once a year so that the omanhenes could ceremoniously restate their allegiance to the asantahene.

The newly united Ashanti army was a study in logical organization based partially upon Osei Tutu's observations of the army of Akwamu. There were four divisions — the van, the rear, and the right and left wings. Each territory of Ashanti had its assigned place in the army and the divisions were led by major omanhenes. All able-bodied male Ashanti could be called upon for military service. With this formidable force the Ashanti drove out the Domaa and engaged the Denkyera in 1699. The Denkyera were defeated and the Ashanti became the dominant power in the interior of the Gold Coast. The Akan tribes, who were conquered in the early eighteenth century, were absorbed

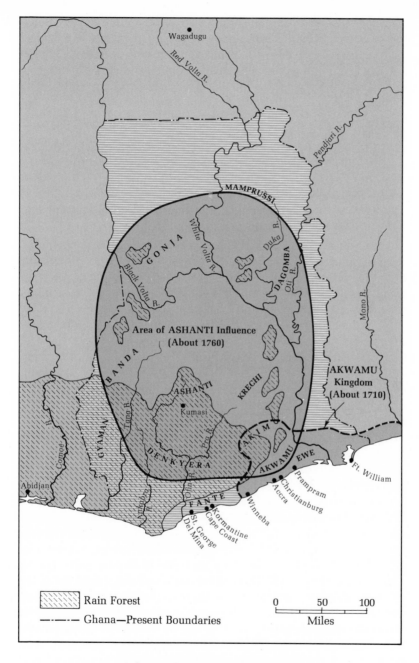

Eighteenth-Century Gold Coast

into the Ashanti confederation, with their rulers becoming omanhenes subject to the orders of the great king at Kumasi.

In the period after 1720 asantahene Opoku Ware extended his empire north at the expense of the Mossi states and also northeastward to control the trade routes to Hausaland. The victorious Ashanti then turned southward in a long series of campaigns against the kingdom of Akim, which had by then absorbed the older, once powerful state of Akwamu. By the time of Opoku Ware's death in 1750 almost all of what is now modern Ghana was controlled directly or indirectly by the Ashanti.

In the extreme south another Akan group, the Fante, had long been in contact with the Europeans. They were as politically divided as their northern kinsmen had been before the rise of the Ashanti. The military success of the Ashanti, however, combined with the obvious willingness of the Europeans to shift their business dealings away from the Fante caused the scattered Fante states to begin to unite. Although the Fante never achieved the degree of cohesiveness of the Ashanti, they became powerful enough to compete with them for control of the coast. There was no full-scale war between the Ashanti and Fante in the latter eighteenth century, largely because of internal conflicts within the Ashanti Union during the long reign of Asantahene Osei Kwame (1777–1801). The Europeans, especially the British, also played an important role in maintaining the Fante against their stronger northern neighbors and kinsmen. The British particularly opposed Ashanti attempts to dominate the coastal areas, and their support enabled the Fante to keep the Ashanti away from the immediate hinterlands of the British trade stations. Much of the history of the Akan peoples of the Gold Coast in the latter eighteenth century is inextricably bound to European developments and will be related in Chapter IV.

The kingdom of Dahomey

The coast of Dahomey became one of the major centers for the trans-Atlantic slave trade in the seventeenth and eighteenth centuries. Because of its importance many European authors wrote detailed accounts of the kingdom. Some of the significant reports were those of the Dutchman Dapper in the seventeenth century and the Frenchman Barbot and the Englishmen Snelgrove and Smith in the eighteenth century. The most quoted source is *A History of Dahomey,* a book written by the eighteenth-century trader Archibald Dalzel. The statement of the Nigerian historian Professor I. A. Akinjogbin that the eighteenth-century history of the area is a mixture of facts, fables, and prejudices is undoubtedly correct and even more true of the preceding five centuries. Nevertheless, a more thorough outline can be drawn of the development of Dahomey than of any other kingdom of the Guinea coast.

In the twelfth or thirteenth century the Adja and other closely related Fon people had moved from the transitional savannah land southeastward into the forest zone. The Adja settled along the banks of the Mono River between Tado and Athieme. In all later legends Tado is considered the point of origin of the Adja. It is probable, however, that these people were related to the early Yoruba clans east of the Okpara River. Other Fon clans had settled in small villages over the entire area north of the Adja. The first major Fon state was Ardra, established in the sixteenth century. Its chief city was Allada, located south of the Lama marshes approximately thirty-five miles north of the coast. In the early seventeenth century quarrels among certain factions in Ardra resulted in the creation of other states, the most important of which were the coastal polities of Jaquin and Whydah and the interior kingdom of Abomey. The growth of Abomey was at the expense of the related but nonunited Fon villages which were soon incorporated into the new kingdom. All of these new states throughout the seventeenth century continued to recognize the theoretical overlordship of Ardra.

The seventeenth century in Abomey was a period of consolidation of royal power. Dako (about 1625–1650) was probably only the head of a particular lineage and his authority depended more on his personal attributes than on any traditional sanctions. His successor Wegbadja (about 1650–1680) began the process of establishing the ruler as the central figure in all areas of life. He established the custom of having the kingship pass in a direct line from father to son rather than according to the normal pattern of from brother to brother. This practice was reserved only for the royal clan and was not strictly primogeniture, since the king, the oracle, and the major officials had to agree on the choice of successor. This innovation did minimize quarrels over succession. Wegbadja also systematically established the principle that royal justice was supreme and only the king had the right to assess capital punishment. He increased his control over the different kin groups by establishing the custom whereby all the property of the head of such a group would on his death revert to the king, who would then return most of it to the new head. Wegbadja also extended the practice of tribute due the king so that he could afford to distribute wealth to his followers. The central religious and political activity of the king, the annual customs, were also begun at this time. The name of the kingdom was also changed during Wegbadja's reign. One story attributes this change to the stubborness of a chief named Dan who refused to give the king land on which to build a new palace. The king had the chief killed, seized the land, and built a palace over the grave. The palace was called Danhomey (the belly of Dan). According to the story, the name was later extended to all the people and shortened to Dahomey.

The history of Dahomey in the eighteenth century is inextricably bound to the slave trade. The kings of Dahomey did not necessarily expand their territories because of profit. Internal pressures and the ambitions of its kings would probably have resulted in attempts to extend their control had there not been a slave trade. However, the trade made the coastal kingdoms of Whydah and Jaquin even more tempting. Allada provided most of the slaves which were sold to Europeans on the coast. Jaquin was the major port for Allada until it revolted in the early eighteenth century. Afterward Whydah became more important, particularly since its king charged Europeans less customs duties than they had to pay at Jaquin. None of the kingdoms of the south, not even Ardra, had as centralized and well-organized a state and army as the rulers of Dahomey. In each of these kingdoms the nobles and country rulers had considerable autonomy, and this disunity was reflected in their military forces. Rivalries between lineage groups prevented the kings from putting into the field anything near their full military strength. European traders living in the coastal kingdoms also contributed to the divisions within those states.

In 1724 King Agadja of Dahomey sent his armies against Ardra. Allada was taken, the king killed, and the town burned. Jaquin almost immediately submitted to the king and agreed to pay tribute. This bloodless victory over Jaquin was not permanent, since in the disorders of the next twenty years European merchants organized the coastal cities, including Jaquin, to

resist Dahomey. Agadja had no immediate plans for the conquest of Whydah. He asked the right to export slaves through
the port and was willing to pay the king of Whydah the usual
fees. Outraged by Whydah's refusal to grant this request,
Agadja attacked and Whydah was conquered in 1727. The royal
court of Whydah escaped to the island of Great Popo and
became the focal point of resistance to Dahomey.

Despite its expansion Dahomey received major setbacks
after 1730. Great Popo and European merchants along the coast
pursued an active policy of resistance. The continual warfare
with Great Popo was disruptive of trade and prosperity to all
concerned and was not ended until 1774. Jaquin was pacified
finally in 1760 when King Tegbesou burned the town and killed
as many of the inhabitants as possible. The greatest threat to
Dahomean power, however, came from the neighboring empire
of Oyo. In the early 1730s Agadja's march of conquest was
halted by a major Yoruba invasion. Yoruba armies returned to
Dahomey at intervals, but they were composed to a large extent
of cavalry and they never completely defeated the Dahomeans,
who retreated into the bush. In 1747 King Tegbesou of Dahomey
ended this direct military intervention of Oyo by agreeing to
pay an annual tribute to the Alafin of Oyo.

In the latter part of the eighteenth century Dahomey
extended its control over the Mahi and Za peoples to the north
of Abomey. These groups, related to the Fon, had only minimal
local political organization and presented a fertile territory for
Dahomean slave raiding. During the struggles with Great Popo
and the Europeans before 1770 a large segment of the slave
trade shifted from Whydah to Jaquin, Porto Novo, and Badagry.
Jaquin was subdued by 1760, but the attempt of Dahomey to
control the trade of the other towns continued throughout the
1780s. Badagry suffered greatly in these wars, but Porto Novo
was protected by its alliance with Oyo and remained in direct
competition with Whydah as the chief slave mart of the coast.
By the end of the century the kings of Dahomey dominated a
wide swath of coast from Badagry west to the Gold Coast. In
the interior they observed a westerly demarcation line with
Ashanti, and in the east they were restricted by the power of
Oyo.

The major factor in the rise of the Dahomeans was their
closely knit political organization. Very few kingdoms in Africa
had such a complex structure as did Dahomey in the eighteenth

century. The king was not viewed by the people as necessarily divine, although the honors paid to him convinced European observers that his subjects believed he was. Notwithstanding the limits that might have been placed upon his godhead, he did possess many qualities of a semidivine. In the seventeenth century the king lived in seclusion, controlled the appointment of the major religious leaders, and authorized the founding of cult houses for each lineage. He alone could authorize human sacrifice, and these were for the greater glory of only the royal house. The king used his special religious position to strengthen his control of the bureaucracy.

There was a bureaucracy of the inside and outside. The former referred to the high court officials and the three grades of royal wives. The leading officials of the state were the migan, who was equivalent to a prime minister; the mehi, who had charge of finance and commerce; the ajai, or first counselor; and the agan, who was in charge of the army. Less important officials directly responsible to the king were the seven great chiefs of the kingdom and the chiefs of the provinces. At almost every level there were deputies to assist the high officials. The army, which was very important, had three deputies to aid the agan in command. These were the sogan, or the master of horses; the posu, or the commander of the left; and the fusupo, or the commander of the right. The very unusual contingent of women in the army were actually the lowest level of the king's wives. They were called akhosi and served many functions in the palace during time of peace. Only in war were they utilized as a military unit.

The king, apart from his semidivinity and appointive powers, also had other methods of retaining supreme authority. One was the use of royal messengers, called the ilari, who traveled throughout the kingdom bearing direct orders from the ruler. Another was the customs, the most important phase of the religious life of the monarchy. The customs were of two types and were probably instituted by King Wegbadja in the seventeenth century. One type, the grand customs, were funeral ceremonies for a dead king which were held years after the ruler's death. Representatives of all classes in the society were sacrificed to demonstrate to the dead monarch that he was still revered and to gain his continued support of the kingdom. The second type, the annual customs, were utilized to remind the people of the king's authority. All the major leaders of the king-

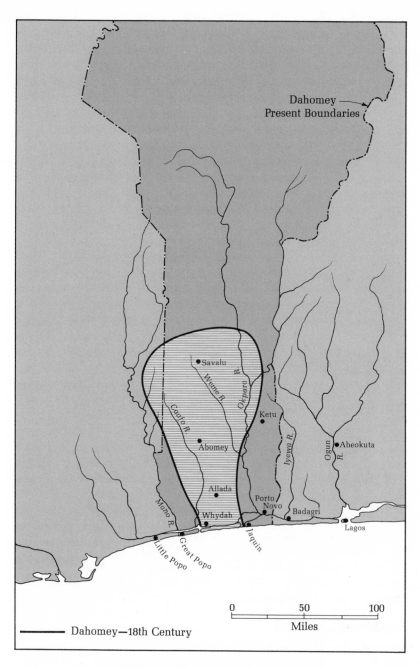

Dahomey
Present Boundaries

● Savalu

Weme R.

Okpara R.

Couffo R.

Ketu ●

● Abomey

Iyewa R.

Ogun R.

● Abeokuta

Allada ●

Porto
Novo ●

Badagri ●

Mano R.

Whydah ●

Jaquin

Lagos ●

Great Popo

Little Popo

0   50   100

Miles

Dahomey—18th Century

Eighteenth-Century Dahomey

dom were required to attend. In one of the complex rituals the leading men of the kingdom surrendered their horses, which would later be redeemed from the king. Thus every year the king symbolically reiterated his supreme position. He also distributed awards for meritorious service at this time and handed down sentences for major crimes. The annual customs were also a time for human sacrifice to gain the continued support of the deceased kings for the dynasty.

Despite centralization and religious sanctions, the rulers of Dahomey at the close of the eighteenth century were still bothered by sporadic uprisings against them. Distance from the center of authority and the new opportunities for wealth and power were open invitations for disobedience and rebellion. The coastal kingdoms where European and Yoruba influence reinforced local ambitions caused the kings great trouble. Whydah was a continuing source of difficulty. The yevogan, or "captain of the whites," was the official directly responsible to the king for the government of the town and trade. His position made him a focal point for dissident factions. King Kpengla's (1775–1789) attempt to rationalize the slave trade to his advantage by collecting higher taxes and requiring payment for slaves in the interior in cowrie shells also caused trouble from many of his subjects, who wanted to deal in European barter goods.

The king's answer to disobedience and defiance was the use of terror. Disloyal villages were plundered and burned and their inhabitants killed. The Dahomean army was one of the fiercest in Africa and treated its enemies in a manner reminiscent of the ancient Assyrians. One example of the hard-line policy that has been recorded by European observers was the taking of Whydah in 1727 when in five days over 5,000 inhabitants were killed. Captured chiefs who had opposed Dahomey were decapitated and their heads carefully preserved in the king's palace at Abomey. Most of the Dahomean rulers were long lived. This factor combined with a generally loyal bureaucracy and a rule of terror enabled Dahomey to preserve into the nineteenth century a unity in the face of European influence that was unusual for West Africa.

Yorubaland and Benin

Evidence for long occupation of the savannah lands of Nigeria was first unearthed on the Jos Plateau. In 1936 a small terracotta head of a monkey was discovered in tin-mining operations

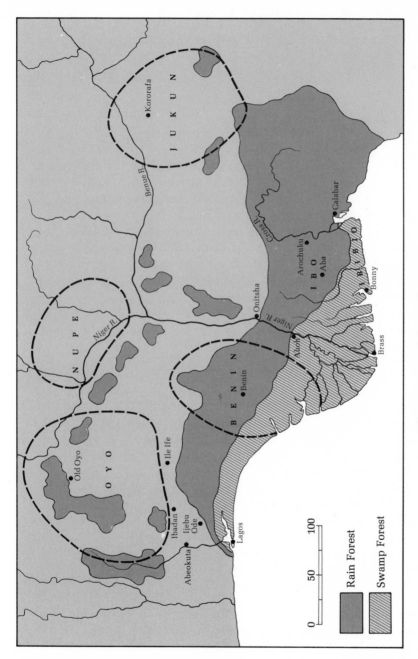

Niger Coast, Eighteenth Century

near the village of Nok. Later discoveries combined with modern
dating techniques have indicated that a highly developed late
Stone Age culture flourished over the entire plateau between
1000 B.C. and A.D. 200. These Nok people were agriculturists
who perhaps also kept herds of goats and cattle. There is evidence that in the later period they also had a rudimentary iron
technology, although stone continued to be the predominant
material for implements. The pieces of art which have survived
indicate that they were extremely gifted artisans. Comparisons
of this art with recently discovered figurines of a Nok type in
Yorubaland and with previously identified works of Yoruba art
suggest a later continuation of Nok culture further south.

Tantalizing as the connections between Nok and the Yoruba
states may be, they are basically conjecture. The history of
Nigeria in the thousand years following the latest identified Nok
settlement is almost a complete blank. This is particularly frustrating, since this is the period when East Indian foodstuffs were
spread throughout Guinea. It appears that during much of this
period the populations of Guinea were in constant movement.
Perhaps the best example of this would be the Bantu migrations.
If either the Greenberg or Oliver theses are correct, the beginning of the Bantu movements from some place in the vicinity
of eastern Nigeria or the Cameroons southeastward took place
in the first segment of this time period. Of equal importance
and equally obscure is the populating of the bush forest and
the fringes of the forest lands directly south of Nok. All that can
be said with accuracy of this latter development is that the political and social organization was on a small scale. Hundreds of
small agricultural villages were created that were held together
by kinship and clan ties.

The impetus toward larger state building was probably
brought from the north and east toward the end of this thou-
sand-year blank period. Of particular interest is the creation of
Ile Ife, the first major state of Yorubaland. Legends in Benin
and Yorubaland ascribe the founding of Ile Ife to Oduduwa.
In some versions he was the son of the supreme god; in others
he was an eastern prince who with his followers conquered the
early inhabitants of the Ife area. Time is not a factor in these
legends. The invasions of Yorubaland by migrants from the
Eastern Sudan could have taken place as early as the eighth
century. The art of Ife indicates that society was highly sophisticated by the end of the twelfth century. Yet one version of the

Oduduwa myth states that his seven sons were responsible for the creation of the ruling structure of the other states of Yoruba-land and of Benin. The city-state of Benin was probably established some time in the fourteenth century. While the stories give clues as to generalized movements, they do not answer the key questions of time, place, and relation.

Ile Ife was regarded as the spiritual home of the Yoruba people long after its place as the strongest political state had been assumed by Oyo. It is reasonable to assume that Ife was the first important Yoruba city, a position it retained for centuries. Its ruler, the oni, stood at the apex of a highly complex theocracy and his influence extended far beyond the territories he actually controlled. In the eighteenth century, for example, the powerful oba of Benin needed the approval of the oni before his coronation. Presumably the religiopolitical system developed at Ife penetrated into the subforests of Nigeria in the period after the twelfth century. The colonies thus formed followed similar patterns of organization, had the same religion, and spoke a similar language.

While the history of Ife at this time is obscure, its art is not. The discovery in this century of a series of naturalistic heads, some done in brass and some in terracotta, make our ignorance of the peoples of Ife even more disturbing. The finest of these heads date to the late twelfth and thirteenth centuries and rank with the best examples of European sculpture. The artists who worked in both media were highly trained and complete masters of their subject matter. The brass heads were cast by the *cire-perdue* process, as were some examples of complete figures of obas. The art of Ife is unique in Africa. Elsewhere naturalism is almost completely lacking, being sacrificed for symbolism. The recently constructed museum at Ife contains enough examples of later work that one can trace the deterioration of naturalism in the fourteenth and subsequent centuries. The later brasses and sculptured works, while technically excellent, show increasing foreshortening of some of the body parts and exaggeration of other features, particularly the eyes and the mouth. It was this form that was transferred, along with the techniques of casting, to Benin some time in the late fifteenth century.

Ife remains a great mystery, as does the early history of states such as Nupe and Borgu. The first Yoruba-type state about which much is known is Benin. The Portuguese first visited Benin City in 1485 and almost immediately established a significant trade with the state via the Benin-controlled port of Gwatto. Descriptions left by these early visitors confirm that Benin was already a great state before their arrival. Just before the Portuguese first arrived the oba Ewuare the Great (about 1440–1473) had encircled much of the city with walls, improved the army, and extended Benin's influence as far south as Lagos, which became a colony of Benin. The area around Benin City was a rich agricultural belt. Benin craftsmen were already well known for their carvings and brass work, and in all probability the state had been in trading contact with the Hausa states in the north for some time.

The earlier history of Benin is largely conjecture, however. The religious association with Ile Ife indicates that the relation at one time had been very close. The people of Benin do not speak a Yoruba dialect, yet their religious, art, and social forms have much in common with the great states of Yorubaland. Benin and Yoruba legends speak of a time when Benin was in difficulty, and a request was made for Prince Oduduwa to send one of his sons to rule over the area. One of the sons, Prince Oranmiyan, answered the call and ruled in Benin for some time. He eventually left Benin with some of the followers and was responsible for the establishment of the Yoruba state of Oyo. His dynasty was continued in Benin, however, in the person of a son. Whether such a story is literally true or not it indicates that at one time, either by invitation or conquest, the royal house of Ife dominated Benin.

The administration of Benin in the sixteenth century was by means of the oba aided by a complex bureaucracy. As was the case in so many large states in Guinea the oba was the center of political and religious life. A check on complete autocracy were the great nobles who in the fifteenth century had acted in the role of kingmakers. In the sixteenth century the town chiefs were raised to a more important role in the state, perhaps as a result of their increasing importance in trade with the Europeans. The leader of the town chiefs, the iyase, was the chief adviser of the oba. Territory owing direct allegiance to Benin was governed by appointed chiefs. The oba gave these chiefs control over noncontiguous lands in order to make it more difficult for any one to build local support to challenge the central authority.

The impact of European trade on Benin was great. Benin

merchants, whose right to trade was controlled by the oba, wanted iron bars, cowries, beads, manufactured wares, and firearms, for which they traded pepper, leopard skins, ivory, and slaves. Benin also acted as a channel for trade with other African states of the interior, particularly the Hausa. In the late sixteenth century slaves became more important for trade, and Benin used the firearms obtained in barter to further extend its empire. Nevertheless, the slave trade was never as important for Benin as for many other states in Guinea. The kingdom of Warri, located southeast of Benin, provided easier access for the Portuguese traders. Portuguese missionaries were active in Warri and their presence as well as their economic interest there prevented Benin from absorbing the territory. In the eighteenth century Benin was even further bypassed because of the greater ease with which Europeans obtained slaves from Dahomey and the Ijo states of the Niger delta.

Captain John Adams, who visited Benin in the latter eighteenth century, noted the movement of the slave trade away from Benin to other areas along the coast. The slave trade and the profits to be gained from it and the relative ease with which guns could be obtained played an important role in the decline of Benin. The obas also had probably overreached themselves in their slave wars of the early eighteenth century. A combination of factors led many of the client states to break away from the control of the obas and, as a result, the Benin of the nineteenth century represented only a shadow of its previous glory.

Even at the height of its power Benin did not attempt to control the major Yoruba cities, since this action would have meant open conflict with the most powerful of the Guinea states, Oyo. The center of this state was the city of Oyo, located in the savannah country northwest of the less important Yoruba city of Ilorin. The early history of the city is largely conjecture, although Yoruba legends ascribe its founding of Prince Oranmiyan, who had previously ruled in Benin. It is known that in the fifteenth century Oyo was no more powerful than its northern neighbors, Nupe and Borgu. Its known history throughout the sixteenth century is one of continual warfare with these states. At one time in this century Nupe took and destroyed Oyo, forcing the Oyo to flee and settle in a new location. In the early seventeenth century Oyo became strong enough to defeat its old enemies and to reestablish the capital city, which remained the seat of government until its abandonment in 1837.

The wars with Nupe and Borgu were probably due to trade rivalry, with each state desiring to control the routes to the north and east. The army of Oyo, like those of its competitors, depended upon light cavalry, which was well suited to warfare in the open country. Oyo modified its army when it began to expand into more wooded territory. Later after trade with Europeans in the south became well established firearms were incorporated into the army. It is impossible to assess accurately the reasons behind the development of Oyo into an empire. However, the growing demand for slaves by Europeans probably was a reason not inferior to internal pressures generated within the state.

The armies of Oyo after negating Nupe proceeded in the latter seventeenth century to bring all of Yorubaland under the control of the alafin, or king, of Oyo. The exact relation between Oyo and Ife is not clear. On a purely ceremonial basis the alafin was still confirmed by the oni of Ife, but how far this titular subjection was allowed to go is questionable. By the opening of the eighteenth century the alafin dominated all of Yorubaland to the edge of the mangrove swamps in the south. His authority extended in the east to the boundaries of Benin. In the west as early as 1698 the armies of Oyo had overrun Great Ardra. In the following fifty years a number of armies were sent by the alafin to assure the obedience of the rulers of Dahomey. From 1747 until 1818 the kings of Dahomey paid an annual tribute to Oyo. In this entire area only Benin, Ijebu, and the Ekiti peoples maintained their separate existence from Oyo. The alafin controlled this vast territory by appointing subkings to rule over the conquered districts. The authority and independence of these subkings varied with the quality and decisiveness of the alafin and their distance from Oyo.

The political and social organization of Oyo was extremely complex. Primogeniture had possibly been the rule at an earlier date, but in the eighteenth century the alafin was selected from members of the royal house. The eldest son of the alafin was given the title aremo and had responsibility over some of the client states of Oyo. To avoid struggles for power the practice grew in the eighteenth century of having the aremo commit suicide on the death of his father. The alafin was believed to be a companion of the deities of the state, the owner of all land, and the giver of justice. He rarely appeared in public; the duties of the state were carried on by his representatives. The Oyo mesi were the main councilors of state who were also ward heads in Oyo. The chief councilor was the basorun, or prime minister. The Oyo mesi had the responsibility of choosing the successor of the alafin and also acted to check misuse of power by the alafin. They could force an alafin to commit suicide if the members were convinced he had exceeded his constitutional powers. The Oyo mesi were themselves constrained from over-use of this control, since one of their members also had to commit suicide with the king. Another counterbalance to the concentration of power in the hands of either the alafin or the Oyo mesi was a powerful secret society, the ogboni, whose decisions were binding on all its members.

The end of Oyo's dominance in Yorubaland came at the close of the eighteenth century. It was long believed that the European slave trade was the primary cause of this collapse, since it held out the chance of great profits to subchiefs and guns provided them the means to resist the alafin. Professor Akinjogbin, however, has pointed out that the demand for slaves did not reach its height until after 1820. It seems more probable that the slave trade was only a contributing cause of the downfall of Oyo. The major reason for the breakup of the Oyo empire was the growing authoritarianism of the alafin's court combined with a breakdown in the central administration.

In 1745 the powerful, strong-willed Gaha became basorun of Oyo. He retained this position for twenty years and utilized the peculiar constitutional instruments of Oyo to concentrate power in his hands. A number of alafins who opposed Gaha and his family were forced to commit suicide. Although this aspect of Oyo's history is not entirely clear, it appears that this period was particularly oppressive for the provinces of Oyo. After Gaha and all his family were killed by a palace revolt led by the alafin it was too late to placate the dissident areas. The Egba declared their independence from Oyo in the 1780s, Borgu followed in 1783, and Nupe in 1786. Although these provinces continued to pay tribute until 1818, the kings of Dahomey were independent in all other matters. By 1800 Oyo, although still a powerful state, had lost much of its empire. The increased demand for slaves after this date combined with the lack of one central authority ushered in a seventy-five-year period of civil war between the competitive Yoruba city-states.

The Ijo, Ibibio, and Ibo

In the delta and eastward from the Niger River lived a large population of many different peoples. British administration in the modern era imposed an order and unity on the area that had never existed before. The three main blocks of people in eastern Nigeria are the Ijo, Ibibio, and Ibo. These divisions are modern classifications and should not be confused with the typical political and social organization of these areas in the period before European occupation. Each group was composed of many separate clans, towns, and villages. Throughout most of the states of Guinea the loose village-oriented political system had given way to rule by a chief over a collection of villages. In turn this system in many cases was only preliminary to the creation of kingdoms and empires. The Ibo and most of the Ibibio perfected and retained into the twentieth century the older decentralized system. The Ijo also clung to this system until the European demand for slaves shifted the economic base of their society and caused the creation of more authoritarian political institutions.

The Ijo speak a Niger-Kordofanian language which is considerably different from the dominant Kwa subgroup of the Ibo and Ibibio. They have traditions of movement into the coastal areas from the north. Perhaps they were refugees from the rule of Benin, but when they moved and under what conditions is not known clearly. The Ijo were resident in roughly their present locations when the Europeans first arrived. They were divided into a number of groups, of which the Nembe, Kalabari, and Itsekiri were the most important. Before the Portuguese arrived the Ijo lived in villages of a few hundred inhabitants along the coastal reaches of the Niger delta. The land occupied by the Ijo was not very productive and could support only a small population. They were fishermen, and due to their geographic location were relatively isolated from the Ibo of the hinterland. The Ijo, however, did trade salt and fish to some of their neighbors for other foodstuffs and iron implements.

An Ijo village was divided into wards or houses that represented one patrilineage. Each ward had a leader, normally the eldest male of the patrilineage. A village head was chosen from one senior patrilineage. The village leader and the heads of wards had religious, executive, and judicial functions. As with many of the forest peoples, their religion was a combination of worship of anthropomorphic deities and natural forces. It was impossible to separate the secular from the religious life of the Ijo. The most important unifying forces among them were age sets, which cut across lineages, and marriage, which linked together various patrilineages.

The slave trade changed Ijo society dramatically. Since the immediate hinterland was too sparsely populated to meet the demand of the slavers, the Ijo, who controlled most of the usable ports in the eastern areas, began to trade and raid into the interior. Firearms obtained from Europeans in part enabled them to dominate this profitable trade. Equally important were the changes in the administrative structure of the important Ijo towns such as Bonny and Brass. The old system of the house was retained, but it became a political and economic unit rather than a collection of people of a given patrilineage. By the eighteenth century the house was in reality a canoe house, denoting the fact that the chief trader or head of the house could afford to equip at least one war canoe and many trading canoes. The authority of the head of the house was supreme, and each freeborn member was required to contribute a significant portion of his revenue to support the considerable overhead of the trade. The town head, whose authority in the old pre-European system had been minimal, now became the king. He and the heads of the canoe houses ruled the growing towns. The power of the monarch varied. Bonny represented perhaps the extreme in autocracy while Brass was more of an oligarchy.

The delta population grew rapidly after the sixteenth century, partly because of natural increase but also because of the influx of slaves. Not all the slaves purchased or captured were sold; many were used as workers by the houses and some became advisers to the rulers and accumulated power and wealth. European merchants encouraged centralization, since they preferred to deal with a few large houses rather than with small, undependable native traders. The Europeans did not challenge the near-monopoly of the interior trade by the Ijo and Ibibio coastal towns as long as the native rulers could supply the requisite number of slaves for purchase.

To the east between the Imo and Cross rivers, extending from Aro country in the north to the sea, lived the Ibibio, who seem to have been relative newcomers to the coastal fringes, having moved there some time immediately before the first Europeans arrived. There is considerable evidence to indicate that some elements had not settled in their present locations until the eighteenth century. They speak a variety of dialects of the Kwa subgroup of the Niger-Kordofanian language family. Today there are six major divisions of the Ibibio — the Efik, Andoni, Eket, Enyong, Anang, and Ibibio proper.

The Ibibio society of the coastal area in the vicinity of the Cross River is reasonably documented, since Calabar was a major slave-trading city. Basically the organization of this city was the same as that of the neighboring Ijo cities, although the Ibibio rulers, or etuboms, never enjoyed the degree of authority held by the Ijo kings. The prosperity of Calabar was based upon the slave trade, and it too had a difinite sphere of influence in the interior. However, the political, economic, and social institutions of Calabar were not adopted by the interior Ibibio; rather, they remained agricultural people and their politics continued to be village-oriented. Presumably they lived in the eighteenth century in much the same way as they did a century later when European missionaries first began to describe their societies.

The basic unit among the Ibibio was the extended family household. A cluster of such households formed a ward presided over by the head of the patrilineage. Male members of the patrilineage formed the nucleus of the ward and held collective rights to land. A group of wards comprised a village under the control of one recognized leader chosen from the ward heads. These villages were separate entities and most of the major decisions affecting the inhabitants were made by the village head in conjunction with an advisory council. The largest meaningful political unit throughout most of Ibibio territory was the village group or town. A village group normally had both a religious and a secular leader. Each leader and his advisers could act on matters of joint concern to all of the villages. This decentralized form of government was not as simple as many European observers believed, however. At each level there were delicate counterbalancing forces that tended to curb authoritarianism and yet allowed the villages to function smoothly. Further complicating the pattern was the existence of age sets, secret societies, and kinship relations between villages based on marriage ties.

Northward of the Ibibio lived the Ibo, an even larger concentration of more diverse people. It is impossible even today to reconstruct what Ibo society was like just fifty years ago.

Certain outlines of that society are known and by extrapolation backward a picture of the Ibo in the eighteenth century can be generally predicated. The term Ibo itself is a creation of British administrators of the twentieth century, since most Ibo people considered themselves to be citizens of a village or, at most, a town. Ibo as a collective term comes from the phrase *ndi igbo*, used by the people who lived along the Niger River, which means simply people of the hinterland. Iboland in the seventeenth and eighteenth centuries was densely populated with hundreds of different villages. Like the Ibibio, the Ibo spoke variants of the Kwa subdivision of the Niger-Congo language family. Today there are two major Ibo languages, Owerri and Onitsha Ibo, although the dialects do not conform with the present boundaries of those Nigerian provinces. There are many more less important dialect forms such as the Nri-Awka, Eluga, and the language of Onitsha town.

Ibo political and social organization was superficially very similar to that of the Ibibio. The basis of the economy was agriculture, and presumably much of the land in the eighteenth century was of good quality. Before the advent of European slave trading there was little organized trade and most of that was on the local level. Political, social, and religious organization was based upon the extended family. In ascending order there were wards, villages, and village groups. The most important political unit was the village, which varied in area from one-half to over six square miles and in population from a few hundred persons to over two thousand. At each political level all freemen participated in decision-making. Secular and religious leaders were chosen because of lineage, age, and ability. Their authority at all levels was circumscribed by custom and by institutions such as age sets and secret societies. In times of danger village groups could combine into a larger armed force, but the strength of their local institutions combined with the geography effectively prevented any long-term coalition.

Scattered throughout Iboland was another group of people who had a special place in the society. These were the Aro, and their population was centered on the site of the great shrine of Aro-Chukwu. The Aro were formed in the early eighteenth century when Ibo invaders pressed in upon the indigenous Ibibio. Neither agricultural group could overcome the other until the arrival of another group, the Akpa, who probably had guns. The Ibo allied themselves with the newcomers and defeated the Ibibio. Instead of killing or driving out the vanquished the conquerors established a confederation of nineteen towns, with each ethnic element having its own sphere. The bases of political action were the clans, with the king of the Aros providing the necessary unifying link between them. The Ibibio had before the confederation established a small shrine by a stream near the town of Ibom. Under the leadership of the new rulers this shrine of the long juju at Aro-Chukwu became the most important religious center east of the Niger. It became for the Ibo, Ijo, and Ibibio what the Oracle of Delphi was for the Greeks. The Aro exploited the shrine of the long juju for their economic and political advantage. Although they used military force against some of their enemies, their hold on the Ibo depended largely on the latter's fear of the long juju. The nineteen Aro towns divided Iboland into spheres of influence and Aro agents were sent to the major villages there. By the opening of the nineteenth century these Aro middlemen controlled all the major trade, particularly in slaves, of Iboland. The shrine itself, apart from the hold it gave over the numerically superior Ibo, was also a major revenue producer, since the priests of the shrine collected large fees from all supplicants.

Iboland, with its large population, its democratic rule by village political structures, and its trade under the control of the Aro, presented to the Europeans of the nineteenth century a confusing mélange. It did not conform to the typical pattern of African state organization and therefore later European administrators and writers tended to dismiss the Ibo as very backward. This idea seemed to be confirmed by the slave records from the eighteenth century onward, since the bulk of slaves transported from the Niger delta area were Ibos. It has been only in the past thirty years that the Ibo themselves and a few scholars have demonstrated how wrong were these naive early reports.

FOUR

Europeans in West Africa

The Portuguese trading monopoly, 1434–1650

Rulers of the Christian kingdoms of the Iberian Peninsula had been interested in North Africa since the eleventh century. Two Muslim dynasties, the Almoravids and Almohades, which briefly halted the Christian reconquest, had come from Africa. Even during the most disturbed periods of Iberian history trade had continued with the Muslim world. In the fifteenth century, although the Mediterranean was still a Muslim sphere, European traders, particularly the Genoese and Venetians, were given specific permission to deal in the rich Eastern trade. The kings of Portugal had sought in vain to break the monopoly of their Mediterranean rivals, and in the early fifteenth century King John I decided to carve out a North African empire at the expense of Morocco. His younger son Henry became the governor of Ceuta after its capture in 1415. For the remainder of his life the austere, dedicated Henry advanced the cause of Portuguese economic interests by encouraging and financing voyages of exploration. There were secondary motivations for his activity in this area, such as bringing Christianity to the unenlightened and crusading against the Muslim infidel. The economic factor, however, was the chief impulse to his sponsorship of early Portuguese explorations.

Abandoning any attempt to force the Mediterranean, mariners under the Portuguese flag began a series of cautious voyages along the coast after 1415. They reached the Canary Islands and began colonization there in 1424. In the 1430s the Portuguese adopted the lateen sail, common in the eastern Mediterranean, to their larger ships. This new technique allowed ships to tack close enough to the wind to sail easily against the prevailing northerly winds. Thus equipped, Gil Eannes rounded the feared Cape Bojador in 1434. There followed in quick succession a series of voyages that brought the Portuguese to the vicinity of modern-day Sierra Leone before Henry's death in 1460. Antam Goncalvez and Niño Tristão explored south of Rio de Oro in 1441, Tristão reached the island of Arguin in 1444, and Aluise Cadamosto and Antoniotto Usodomare investigated the Gambia River by 1456. Fernão Gomes' ships crossed the equator in 1475, Captain Diogo Cão investigated the mouth of the Congo River, and in 1487 Bartholomeu Dias rounded the Cape of Good Hope. Two years before the close of the century Vasco da Gama sailed along the East African coast and from there across the Indian Ocean to India. Islamic control of the Eastern trade was thus broken and the Mediterranean ceased to be the highway of commerce for the luxury items so in demand in Europe.

Long before the voyage of Vasco da Gama the Portuguese were attempting to extract profit from their discoveries. They established factories, and wherever necessary, forts in key places along the Guinea coast which enabled them to trade for desired African goods. Arguin, an island just below Cape Blanco, flourished as a trading center for almost seventy-five years. Santiago Island in the Cape Verde group became very important to the early Portuguese ventures along the upper Guinea coast. Other important Portuguese factories in this region were Rio Fresco near Cape Verde, Cacheo near the Rio Grande River, and Mitombe in what is now Sierra Leone. Settlers, freebooters, and priests followed the merchants and soldiers and thus small Portuguese populations became residents near the trading stations. The wealth imagined for most of the upper Guinea coast proved illusory, and in the sixteenth century the Portuguese began to ignore these areas and concentrate their efforts on the more profitable Gold Coast and the Congo-Angola complex further south.

The Mina coast very early became the center of Portuguese activities. Here the traders discovered the answer to the dreams of a gold-starved monarchy. The presence of well-organized Akan states, however, made trading sometimes a difficult and dangerous occupation. In 1482 Portuguese traders constructed the first portion of their most imposing fortress in West Africa, São Jorge da Mina. All later Portuguese factories along the Gold Coast were also fortified and because of the danger movement between them was by sea or if by land with an armed escort. The island of São Thome also played an important part in Portugal's West African ventures. Settled in the late fifteen century from the mainland, it had become within twenty-five years valued for its plantation cultivation of sugarcane. Slightly later the islands of Principe and Fernando Po also began to produce sugarcane. Much less important to the Portuguese but still of significance in the slave trade until 1520 was the station of Gwatt, located within the boundaries of the kingdom of Benin.

The Portuguese were mainly concerned with obtaining as much gold as possible. Trade in ivory, pepper, and slaves in the early sixteenth century were all subservient to this primary interest. Along the Gold Coast they were constrained to deal with African middlemen, since the inland Akan states were too powerful to be brought under Portuguese control. Nevertheless, it is estimated that in the early sixteenth century traders near São Jorge da Mina provided Portugal with over one quarter of a million dollars annually in gold.

In this very early period of consolidation the Portuguese were challenged by only one other European power. Merchants from Castile were active in the Canary Islands and on the Guinea coast during the latter fifteenth century. Increasing this potential rivalry were the claims of Portuguese kings to the throne of Castile. There was open warfare between the two states from 1475 until the Treaty of Alcaçovas in 1479 settled many of the differences between the two powers. By this agreement Portugal renounced its claims on Castile and the Canaries and received Castilian promises not to intervene in the Azores, Cape Verde Islands, and on the mainland of Guinea. The New World soon absorbed the attention and energies of Castile, and the Treaty of Tordesillas of 1494 guaranteed Portuguese possession of the new territories east of the 46th meridian while Spain was granted the monopoly of the New World west of that line.

Portuguese trade in African slaves was almost as old as that country's earliest southward explorations. Goncalvez in 1441 brought back twelve captives to Lisbon, and thereafter every Portuguese captain followed the practice of seizing slaves for the return voyage. In 1456 Cadamosto reported systematic raiding off the Cape Verde coast of fishing villages for slaves. By the close of the fifteenth century the Portuguese operating from Arguin had stopped raiding and had begun to trade with the Sanhaja Berbers for captives. Horses, silk, and manufactured items were key wares in the trade. The rate of exchange varied considerably, but a good horse could bring in return as many as fifteen slaves. Some slaves obtained in the northern trade were shipped further south to the Mina coast and traded to the Akan for gold. This practice emphasizes the early unimportance of slaves in comparison with gold.

There was no significant demand for slaves in Europe during the fifteenth century. Africans taken by the Portuguese in this period were used as domestics or preserved for their curiosity value. Other European states, concerned with the multifold problems of incipient nationalism, feudalism, and dynastic quarrels, were uninterested in Africa and viewed slavery with abhorrence. In the early sixteenth century a proclamation of the French government stated that no slavery was permitted in France, and as late as 1607 a French policy statement was isued similar to the Mansfield dictum of 1772 in England. According to this policy all slaves who set foot on French soil were presumed to be free. Similar sentiments were expressed by English officials. Richard Jobson, a factor on the Gambia River in 1623, scornfully rejected an offer to purchase slaves with the statement that Englishmen did not buy and sell other men.

Many of these noble sentiments when expressed by church and secular officials were already at variance with reality. The change in attitude toward slavery that came about in the sixteenth century was a direct result of Spanish exploitation of their new territories in the West Indies. The indigenous Indians of the islands were either so hostile that they were exterminated or when pressed into labor gangs to work the mines they died in great numbers from overwork or disease. Mining operations and the newly established sugar plantations demanded a larger number of docile laborers than could be supplied by the enslavement of Indians. In 1501 the first foreign slaves, most of them white, were transported to Hispaniola. However, in 1518 the first shipload of slaves was brought to Hispaniola directly from Africa. Plantation crops of tobacco and sugar were systematically extended to all the Spanish territories of the West Indies in the sixteenth century. The Spanish crown licensed the importation of an ever-increasing number of slaves from Africa to the islands to meet the continuously inflated demands. In addition, direct voyages from Africa were relatively simple because of the prevailing westerly winds and currents.

Conflicting Portuguese and Spanish political goals, which might have restricted the supply of slaves, were resolved in 1580. When Portugal regained its independence the combined empire controlled the sources of supply and the areas of greatest demand for slaves. The first major licensed monopoly for importation of slaves to the New World was granted to Pedro Gomes Reynal in 1593. For the sum of 900,000 ducats Reynal guaranteed to provide 3,500 live slaves from Africa every year for nine years.

Other areas of the New World were undergoing a similar agricultural revolution. Brazil by the middle of the sixteenth century, although the full exploitation of its mineral and agricultural potentials was far in the future, was demanding slaves to clear the land and work its mines. Portuguese settlers early in the sixteenth century introduced sugar culture to the islands of São Thomé, Fernando Po, and Principe. These planters also demanded slaves to work their rich plantations. Thus in less than one hundred years the world's economic situation had altered completely. Negro slaves, who were of only nominal value in 1500, had become indispensable to the maintenance and development of this new plantation economy. The Portuguese, who had a theoretical monopoly on the slave trade in the sixteenth century, found it increasingly difficult to supply the needs of all the new areas. In the early seventeenth century when their country was joined to Spain and its European policies the Portuguese had the additional, ultimately insoluble, problem of protecting their monopoly from the incursions of the English, French, and Dutch.

England in the early sixteenth century was recovering from almost a century of civil war. Its maritime fleet was inferior to those of the Spanish and Portuguese and its entrance into world trade was conditioned by its economic ties with the Spanish Netherlands. The first English trading voyage to the Guinea coast was undertaken by William Hawkins in 1530. Hawkins and later captains were interested not in slaves but in gold, ivory, and pepper. Technically the English were inter-lopers but profits up to ten times the investment made the Guinea trade increasingly important. Demands by the planta-tions of the Spanish empire for slaves caused William Hawkins' son to undertake the first English slaving voyage in 1562. John Hawkins' three ships carried approximately 300 slaves from Africa to the West Indies, where the Spanish planters eagerly purchased the illegal cargoes. Hawkins made two other slaving voyages in the 1560s.

Spanish commitments to the religious wars in Europe had far-reaching consequences. In the course of these disturbances a new nation, the Dutch Republic, was created out of the old Spanish Netherlands. Further, Philip II's attempts to subvent the English monarchy broke the centuries-old trading links with England. English mariners, encouraged by Queen Eliza-beth, attacked the Spanish empire on all the oceans and later in the seventeenth century established English colonies in the West Indies and North America. The English seized Bermuda in 1609, St. Christopher in 1623, Barbados in 1625, and after-ward moved to the leeward chain of islands. From 1609 onward English colonists were planted in the North American colonies. In this manner England created its own slave-utilizing empire. In 1588 Queen Elizabeth to capitalize on slave trade granted exclusive rights for a period of ten years to certain English merchants trading in West Africa. In 1598 and again in 1618 the English government granted new concessions to other mer-chants. The 1618 monopoly was given to thirty London mer-chants who called themselves The Company of Adventurers. While none of these companies ever gained the riches that their investors or royal sponsors imagined, they nevertheless repre-sented solid mercantilistic inroads on a trading territory that had previously been a Portuguese monopoly.

The French in the latter sixteenth century also became interested in West African trade. By 1560 merchants of Dieppe had established a regular trade with Senegal and areas immedi-ately south of Cape Verde. French efforts after this date became concentrated on the Senegambia region. In 1612 an attempt to plant a colony on the Gambia River failed and thereafter French merchants preferred to trade further north near Cape Verde. Although the Portuguese still traded in the Senegambia, the area had ceased to be of great importance to them, since most of their wealth came from the Gold Coast. Thus these early French ventures did not drastically interfere with Portuguese trade.

The entrance of the Dutch into competition for world trade, however, dealt the Portuguese blows from which they never recovered. The Dutch Republic was the result of the revolt of the northern areas of the Spanish Netherlands against the centralized policies of Philip II. The revolution which began in 1572 had, with the aid of England and some of the German states, by the close of the century created a new major maritime power. The most vulnerable parts of the Spanish empire were the Portuguese possessions, and the Dutch captains concentrated on these. Portuguese naval power in the spice-rich Indian Ocean area had been all but destroyed by 1610. Dutch traders were active in West Africa earlier. In 1612 the Dutch constructed a trading base on Mouri in the Senegambia and five years later built two forts on the island of Goree near Cape Verde.

Dutch dominance over the Atlantic carrying trade began with the creation in 1621 of the Dutch West Indies Company. The focal point of this company was the New World. By 1637 the Dutch had conquered a good part of the settled areas of Brazil. To gain the maximum profit from Brazil they sought to encourage the development of the tropical plantations owned by Portuguese planters. Such growth depended upon a steady supply of slaves. The Dutch, therefore, embarked upon the conquest of the major Portuguese trading stations in West Africa. In 1637 São Jorge da Mina (renamed Elmina) was taken, and by 1642 all of the Portuguese forts along the coast were in Dutch hands.

After Portuguese independence from Spanish control had been effected in 1640 a counteroffensive was mounted against the Dutch. São Thomé and Loanda were recaptured in 1648 and the Dutch were finally expelled from Brazil in 1654. However, the Dutch retained possession of Arguin, Goree, and the Mina coast. By the middle of the seventeenth century other states had taken advantage of the breakup of the Portuguese monopoly. In the 1640s Dutch capital financed the creation of the Swedish African Company which established stations along the Gold Coast. In 1647 the Swedish forts along the Mina coast were transferred to Denmark. English merchants after the debilitating civil war at home became extremely active in world trade after 1650, and the French, guided by Louis

XIV and his finance minister Colbert, became more interested in colonies. Even states such as Brandenburg and Courland established stations in West Africa. Trade with West Africa after 1650 became extremely competitive and the area more than at any previous time felt the destructive efforts of a century of European wars.

The period of rivalry: 1650–1763

From the beginning European trade efforts in Africa and the New World were closely connected with the foreign economic policies of individual states. The dominant economic theory was mercantilism, which viewed trade and colonies as another method of securing political advantage for one's own state against other European nations or dynasties. Thus all trading companies in Africa in the sixteenth century were given trading monopolies by their governments. The chartered companies were granted vast prerogatives. Some, like the Dutch West Indies Company, were given authority in both Africa and the New World. Mercantilism in its pure sense was never operative even in the sixteenth century, and the close association of the trading companies with their governments served to hasten the demise of monopoly. This was a period of dynastic rivalry and religious differences in Europe. A succession of European wars in the seventeenth and eighteenth centuries were duplicated in the West Indies and Africa. Forts, stations, supplies, and ships of the rival companies became political targets, and this combined with the cost of maintaining permanent stations made the African ventures, even at the height of the slave trade, unprofitable for the large companies.

The degree of competition and lack of profits is illustrated by the numbers of companies active on the coast of West Africa in the earliest period. The English crown had recognized different groups of merchants to trade along the coast in 1588, 1618, and 1631. The commonwealth chartered a Guinea Company, and this in turn gave way to the Royal Adventurers, which was recognized in 1660. This latter company was organized specifically to provide slaves for the plantations of the New World. Its failure resulted in the creation in 1672 of the Royal African Company. There was lengthy litigation with the stockholders of the previous company before the Royal African Company legally became the sole English trading company in West Africa.

The French followed the same general pattern, with four short-lived companies created between 1634 and 1658. In 1664 Colbert organized the French West Indies Company, which was given the monopoly of all French trade in the Indies and of all slave carrying from the west coast from the Cape of Good Hope northward. The ambitious scheme collapsed in 1672 and subsequently there was formed a Senegal Company and then a Guinea Company to exploit the West African trade. Finally in 1696 the Royal Senegal Company was organized. By this time France had concentrated its efforts on the Senegambia region and in the early eighteenth century the company prospered. There were, however, two major resrictions upon any French company at this time. From the Senegambia enough slaves could not be obtained even to supply the French plantations of the West Indies. More crucial were the adverse effects of the continuing wars with England. In the latter half of the eighteenth century France lost most of her colonial empire and everywhere her trade and prosperity were on the wane.

The first three quarters of the seventeenth century witnessed the quick rise to prominence of the Dutch in world trade. They swept the Portuguese from the Indian Ocean and captured the bulk of Portugal's holdings in West Africa. For a brief time the Dutch even controlled Brazil and the rich sugar-producing islands of São Thomé, Principe, and Fernando Po. The government of the Dutch Republic chartered two companies to exploit world trade. The East Indies Company operated in the vast territory east of the Cape of Good Hope, while the trading monopoly for the Atlantic area was given to the West Indies Company, which was formed in 1621. Even after the Portuguese had recovered the islands in the Gulf of Guinea and their stations in Angola the Dutch maintained a virtual stranglehold on the Guinea trade.

The Dutch base of operations in West Africa was Elmina on the Gold Coast, although they held stations as far north as Cape Verde. Furthermore, the Dutch had the largest and best designed merchant fleet in Europe, and thus they controlled the bulk of the carrying trade to even the theoretically closed markets in the British, French, and Spanish empires. This maritime dominance was challenged by England in the latter seventeenth century. The first navigation acts instituted by the commonwealth led in 1652 to a two-year naval struggle between England and Holland. Two more wars followed in 1665–1667 and 1672–1674. Neither antagonist won a clear-cut victory in these wars, but the English navigation acts remained in force and the economic drain of the wars combined with those essayed by Holland against Louis XIV proved too much for the Dutch. The Dutch retained their stations on the Gold Coast and in the West Indies, but dominance of the carrying trade passed to England. In the early eighteenth century England's control of the seas was challenged by France as an adjunct to the European conflicts of the two states. This costly rivalry continued through the entire century, melding into the Napoleonic wars of the early nineteenth century. By 1763, however, the French had already lost their race with England for colonial supremacy in India, North America, and the West Indies. Further, in the eighteenth century England had developed efficient methods of government finance, while the administrations of Louis XV and XVI in France were rushing headlong into bankruptcy and revolution.

In Africa the Royal African Company's profits were drained by the cost of upkeep of forts, small native wars, and the succession of costly European wars. More fundamental than any of these factors in the demise of the monopolistic company were the numbers of free traders who became active in the trade in the eighteenth century. Parliament after the revolution of 1688 was hostile to the maintenance of monopoly, and in 1698 trade with West Africa was thrown open to all English merchants. The Royal African Company, charged with the upkeep of forts and defenses, was allowed to assess a ten percent duty on all goods sent to and from West Africa. This measure was not sufficient to allow the Royal African Company to keep pace with its smaller competitors, however, and after 1730 the company depended upon an annual subsidy from parliament to operate. The War of the Austrian Succession and the cancellations of the parliamentary subsidy in 1747 brought an end to the company and parliament made its bankruptcy official by a divesting act in 1752. Its place in African trade was taken by a regulated "Company of Merchants Trading to Africa." This company represented the interests of all English traders and was forbidden to carry on trade in its corporate capacity. It could only make rules for the conduct of trade and was given an annual subsidy by parliament to maintain the English coastal forts. Otherwise the English free traders had a clear field for their operations in West Africa.

Trading areas of West Africa

The slave trade was not pursued with equal intensity in all parts of West Africa. A brief survey of the main geographic segments of the coast will indicate the areas of greatest interest. No company ever managed to gain a predominant position in the trade along the windward coast from Goree Island south to Sherbro Island. In the northern section the French became dominant after taking Goree from the Dutch in 1677. They were never able to gain a monopoly of the Gambia River trade, however, because the English, established on James Island, effectively blocked these ambitions. From 1765 to 1783 England ruled the entire coastal area from the Gambia north to the Senegal River. The French regained their predominance in the Senegambia only after the Treaty of Versailles. South of the Gambia the Portuguese had a few stations such as Bissau and Bulama. In the eighteenth century English independent merchants had built temporary stations and enjoyed relatively good relations with the natives of Sherbro Island and the adjacent coast of Sierra Leone.

The Grain and Ivory coasts were important in the early sixteenth century for the pepper and ivory that could be obtained by barter with the natives. Many factors combined, however, to minimize trade with this section of the coast. There were few good harbors, and strong coastal currents and frequent storms made trading ventures dangerous. The political organization of the native peoples was such that they could not supply large numbers of slaves. There were so many other places in West Africa to trade where these problems were absent that only a few Europeans, mostly French, bothered with the Grain and Ivory coasts. French missionaries established a station at Assini in 1687 and a few traders settled there, but the post was abandoned eighteen years later. Thus in the eighteenth century the small volume of trade from this portion of the coast was handled by a few itinerant merchants hoping to fill out a cargo without the competition of the larger companies.

Reference has already been made to the importance of the Gold Coast as early as the fifteenth century. All European companies interested in trading with the Akan people were constrained to follow the Portuguese example and build forts. From these fortified enclaves European merchants traded in various fashions with the neighboring Ashanta, Efutu, and Ga clans. At the opening of the eighteenth century the Dutch West Indies Company, with its headquarters at Elmina, controlled ten forts from Axim in the west to Barracoe in the east. The English established their first forts at Kormantin in 1631 and in 1664 captured Cape Coast Castle from the Dutch and made it their headquarters. By the close of the seventeenth century there were nine English forts along the coast. In the western region there were two small forts operated by Brandenburg until 1709. The Danes were also very active, particularly among the Ga people east of Accra. Trade in gold remained important throughout the eighteenth century, but the major lure of the Gold Coast, as elsewhere, was slaves. The development of the Ashanti Union in the seventeenth century changed the relation of the Europeans to their suppliers. Instead of dealing with scattered, moderately powerful states they now had to depend upon the goodwill and cooperation of one of the most powerful African nations. The Ashanti controlled the supply of slaves for the coast. The history of the Gold Coast for two centuries after the creation of the Ashanti Union is the story of European conflict with this powerful polity.

The ever-increasing demand for slaves led the chartered companies and individual traders to expand their search to include areas other than the older, established ones. Thus by the end of the seventeenth century efforts were concentrated on the coastal strip from the Gold Coast eastward to Badagry. The Portuguese had done little in the way of trading with the native peoples in this territory, but European traders in the late seventeenth and throughout the eighteenth century took so many slaves from this area that it was given the name Slave Coast. The most fruitful territory for pursuing the trade was controlled in the eighteenth century by the king of Dahomey and the alafin of Oyo and their representatives. These rulers with few exceptions did not allow even the large companies to establish permanent fortified bases. European traders were permitted to construct only mud and thatch buildings for their living quarters and the depots where slaves could be collected. Even with such precautions Europeans by allying with dissident elements at Jaquin, Whydah, and Little Popo were a continual problem for the kings of Dahomey.

In the latter eighteenth and well into the nineteenth century many slave traders had been forced by recurring crises

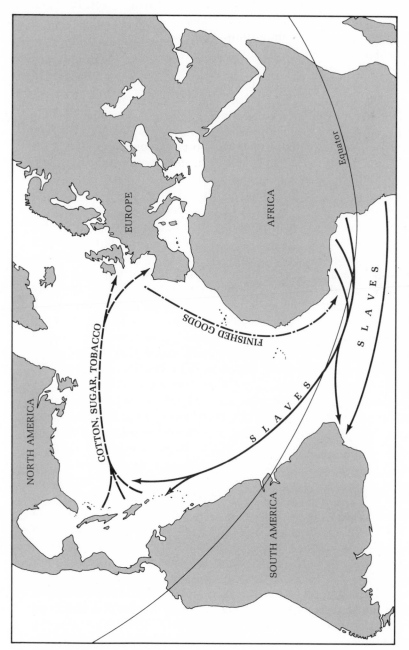

The Triangular Trade

within the kingdom of Dahomey to trade further east. Badagry, Lagos, and the Ijo and Ibibio states east of the Niger delta became increasingly important. Trade with Badagry and Lagos prospered as long as the kingdom of Oyo remained the power along the coast. However, with the waning of Oyo trading with the Yoruba became more complex and dangerous.

The rise of slaving as an important industry east of the Niger River resulted in the conversion of former small fishing villages into highly centralized, powerful trading polities. The most important of these were the Ijo towns of Bonny and Brass and the Ibibio state of Calabar. Europeans, the bulk of whom were English, were under the same kinds of restrictions along the Niger coast as in Dahomey. The recruitment of slaves from the interior, either by raiding or purchase from the Aro or Hausa, was rigidly controlled by the kings and the heads of the canoe houses. There was no disagreement on this point between the European and native merchants, since by the time the Niger districts became important no slaving consortium was interested in building and maintaining costly forts. Europeans were thus more responsive to native pressure and were not as much in control of the bartering situation as in some other areas. Nevertheless, the supply of slaves, which seemed almost inexhaustible, and the political stability of the coastal states made up for this inconvenience. The problem of providing places to keep slaves after their purchase was solved by temporary slave pens (baracoons) or by the use of hulks moored in the rivers. By 1800, with the exception of Angola, more slaves were being sent from the eastern coast of Nigeria than from any other part of Africa.

The methodology of the slave trade

The methodology of the trade varied greatly with the area of recruitment as well as with the time period. Policies in the Niger delta region in the late eighteenth century were very different from those on the Gold Coast in the seventeenth century. The activities of a factor representing a large monopoly company would be different from those of a captain of a vessel sponsored by a small independent company. Many of the differences in technique were responses to the various African people who represented differing attitudes and demands. Despite the research that has been done on the slave trade, there is still a tendency to view the African's role as passive, meekly surrendering to the will of avaricious European traders. The factors and slavers were harsh and cruel, but, except in a few areas they did not control the internal trade. Collection of slaves from the interior was almost exclusively in African hands. The continual flow of slaves to coastal areas was determined by the operation of complex political and economic arrangements between interior African states and the African middlemen who dealt directly with the Europeans. Powerful kingdoms such as Ashanti, Dahomey, Oyo, and Benin zealously guarded their prerogatives from interlopers.

European merchants along the Gold Coast were in a more fortunate position than their counterparts elsewhere. They could defy the kings of Ashanti and be protected from military retribution by the strong walls of their forts. Nevertheless, the Ashanti could punish individual European nations by diverting slaves away from the trading stations of their enemies to those of their friends. Merchants along the Gold Coast could also accumulate more slaves, which were held in the forts pending the arrival of appropriate ships to take them away. This system obviated the problems of indifferent and irregular supply and minimized turnaround time for the slave ships. Elsewhere along the coast slave captains either dealt directly with African middlemen for their cargoes or used resident agents to make their purchases, holding the slaves in baracoons until the arrival of ships. In either case the Europeans were at the mercy of the African, who was not reluctant to press his advantage. One of the few permanent forts east of the Gold Coast was São João Baptista de Ajuda, constructed by the Portuguese at Whydah in 1721. In eighty-four years of operation it had twenty directors, six of whom were expelled by the kings of Dahomey. The fort in the same period was invaded twice and burned three times.

Where there was no real danger to European traders their activities were still restricted in any number of ways as the Africans sought to increase their profits. The most obvious method was by the pricing of slaves. There was no fixed price per slave along the coast but rather the price set according to demand, and African merchants would charge all the market would bear. The Africans also charged for other necessary services they rendered. Individual captains who had to deal with chiefs or middlemen directly found that not only time and patience were needed but also presents for the chiefs. In some better-organized states the rulers had developed the tax and tribute systems to a very fine art. James Barbot reported that at Great Ardra the custom was to pay the king up to the value of fifty slaves in goods for the right to trade. A similar system of "comey," or tax for permission to trade, was established in all the Niger delta states. In addition, merchants had to hire canoes and canoemen to transport slaves, and they were charged for water, wood, and food. Barbot reported some of the costs involved in revictualing a ship engaged in the trade at Calabar in 1699. Among other items, he needed 50,000 yams, for which he was charged one iron bar for 150 slave yams, or sixty king's yams. Considering that in many places a healthy slave could be obtained for forty bars, this meant that the minimum expenditure for the yams was the equivalent of approximately nine slaves. Other prices at the time were eight to ten bars for a cow, one bar for a goat, and seven bars for a length of wood.

Even in peaceful areas where there was no European war to disturb business the African trade was a very complex procedure. The economic historian Karl Polanyi has pointed out that traditional African trade was an import-oriented system designed to obtain needed staple items. In most cases this system involved barter, an exchange of one unit for another. In contrast, the European system from the seventeenth century onward was export-oriented and designed to gain profit in money terms. The African method prevailed and the European merchants came to accept the relation between two staple items. These barter items had then to be recalculated in terms of money or gold.

Although there were well over one hundred trade items used, the most common European goods were iron bars, rolls of tobacco, gold, cowrie shells, platilles (folded white linen), and barrels of brandy. A feature of the trade of the seventeenth and eighteenth centuries was the use of "sortings," or bundles of various types of goods which were calculated to be the equivalent of one ounce (480 grains) of gold. These sortings were selected to please the tastes of African merchants, and their composition varied greatly depending on time, place, and the initial cost of the articles. The practice of marking up costs of these sortings one hundred percent was soon adopted by almost all European traders. There was thus created an artificial currency unit called the trade ounce, or in French areas *once*. The trade ounce could be further subdivided and its value expressed in other terms such as bars, cowries, and actual value in gold.

The following table partially extrapolated from Archibald Dalzel gives the approximate values for the Dahomean coast in 1793:

40 cowries	=	1 tockey	=	1⅕ d			
5 tockeys	=	1 gallina	=	6 d			
5 gallinas	=	1 ackey	=	2/ 6d			
4 ackeys	=	1 cabess	=	10 s	=	2 bars	
4 cabess	=	1 ounce	=	40 s	=	8 bars	=	16,000 cowries

The money value expressed above is that of the trade ounce. The real European value for a gold ounce was 32,000 cowries.

The artificial system gave the European merchants initially much greater profits and a larger cushion against losses. However, the Africans soon compensated for this by demanding more for a normal slave. In Dahomey, for example, a good slave could be purchased in the 1690s for approximately £5.

After 1704 the equivalent slave cost 80,000 cowries, or five trade ounces, which represented a doubling of the cost of ten years before. Thus the Africans effectively balanced the cost of slaves in terms of gold.

As previously noted, different products were needed to conduct trade along various sections of the coast. Barbot reported that along the Slave Coast cowrie shells made up about half the trade supplies of European merchants. The other half consisted of various manufactured products. When cowries were in short supply the Europeans tried to stress European goods. One reason for the shift of trade eastward to Porto Novo and Badagry in the eighteenth century was the attempt by one king of Dahomey to establish a full cowrie currency. Sortings of various kinds, iron bars, and brandy were the important elements in the Niger delta trade.

The most popular item of trade along the Mina coast was Brazilian tobacco from Bahia. The Dutch in the seventeenth century allowed a direct trade from Bahia to this area on the payment of a ten percent duty on imported goods. The Portuguese required Brazilian merchants to send the best tobacco to Lisbon, keeping only the third grade for their use in the trade. This inferior leaf was rolled into ropelike forms and liberally treated with molasses to preserve it. The resultant flavor made it a great favorite with Africans and this gave the Bahia merchants a distinct advantage over all other traders. The African merchants preferred this item even to gold. Normally one roll of tobacco was worth one ounce of gold and in the 1750s at peak times a prime slave could be obtained for six rolls of this tobacco. The popularity of this single item can be seen in the volume of direct trade between Bahia and West Africa. In the last thirty years of the eighteenth century 386 tobacco ships left Bahia for the Mina coast.

Pricing aside, the method of trading for slaves remained consistent. Where companies could afford factors these representatives purchased slaves from their African counterparts and kept them in baracoons until ships arrived to take them away. These officials were also responsible for overseeing a large and complex credit system. Trade supplies would be loaned to African traders who would actually gather the slaves. Where there were no resident agents captains or supercargoes would do the bartering. One major problem for the European was to establish criteria for a normal or standard slave. Once this had been done the buyer would be recompensed for any deviation from this norm. All slaves were examined as thoroughly as possible by the buyers and in some cases by medical officers, since the long, harsh voyage put a premium on young, healthy slaves. Once the selection had been made and accounts rendered, the slaves were branded, usually on the chest, with the device of the particular company. William Bosman, taking care for the delicate sensibilities of his readers, reported in the eighteenth century that "we take all possible care that they are not burned too hard, especially the women, who are more tender than the men."

After the marking was completed the slaves were either taken to holding areas or directly to the ships. All types of vessels from 50 to 400 tons were used in the trade. The most common type of ship was a snow, a sturdy craft of between 125 and 150 tons. The larger English frigates were licensed to carry about 450 slaves, but overloading of one hundred percent was ordinary. The voyage from West Africa to the New World took between six and ten weeks. The crowded and unsanitary conditions combined with the sadism and brutality of ship officers took a large toll of the slaves. Most captains, however, were very concerned about their loss rates, since a consistently high rate cost the owners money and would jeopardize the captain's career. In the seventeenth century losses of over twenty-five percent were not uncommon. In the eighteenth century most captains followed policies of watching diets and bringing slaves on deck to force them to exercise. Even with greater care the attrition rates continued to be very high.

Volume and effects of the slave trade

The simple, direct, and important question of how many human beings were transported from Africa cannot be answered, although a number of attempts have been made to fix the approximate numbers involved. None of these satisfies, since in order to construct a figure certain sweeping assumptions must be made concerning the average number carried by company and private traders during a specific period. By establishing average figures and then backplotting a total number can be assigned. The initial assumptions of average numbers carried by Portuguese, French, British, and Dutch ships are educated guesses based upon available data. However, record-keeping was not that important during the earlier periods. During the latter seventeenth and early eighteenth centuries when private traders were unlawfully invading monopoly areas it was not advisable to maintain good records. As an example of the potential difference between data maintained by different agencies, witness the records of Barbados between 1698 and 1708. The port records indicate that separate traders brought in 7,218 slaves and that the Royal African Company imported 5,982 for a grand total of 13,200. The naval officers' list for this same period shows that 34,583 slaves had been brought to Barbados. The difference of over 20,000 in the two lists can perhaps be accounted for by slaves brought by separate traders and never recorded by shore authorities. But which figures are correct?

Nevertheless, some comparatively accurate statistics do exist and they cast light on the magnitude of the trade. The Spanish territories in the New World, which were the greatest buyers in the sixteenth century, required an average of approximately 4,000 slaves per year. This low figure is in sharp contrast to the numbers demanded by seventeenth- and eighteenth-century markets. The asiento, or permission to supply the Spanish empire with slaves, was obtained by the French Guinea Company in 1702. This agreement called for 48,000 slaves to be

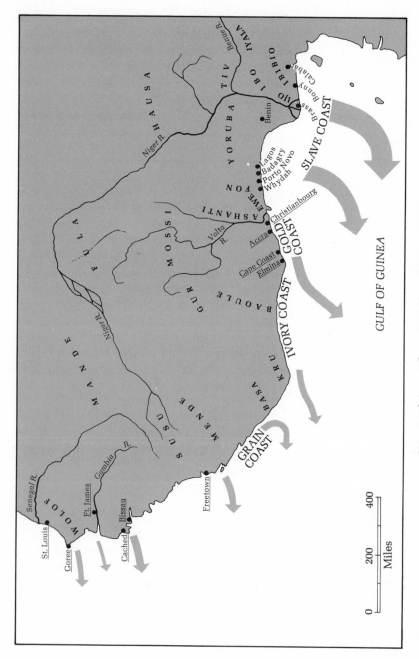

West African Slave-Trading Areas, 1880

delivered over a ten-year period. In 1713 the asiento passed to Britain, which promised delivery of 4,800 slaves annually for the Spanish territories for thirty years. That this was a very small portion of the total number transported in this period can be seen from the statistics for the French Indies Company, which delivered 136,000 slaves in the years 1722–1741.

By the eighteenth century Britain was the most important trading nation. A random sampling of figures will give some indication of the degree of its involvement. Liverpool, which became the chief British port for the slave trade in the early seventeenth century, had a total registered tonnage of 18,000. By 1792 the total had grown to 250,000 tons. In the period 1795–1804 10,000 Liverpool ships transported over 300,000 slaves. London ships in the same period had carried 46,000 slaves and Bristol-based ships over 10,000.

It is almost equally impossible to arrive at satisfactory loss figures. Despite the concern of captains and their superiors with minimizing deaths, the rigors of the crossing and the implicit cruelty in overcrowding caused many slaves to die in transit. It is probable that death rates on Portuguese and Dutch ships were higher than on British and French vessels. Nevertheless, losses of up to thirty-five percent were not uncommon on British slave ships. There was also considerable fluctuation in losses from the sixteenth through the eighteenth centuries. Despite this variation, a reasonable estimate would be that for every four slaves delivered one died in transit. The estimates, however inadequate, of the total number of slaves delivered vary from eight million to twenty-five million. Adding the loss factor, we find that between nine and one-half million and thirty million persons were uprooted from Africa and carried toward the New World in the four centuries of the trade. The bulk of these slaves had been purchased in West Africa.

Earlier interpretations of the direct role of the slave trade in stimulating the large new political structures of West Africa are now under scrutiny. It seems reasonably clear that the impetus toward creating larger, more authoritarian polities in some areas predated the coming of Europeans. The Western Sudanic states extending from the Atlantic to Bornu, developed in the European Middle Ages, could have acted as models for the intermediary and forest states. Centralization had occurred among the Wolof and Yoruba states before the slave trade became important. Development of the later empires of Ashanti, Dahomey, and Oyo, although stimulated in part by the slave trade, took place largely as a result of internal forces which had little connection with the trade. This is not to say that there was no relation between the desire of rulers to dominate a profitable sector of the economy and the construction of larger states. The development of Bonny and Brass indicates how older institutions were transformed to exploit the new economic opportunities. What must be said, however, is that the slave trade was only one of a series of related forces that shaped the development of African states at this time.

Another question that is currently being examined is the degree to which the slave trade retarded African development. Although it is impossible to state with any accuracy the number of persons removed from West Africa, the percentage of annual removal from any one area was probably not more than two to three percent. Territories such as the Slave and Gold coasts, which supplied large numbers of slaves, had and still have very dense populations. On the positive side the trade in human beings stimulated economic activity, instituted proto-money economies, and introduced European methodology as well as European goods to the coastal states. It is not possible to know to what degree these developments were offset by the loss of young and active members of certain societies over successive generations. It is known also that certain religious and political institutions were warped to complement the needs of the trade and therefore became debased. Military skill in some locales became more important than the traditional, often delicately balanced political systems. There was also a loss in skills as inferior European goods replaced local wares, and some traditional art created out of the new environment was inferior to that which had gone before. Perhaps the most debilitating effect of the trade was that Africans concentrated almost exclusively upon only one export article. Almost all West African societies experienced severe economic and political strains in the nineteenth century when Europeans, reversing their previous positions, attempted to end the slave traffic. In human as well as political and economic terms the trans-Atlantic slave trade had a far greater effect upon the societies receiving slaves than upon the African territories that supplied them. Much more research will have to be done before the actual effect of the slave trade upon any African area can be more definitely stated.

Eighteenth-century antislavery movements

Opposition to the traffic in human beings persisted in Europe throughout the seventeenth and early eighteenth centuries. These voices of protest, however, were almost drowned by the flood of philosophical and neoreligious arguments that equated slavery with the civilizing mission of Western man. A number of factors operating in conjunction with one another made the position of the slavers and slave owners seem virtually impregnable through the 1750s. The most obvious prop to the institution was the profits of the system. Although slave merchants made excellent profits from the direct trade, they were only part of the economic underpinning of the system. Absentee landlords had a tremendous investment in plantations in the West Indies, which needed slave labor in order to continue to function. In 1797 it was estimated that the British had invested over seventy million pounds in their possessions in the West Indies, and their annual income from sugar was approximately six million pounds. However profitable the British West Indies were, some French, Dutch, and Spanish possessions were economically more valuable. The French island of Santo Domingo was the most important single producer of sugar. The Dutch territory of Guiana and the Spanish islands of Trinidad and Cuba were also richer than any part of the British West Indies.

The nature of European governments also made it difficult for the opponents of slavery to translate their programs into action. Britain, which had evolved the framework of parliamentary democracy, was by far the most responsive to popular pressures. But the Whig and later the Tory oligarchies in Britain in the eighteenth century were far from representative of even the middle class. Parliamentary reform, long overdue, was postponed for almost half a century by the long wars with revolutionary France. European monarchs and nobles cooperated with factions that had an economic stake in the West Indian plantations to assure the continuance of the slave trade.

Nevertheless, very early there were organizations as well as individuals who opposed the trade. In the North American colonies Massachusetts in 1641 outlawed slavery except for captives taken in war or those persons willing to be sold. In 1652 Rhode Island placed a limit on the length of time a slave could be held. The Society of Friends condemned the slave trade and its members were constrained from buying or selling slaves.

The Friends in the early eighteenth century tried in vain to get the Pennsylvania assembly to declare the importation of slaves illegal. In 1761 the assembly did set a duty of ten pounds per slave, which for all practical purposes ended the slave trade to Pennsylvania. Nor were the protests against slavery confined to the northern colonies. The Virginia assembly's restrictive measures were overruled by the royal governors. By the end of the Revolutionary War importation of slaves was legal only in Georgia and North Carolina. In the latter colony importation was subject to a heavy duty. In 1798 Georgia finally prohibited the entry of foreign Negroes. Thus by the close of the eighteenth century the United States had all but closed its doors to the human traffic. However, the invention of the cotton gin and the importance of cotton as a crop within a short time reversed the trend for abolition in the South. In 1792 the southern states exported 138,000 pounds of cotton. By 1800 this total had grown to eighteen million pounds. Illegal slave trading was openly condoned by southern authorities after 1793.

In Britain the Society of Friends was soon joined in its opposition to slavery by the new religious force of Evangelicalism. Begun by the Wesleys, this movement within the Established Church called for a return to simple biblical Christianity with few frills and a maximum of moral commitment. By the close of the century the movement had ceased to be restricted to the radicals and lower classes and had become the faith of the most respected middle classes. Evangelicalism stressed the preaching of the Word to all men and thus gave rise to the Baptist Missionary Society (1792), the London Missionary Society (1796), and the Church Missionary Society (1799). Dedicated missionaries sponsored by these organizations had a profound influence on African development in the nineteenth century. Other Evangelicals opposed slavery and the trade in human beings not only for its inhumanity but because it was against the laws of God.

Some rationalists also lent their efforts to end the slave trade. There had developed in Britain and France a mass of political theory and literature based on the concept of the "natural" man. From the time of Defoe through that of Rousseau men in a state of nature had been extolled as living lives of purity. Only civilization with its artificial forms corrupted this natural goodness. The slave trade was an excellent example of simple, good natives being sullied by their contact with European culture. It is impossible to assess the influence of rationalists in the antislavery crusade. However, it is worth noting that men such as Mirabeau and Lafayette in France and the younger Pitt and Charles James Fox in England, who were invaluable in the drive against the slave trade, were rational humanitarians.

Although there had been protests against slavery before, the first major victory in the long struggle for abolition was struck by Granville Sharp. In 1765 at the age of thirty Sharp found a slave in London who had been severely beaten by his owner and turned out on the streets to die. Sharp nursed the man back to health, only to have the slave, on his recovery, kidnapped by his owner and sold. The owner, a Barbados lawyer, brought a charge against Sharp for stealing, but the suit was dropped. This sequence of events confirmed Sharp in his life's work and also indicated the first place where institutional slavery could be attacked. Sharp was convinced that the 14,000 slaves resident in England were being held contrary to the English common law. He attempted to test this thesis five times before 1770 and each time the case was decided on minor points rather than on the crucial issue. In 1769 Sharp found another slave, James Somerset, who had been abandoned by his master because of illness. Sharp sent him to a hospital and on Somerset's recovery found employment for him. In 1771 Somerset was claimed by his master and was imprisoned. Sharp brought the case before the court of the king's bench. Lord Chief Justice Mansfield, acting on this case in 1772, rendered a landmark judgment that slavery was repugnant to the English common law and that "as soon as any slave sets foot on English ground he becomes free." Thus by one decision 14,000 slaves worth £500,000 gained their freedom. But the Mansfield decision did not apply to the empire and said nothing about the legality of the trade.

The next important figure in the abolition movement in Britain was Thomas Clarkson. In 1785 at the age of twenty-five as a student at Cambridge University Clarkson won a prize for an essay on the subject of slavery. Soon afterward he came to believe that he was divinely called to work for abolition. In 1787 along with Sharp, Josiah Wedgwood, and others he created the Society for the Abolition of the Slave Trade. This agency acted in the latter years of the eighteenth century primarily to gather information and through publications to alert the British public to the magnitude of the cruelties of the slave trade.

None of the men who formed the society had the necessary contacts within the power structure to influence legislative reaction. This was to be the objective of the young man recruited to the cause soon after the society's creation. William Wilberforce, the son of a wealthy Yorkshire merchant, had entered parliament at the age of twenty-one and until his conversion to Evangelicalism was as worldly and bored as any of his parliamentary contemporaries. Once enlisted in the cause he became a tireless worker and utilized all of his contacts to further abolition. Wilberforce was a close friend of Prime Minister Pitt, who privately encouraged Wilberforce's efforts. Pitt, with his responsibilities and particularly with the problems attendant on the French revolution, could not make emancipation a government project. Sheridan and Charles James Fox were two other parliamentary leaders sympathetic to Wilberforce's activities.

The strategy of the abolitionists was to attack the slave trade first, hoping to mollify the West Indian interests on the subject of slavery. Books, pamphlets, and petitions were all used to support parliamentary action against the trade. In 1788 the first positive legislative step was achieved by the enactment of a law establishing the legal number of slaves carried on ships. The limit was supposed to be five for every three-ton weight of the vessel. In 1790–1791, prodded by Wilberforce, parliament conducted long, detailed hearings on the slave trade.

A combination of factors halted parliamentary action. The French revolution had begun to change moderate attitudes into more conservative views. Any reformer in the 1790s was likely to be viewed as tainted with Jacobin ideas and therefore an enemy to English "liberties." The revolt of slaves on Santo Domingo, which cost the lives of over 2,000 French residents, reinforced the arguments of those with West Indian interests against parliamentary tampering with such a volatile subject as slavery. In Jamaica, where the Negro population of 400,000 outnumbered the white settlers by a factor of eight to one, there had been a series of wars with the maroons, who were runaway slaves living in the interior of the island. The final war between the whites and maroons occurred in 1795 when the authorities used fierce bloodhounds in their campaign. Many maroons were captured and exiled to Nova Scotia.

Far more important in blunting abolitionist efforts was the upturn in the fortunes of the sugar planters in the 1790s. Sugar interests had always enjoyed a preference on the British market but had serious competition elsewhere with French and Spanish sugar, which was more plentiful and cheaper. The rebellion on Santo Domingo and the disturbances of the French wars elsewhere in the Spanish and French West Indies meant a lessening of such competition. Thus the last decade of the eighteenth century was a period of great prosperity for the British planters. In 1797 the value of investment in the British West Indies amounted to seventy million pounds, and one eighth of all British shipping was registered to West Indian ports. The planters and their supporters in parliament were not likely to approve any measure that might threaten this prosperity.

In 1791 Wilberforce and his supporters introduced a motion to abolish the slave trade which was defeated by a vote of 163 to 88. Undaunted, Wilberforce introduced similar measures with each new session but with no success. The nearest claim to victory came in 1793 when the Commons approved by a vote of 193 to 125 a statement that the slave trade ought gradually to be abolished. Wilberforce and the Evangelicals had, however, laid the groundwork in the eighteenth century for later victory. In the early nineteenth century sugar from India and Mauritius began to enter the English market. The West Indian planters and their parliamentary representatives became divided. Under these conditions Charles James Fox, who headed the ministry briefly after the death of Pitt, made the abolition of the slave trade one of his principal concerns. The parliamentary resolutions sponsored by Fox prohibiting commerce in slaves were approved in 1807 and took effect on January 1, 1808.

The upheavals in France after 1789 brought a succession of governments to power. All, however, were imbued in varying degrees with rational humanitarianism. The Declaration of the Rights of Man raised important questions concerning slavery. Did these lofty ideals apply also to Negro slaves? In the earliest stage of the French revolution Mirabeau and Lafayette were in favor of early abolition of the trade. Radical statements by Vincent Ogé, a Negro from Santo Domingo, frightened the deputies and they refused to pass the bill introduced by Mirabeau which would have outlawed the trade. The subsequent revolt in Santo Domingo again postponed any definitive action by the French. In 1794, however, a decree of the national convention abolished slavery in all French colonies. The institution with the attendant trade was reimposed by Napoleon in 1802.

As already noted, by the turn of the century in all of the states in the United States the importation of slaves was forbidden or the trade was heavily taxed. Nevertheless, there was considerable debate on the question at the Constitutional Convention. Conservative views prevailed and section 9 of Article I of the Constitution specified that Congress could not pass any laws prohibiting the trade before 1808. All that the federal government could do until then was to impose a maximum tax of ten dollars per slave imported. Long before President Jefferson on March 2, 1807, signed the bill prohibiting the trade (to take effect on January 1, 1808) cotton culture had changed the attitudes of southern planters and politicians.

By 1800 there was a growing revulsion against the traffic in human beings, particularly in Great Britain. However, little concrete legislation had been passed limiting the slave trade. The small portion that had been enacted did not provide for the strict policing of the new codes. Abolition of the trade and its enforcement belonged to the next century and proved more difficult than ever envisioned by the Evangelicals.

Before closing this brief discussion of the antislave trade movement one must note a concurrent issue that agitated the Evangelicals. This question concerned the best method of caring for slaves once they had been emancipated. Presumably when the antislavery forces became successful this minor problem would become a major one. A significant number of abolitionists believed that the Negro should be assisted in every way to return to Africa. Most of the supporters of these ideas knew little of Africa and made certain assumptions that proved in time to be false. The back-to-Africa movement, however, was sponsored by Christians on both sides of the Atlantic and had an important effect upon the thinking of philanthropists well into the twentieth century.

A proposal by the naturalist Henry Smeathman to conduct free Negroes to West Africa and there establish a colony was seized upon by many Evangelicals as a way to solve the growing problem of the blacks in England. The British government also promised to support financially any resettlement attempt. The first venture at such colonization was begun in 1787 when 411 ex-slaves departed Britain for St. George's Bay in present-day Sierra Leone. Upon arrival a strip of coastal land was purchased from a Temne chief, King Tom, for trade goods valued at slightly over fifty-nine pounds. The settlers immediately went to work to build rough houses and clear the land adjacent to the first town, which was named Granville Town in honor of Granville Sharp. They soon discovered their inadequacies within this hostile environment. Few were skilled agriculturists, none was familiar with low-fertility African soils, the Temne people were unfriendly, and promised supplies from England were not forthcoming. Disease also took a frightful toll. By the beginning of 1788 less than 150 of the original settlers were still alive. A small number of other settlers arrived in Granville Town in 1788 as reinforcements, but all the work and effort of the colonists went for nothing when the Temne took the town and scattered its settlers in 1790.

In Britain Sharp, Wilberforce, and the banker Henry Thornton had formed a joint stock company to further pursue the planting of colonies of free slaves in Africa. This corporation was called at first the St. George's Bay Company and was later renamed the Sierra Leone Company. The direction for recruitment of new colonists came from Thomas Peters, a Negro who had received his freedom by serving loyally in the British army during the American Revolution. Migrating, as did so many other Negro loyalists, to Nova Scotia after the war, Peters discovered that the government would not keep its promises for free land. Peters sailed for Britain as a spokesman for his fellows and there met the officers of the Sierra Leone Company. Promised land in Africa, he agreed to return to Nova Scotia to recruit colonists. The company, supported in this venture by the British government, eventually landed over 1,100 new settlers, most from Nova Scotia, in 1792 near the former site of Granville Town. The new settlement was named Freetown.

The settlers who had been promised free land discovered that the presence of the hostile Temne prevented widespread distribution of land. Eventually when land became available the company expected the settlers to pay quit rents for their plots. Fever was a constant companion, the Temne were unfriendly, and in 1794 French naval forces took and burned Freetown. The miraculous survival of the settlement was due to a great extent to the efforts of the first two governors, John Clarkson and after 1794 Zachary Macaulay. The latter understood very well the grievances of the colonists against the company. However, the new colony was slowly draining the limited resources of the company and alternate sources of revenue were looked for to help defray expenses. An attempt to charge the settlers for school fees resulted in an abortive rebellion by some of the settlers in 1800. The governor, aided by the timely arrival of maroons from Jamaica, put down the uprising. The future of the venture remained in doubt in the years immediately after the abortive revolt. Success of the colony was guaranteed only by the decision of the British government to use Freetown as its major naval base for the West African antislavery patrol. In 1808 Freetown, with a population of approximately 2,000, became a British crown colony. The inhabitants served as the nucleus for the later development of the distinct creole population and culture of Sierra Leone which played an important role in the later development of British West Africa.

FIVE
Central Africa

Bantu empires in the Rhodesias

Archeologists and anthropologists have done more work in Zambia and Rhodesia than anywhere else in Central Africa. Although much more will have to be undertaken before any conclusive statements can be made about the pre-European period, a tentative picture does emerge of a late Stone Age Bushmanoid people who were gradualy supplanted by Bantu. At first the Bantu who crossed the Zambesi River came in small numbers and lived in harmony with the scattered indigenous hunting people. These early Bantu settlers are associated with a particular type of pottery called channeled ware. Such pottery remnants are closely related to examples found further north in Ruanda, Burundi, and Kenya. Channeled ware in these northern areas has generally been dated earlier than the Rhodesian finds. Since this type of pottery has been found at later dates in association with iron, it is presumed that the Bantu and iron technology moved from eastern Africa into the Rhodesias. It is possible, judging from the Carbon 14 date at Machili (A.D. 99–212), that the Bantu were present in the Rhodesias before the arrival of iron. However, J. D. Clark and Brian Fagan, who have done considerable work in the area, consider iron to have been introduced to the Zambia area by Bantu in the first century and to Rhodesia in the fourth.

The small Bantu clans in the first millennium of the Christian era were primarily agriculturists. Cattle were kept but this occupation did not become predominant until toward the end of this period. When the Bantu did adapt themselves to cattle tending their relations with the non-Bantu changed. Population pressure, human and cattle, on the land increased and the non-Bantu were driven further south or to more inhospitable territories. Some time in this period the clan organization among some Bantu was strengthened and chiefs began to emerge. Presumably there was constant movement of new Bantu groups from the north and a splitting off of new groups from older, more settled communities. By the twelfth century the ancestors of the Sotho, Nguni, and Shona Bantu were already present in the Rhodesias.

These early Bantu had already discovered gold and begun to exploit it, perhaps trading with Arabs at Sofala. They had also begun to build stone forts on hilltops, utilizing dry stone-working techniques similar to those developed earlier in Ethiopia. The earliest construction at Great Zimbabwe dates from the eleventh century. Discovery of these ruins in the late nineteenth century by Europeans led to considerable speculation concerning who built them. Arabs and Phoenicians were both considered, since it was not believed that Africans possessed such technical knowledge. It is now known that all the ruins — hill forts, smaller town sites, and Great Zimbabwe — were constructed by the Sotho and later the Karanga and Rozwi Bantu. Great Zimbabwe in its finished form was built on level ground and was surrounded by a massive elliptical exterior wall. Inside this enclosure were other secondary walls and some stone buildings. The most intriguing of these was the solid conical tower dating from the later or Rozwi period. In all the buildings rough-hewn stone was used without mortar. There were no arches or vaulting, and in all probability the roofing material was either thatch or daga, a cement-type earth made from anthills. Most of the construction was done after the Karanga Bantu moved north and their place taken by Rozwi Bantu.

Sotho Bantu seem to have been the dominant population in Rhodesia through the twelfth century. However, at about that period a group of patrilineal clans of Shona Bantu crossed the Zambesi and within a century became the overlords of the territory between Zimbabwe and the Matopo hills. Some of the Sotho were forced further south where they joined the Bantu already living across the Limpopo River. Other Sotho stayed behind, intermarried with the Shona, and taught them the techniques of gold mining and smelting. It is obvious that the Shona were in trading contact with the coastal Arabs.

The details of Shona consolidation are unknown, but at the beginning of the fifteenth century one segment, the Vaka-ranga, had evolved a highly complex centralized political and military system. All of the elements of a Sudanic state organ-ization, as described by Roland Oliver, were present. The king had supreme, semidivine powers and ruled over the scattered Karanga clans by means of an efficient, appointed bureaucracy superimposed over the traditional local system. The Karanga king was treated by his subjects with the awe deserved by a person who communed with the spirits. No common people ever saw him, since he gave audience from behind a curtain. Members of the court imitated his actions. If he coughed, so too did they. All persons approached him by crawling on their hands and knees. When the king reached old age or had a serious infirmity he was supposed, for the good of the kingdom, to take poison. The new moon had special meaning for the rulers of the Shona. This was the time when the kings com-muned with their ancestors. A royal fire was kept burning for as long as the king lived. All other chiefs and great vassals also had fires, which were rekindled once a year from the king's fire after the special new moon ceremonies in May. When the king died all fires were put out, to be started again when the new ruler assumed his position. The spirit of the dead king was sup-posed to enter the body of a lion. These animals, therefore, were sacred and could be hunted only by a king.

The bureaucracy, as later described by the Portuguese, resembled in outline the ruling mechanisms of other Sudanic-type states. The capital of the kingdom was where the king and the court were located. In the royal enclosure were the chancel-lor of the kingdom, the court chamberlain, head drummer, military commanders, and all other high officials necessary for running the vast empire. The queen mother and the nine prin-cipal wives also had their own courts within the royal enclave. Lesser wives, concubines, and waiting women brought the number within direct range of the king's palace to many thou-sands. The ruler also appointed vassal kings and governors of provinces, usually from the numbers of royal relations. Their duties were to keep order, enforce the king's will, deliver men for the military, and collect and report the necessary tribute from their areas to the king.

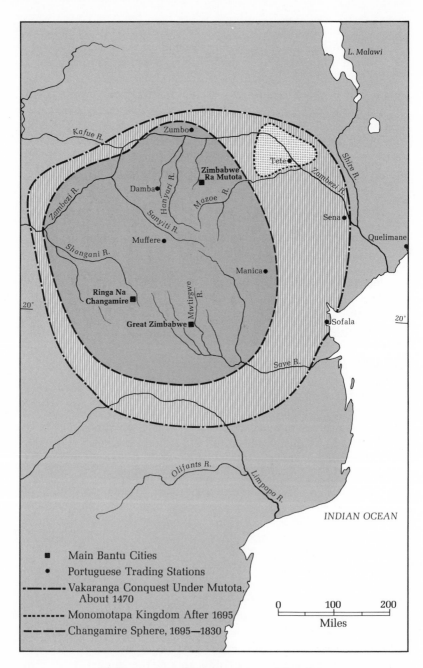

Main Bantu Cities ■

Portuguese Trading Stations ●

—·—·— Vakaranga Conquest Under Mutota, About 1470

········· Monomotapa Kingdom After 1695

— — — Changamire Sphere, 1695—1830

L. Malawi

Kafue R.

Zumbo●

Tete●

Shire R.

Zambezi R.

Zimbabwe Ra Mutota ■

Damba●

Hanyani R.

Mazoe R.

Sanyiti R.

Sena●

Quelimane●

Shangani R.

Muffere●

Manica●

Ringa Na Changamire ■

Mtwtirgwe R.

Great Zimbabwe ■

●Sofala

Save R.

20°

20°

Olifants R.

Limpopo R.

INDIAN OCEAN

0   100   200
Miles

Vakaranga and Monomotapa Kingdoms

In approximately 1440 the small Karanga kingdom centered on Great Zimbabwe began to expand northward. The reasons for this movement are unknown, although lack of salt in the southern areas has been given as one cause. It is doubtful that this was the dominant factor, however, since the Karanga, who controlled gold mines and were engaged in trade, could have obtained sufficient supplies of this material without conquest. A more likely explanation is that the political and military reforms within the state combined with- the vision and ambitions of King Mutota impelled this people toward expansion.

The Karanga armies, called by some of their enemies korekore, or locusts, swept northward. King Mutota, who launched this movement, was called the mwene mtapa, or the great plunderer, by his subject peoples. This title was understood by the Portuguese a half century later to refer to a title of respect for the ruler. Rendered as Monomotapa, it was used to signify both the ruler and the kingdom. By the time of Mutota's death the Karanga had conquered all of what is now Rhodesia except the eastern portion. Mutota's son Matope continued the wars, and by 1480 the Monomotapa empire had been extended to control the Zambesi River from the Kariba gorge to the Indian Ocean and an undefined area of the coast south of the Zambesi delta.

The center of the kingdom also moved north, and the leading city became Zimbabwe Ra Mutota, located on a tributary stream to the Zambesi approximately 150 miles above Tete. The kingdom was organized into provinces, each under the rule of an appointed governor, usually a son or close relative of the king. The territory nearest the king's town was administered directly by the ruler and his central bureaucracy. The great distances between the Monomotapa's court and the outlying portion of the empire made it difficult to maintain authority. The lack of tribal homogeneity also caused the king many problems. Even before the death of Matope the empire began to break apart. The area of original habitation near Great Zimbabwe, called Guniuswa after 1480, was ruled by a grandson of Mutata named Changa, who was quick to take advantage of the divisiveness within the empire to carve out his own kingdom. Perhaps encouraged by Arab traders, this ruler declared the southern part independent and gave his name to the new kingdom of Changamire. The dominant Bantu people in the south were a segment of the Shona who called themselves Rozwi.

By the time the Portuguese became well established at Sofala the Monomotapa had lost to the Changamire over one half of the area controlled by the first two rulers of the Karanga empire.

The later history of the Monomotapas is inextricably tied to Portuguese political and economic movements on the lower Zambesi. There existed within the Karanga empire a complex, well-developed trading system. Most of the exterior trade was controlled by Arab traders resident within the empire. The numbers who lived and traded under the jurisdiction of the Monomotapas are unknown but obviously were very large. The Arabs traded guns, cloth, and manufactured wares for gold, ivory, copper, and slaves. The Portuguese were not content merely to supplant Arab power in coastal cities such as Sofala. They also wished to gain if possible the sources of the valuable native items, particularly gold. By the middle of the sixteenth century the Portuguese were firmly in control of the river ports of Sena and Tete. Their agents were also active in the Monomotapas' territory. In 1575 they tried to rid themselves of much of their trade competition by a treaty with the Monomotapas which expelled the Arabs from the territory and also gave the Portuguese valuable mining concessions.

From the favorable vantage point of having many traders and priests in the lands of the Monomotapas and controlling the import of desired goods the Portuguese moved toward direct interference in political affairs. In the early seventeenth century the Monomotapa Mavura Philippe became a vassal of Portugal. In 1652 when a new ruler attempted to declare independence from Portuguese control he was killed and deposed by his younger brother, who had been given Portuguese help. This interference with the normal government of the empire resulted in large segments of the empire becoming all but independent of the Monomotapas. The chief beneficiary of these losses were the rulers of Changamire.

The Portuguese attempted to dominate Changamire but largely because of three factors were never successful. The first was simply distance. The chief town of the Rozwi, Ringa na Changamire, located near the Shangoni River, was over 400 miles in the interior from Sofala. Another reason was the continued strength of the Changamire rulers. Finally, the Portuguese drive for empire had slowed considerably by the seventeenth century. They had lost the bulk of their Indian Ocean empire and were not powerful enough to mount a major offensive against a strong interior kingdom such as the Changamire. There was continual trade between the Rozwi and Portuguese, but normally through trade fairs and after 1760 trading caravans. In all cases trade was conducted according to rules established by the rulers of Changamire, and the Portuguese were never able to subvert the kingdom.

In 1692 the Monomotapa combined with the Changamire ruler to try to expel the Portuguese from the interior. This campaign was moderately successful in its objective, but was ultimately a disaster for the Monomotapas. King Domba of the Changamire, after witnessing the weakness of his brother ruler, incorporated the bulk of the Monomotapas' northern areas into his empire. From that time forward the Monomotapas were merely Portuguese-controlled puppet rulers who ostensibly ruled the area between Tete and Sena. The Changamire kingdom continued to prosper in relative isolation. Most of the major stone buildings at Great Zimbabwe and elsewhere in Rhodesia date from the Changamire period of the late seventeenth and eighteenth centuries. Rozwi hegemony over the area south of the Zambesi continued unimpaired until the Nguni invasions from the south in the early nineteenth century.

Luba-Lunda kingdoms

The most widespread culture and complex settlement patterns in the Congo basin were those of the Luba-speaking people. Their origins are as obscure as those of any Bantu people, but observers have hypothesized that small Luba clan groups were living in the region of Lake Victoria in the tenth or eleventh century. Probably for a combination of reasons these groups began to move southward along a route west of Lakes Kivu and Tanganyika and away from the deep forest areas, settling in a region between the Lualaba and Bushimaie rivers. The Luba were agriculturists and hunters and probably had domesticated small animals but they kept no cattle. Probably the Luba clans were associated with one another in a very loose political federation. Before the first contacts with the Portuguese in the late sixteenth century fragmentation of the Luba had already occurred. These offshoots all carried different names and had differing customs. The territories to the east, west, and south where they migrated were sparsely inhabited. The scattered Bushman-type population was either killed or

Movement of Bantu in Central Africa, 1500–1800

driven away by the Luba. By the early seventeenth century one Luba group had moved westward and made contact with the Portuguese before settling down in the Kasai.

The late sixteenth- and early seventeenth-century displacement of the Luba was not accomplished in isolation. This was the same period when the Lala, Maravi, and Luyi were also migrating. The interconnections of these groups is unknown, but it is not unreasonable to assume that the movement of one group affected other semisedentary Bantu people. In the latter part of the seventeenth century far-reaching changes occurred among the central Luba. There is no definite evidence of what happened, although Oliver suggests that some ivory hunters, probably armed with guns obtained from the Portuguese, seized power. Traditional accounts tell the story of a woman, Lueji, and her husband disputing with her brothers over the control of a Luba clan. One brother and his adherents went west and settled near the Lui River; another group moved southwest to the upper Zambesi where they took the name of the Lovale. Meanwhile Lueji's husband was consolidating his control over neighboring clans and these semiunified groups took the name Lunda. The traditional accounts need not be in conflict with the idea that the Lunda kingdom with its strong centralized government was founded on ruthless leadership combined with the possession of guns.

A grandson of Lueji took the title of mwato yamvo, lord of wealth. His position within the kingdom was secured by the religious and social sanctions associated with a Sudanic-type state aided by an efficient bureaucracy and large army. In the early eighteenth century the Lunda armies, expanding to the west, reincorporated many of the Luba elements that had established themselves along the Lui River. Later the mwato yamvo's army turned eastward to the Luapula Valley where earlier Bantu groups lived. After 1740 one of the Lunda generals conquered the territory, took the title of Kazembe II, and established his own kingdom. It is certain that Kazembe's army had some firearms before moving into the Luapula Valley. The Lualaba River became the border between the two Sudanic-type states. In the latter part of the eighteenth century this new kingdom of the Kazembe's rivaled in power and wealth the older Lunda empire of the mwato yamvo even though the Kazembe rulers continued to recognize the mwato yamvo as superior.

In the latter part of the seventeenth century another Luba group added to the flux prevalent in the Congo. The Bemba resident at the beginning of this period near the Lualaba River started a migration which did not cease for a century. One large segment of this group crossed into the Luapula Valley and in the middle of the eighteenth century lived next to the Lunda of Kazembe. Perhaps for this reason their stay there was short, and a further migration took them north of Lake Bangweulu. Here sections split off, eventually forming the Chishinga and Unga groups and also the Bisa, who migrated southwestward from the lake. Another section moved eastward across the Luangwa River and became known as the Senga. The main body of the Bemba reached the Luangwa Valley around 1760 and upon encountering the Cewa retreated and finally settled down in the territory between Lakes Bangweulu and Tanganyika.

A final major migration should be noted in connection with the Luba-Lunda people even though the Bantu involved did not necessarily belong to that group. These were the Luyi, or river people, who later were given the name Lozi. Their place of origin is obscure, though perhaps it was somewhere to the west of the original Luba settlers along the tributaries of the Congo. In the late seventeenth century they too migrated southward, eventually stopping in the upper Zambesi Valley where they drove out many of the older settlers. In their movement the Luyi had become skilled cattle herders as well as competent farmers. In the eighteenth century they absorbed many of their neighbors into their political system, which was a loose federation. This was a well-organized and peaceful polity and at one time was composed of over twenty distinct groups. The Luyi prospered in the upper Zambesi until a more militant group of Bantu, the Kalolo, fleeing the disorders in southern Africa in the 1830s, destroyed their hegemony.

Lake Malawi people

The southward migrations of Bantu from north of Lake Tanganyika were responsible for populating the Lake Malawi and Shire highlands area. The Portuguese in the early seventeenth century noted that most of the inhabitants westward of the lake called themselves Maravi, and it was estimated that they had been in those locations for a hundred years. If this is true, then the Maravi movements predated the Luba explosions into the central and southern Congo by a considerable time. The Maravi migrations, however, continued in the seventeenth century, with some groups settling along the extreme southern shores of Lake Malawi.

In the eighteenth century there was a further exodus of Maravi to the west of Lake Malawi where they formed a distinct group of tribes called the Cewa. There were at least four major subdivisions to the Cewa. One group remained to the south of the lake on the Shire River near present-day Blantyre; another at midcentury crossed the Luanga River where the Bemba drove them back to the territory near Kasungu. A third segment established itself eastward to the vicinity of modern Fort Jameson, and the fourth settled along the Kopche River. A portion of the original Maravi remaining near Lake Malawi developed differently from the Cewa and took the name Nyanja, or lake people. Intermarriage between the Cewa and resident Lala people to the west after 1800 resulted in the formation of yet another tribe, the Nsenga.

These varying Maravi peoples never evolved aggressive, large, expansive polities. Maravi chiefs did not succeed in overturning the political system based upon the family where the chief's power was counterbalanced by religious and social customs. These lake tribes did not absorb the cattle culture that became the common feature of so many southern Bantu. They remained primarily agriculturists, keeping a few small animals and supplementing their food supply by hunting. As early as the seventeenth century they were trading with the Portuguese based at Quelimane and also with the kingdom of the Monomotapas. The Maravi in the nineteenth century paid for their peaceful, nonaggressive way of life when they became the prey of the Ngu'ni, Yao, and Arab slave raiders.

East of Lake Malawi were the Makewa and Yao. There are practically no traditions of origin for the former group. The Portuguese in the early seventeenth century reported them living in approximately their present location in Mozambique. The Yao lived immediately south of the Rovuma River between Lake Malawi and the Indian Ocean. In all probability the Yao acted as middlemen in the trade with coastal-based Arabs before the arrival of the Portuguese. In the nineteenth century groups of Yao moved further south along the eastern lake shore and played an important role in the slave trade and the disruption of the Maravi agriculturists.

The kingdom of Kongo

Bantu people were living along the coast and the immediate interior near the mouth of the Congo River well before the fourteenth century. How long they had been there and from whence they came are at the present time unanswerable questions. Oliver suggests that the founders of the Kongo kingdom might have been an offshoot of the Luba from the Katanga who migrated there in the late fourteenth century. However, Jan Vansina, although he does not speculate on the earliest migrations, tends to refute this northward movement by placing a number of Bantu polities north of the Congo at this time and assigning to one of these the impetus for creating the Kongo kingdom.

According to Vansina, the son of a chief of a small Bantu group and his followers crossed the Congo River in the fourteenth century and imposed their rule over the inhabitants of the Kongo plateau. This ruler, Wene, took the title of manikongo, divided his conquests into provinces, and further extended his domains by incorporating the preexisting kingdoms of Mpangu and Mbata. By the time of the arrival of the Portuguese the Kongo kingdom, divided into six provinces, extended from the Congo River south to the Loje River and almost as far inland as the Kwango River. The kingdom of the Manikongo did not extend far north of the Congo River and had not absorbed the other Bantu states such as the Loango into his domain.

Early Portuguese accounts show that the organization of the Kongo state was similar to that of the neighboring kingdoms, although it was more centralized. The basic unit was the village, with the heads chosen according to matrilineal standards. Above the village level were the districts, with officials appointed either by the king or rulers of the provinces. Districts were grouped together into six provinces, each with a governor selected by the manikongo. As was the case within Sudanic-type states elsewhere, the king was the focal point for the entire system. He was in theory absolute over the lives and property of his subjects. By his powers of appointment and removal he determined policy throughout his territories. The bulk of the detailed work was handled by a central bureaucracy resident at the king's town, Mbanza. There was no regular army, only a personal bodyguard for the manikongo. However, all able-bodied men were subject to military duty on command of the king.

The manikongo was also in firm control of the economy of his territory. The Kongo people knew iron- and copperworking techniques and were skilled in making pottery, clothing, and mats from raffia. The rulers were able to divert trade and profits in these goods to their advantage. Governors of provinces were required to collect taxes and tribute in their territories and render their accounts to the manikongo every six months. The basic currency of the kingdom was cowrie shells. The source for most of these shells was the island of Luanda, which belonged to the king.

One facet of the political life of the Kongo which was different from that of many Sudanic-type states was the method of choosing the manikongo. There was no clear rule for determining succession. Before 1540 all male descendants of the line of Wene, the first king, could seek the throne. After 1540 aspirants had to be of the line of Afonso I. A new manikongo was chosen from all claimants by an electoral board composed of the great nobles of the kingdom. This method of selection was by its nature divisive and in the sixteenth and seventeenth centuries, combined with the diverse Portuguese interests, proved disastrous to the kingdom of Kongo.

In 1492 the Portuguese navigator Diogo Cão made contact with the kingdom of Kongo. From that time on the history of the kingdom is inextricably bound to the Portuguese overseas adventure. Under Portuguese influence the entire kingdom changed and its kings consciously attempted to create a state modeled upon those of feudal Europe. Because in the sixteenth century the impetus for this change rested with the Portuguese, the later history of the Kongo is considered in the section devoted to European activities in Central Africa.

Adjacent to the kingdom of the Kongo were a number of other Bantu polities. South of the Loje River were the Mbundu kingdoms of Dembo, Matamba, and Ndongo. According to Vansina, the Mbundu were of Lunda origin. The most important of these states for the Portuguese in the sixteenth century was Ndongo, which had been formed as a small state in the latter fifteen century by a wealthy smith who managed to have himself proclaimed its king, or ngola. By the middle of the sixteenth century the ngola controlled the territory between the Dande and Cuanza rivers, although Ndongo was a tributary state of Kongo. Some Portuguese traders from São Thomé had made contact with the kingdom before 1550, and it was partially for this reason that Ndongo gained its independence. Portuguese advisers to Manikongo Kiogo convinced him to punish the ngola for breaking the royal monopoly by trading directly with the São Thomé merchants. In 1556 the ngola defeated the Kongo armies and thus became totally independent of northern control. Almost immediately afterward the ngola made the fateful decision to invite more Portuguese to come and settle within his kingdom. The positive answer to this request marked the beginning of an epoch of war and bloodshed for Ndongo which left the kingdom devastated.

The Portuguese and the kingdom of Kongo

Diogo Cão in 1482 landed on the south bank of the Congo River and sent a deputation of four men to Mbanza, the capital of the kingdom of Kongo. Upon learning that his envoys were being held by the manikongo, he seized four Africans as hostages. These Africans were taken to Portugal and given excellent treatment to convince them of the power and wealth of Portugal in order to use them to obtain a favorable treaty with the ruler of Kongo. Cão returned to Kongo in 1484 and the captives acted as mediators to secure friendly relations between the manikongo and Portugal. Thus began one of the most bizarre episodes in the history of relations between Africans and Europeans. Implicit within the early Portuguese expansion had been the hope of Christianizing the pagans and combating the infidel. In Kongo the Portuguese attempted to put these philosophical concepts into action. In 1490 three ships containing priests, artisans, and soldiers were sent to Kongo. In the following year King Nzinga Nkuwu was baptized and took the name John I.

The stresses upon a Sudanic-type kingdom when the king and his leading advisers abandon the traditional religion are very great. In Kongo the anti-Christian feelings of traditionalists resulted in a brief civil war after the death of Nzinga Nkuwu in 1506. However, with Portuguese aid the faction favorable to Europeanization won and the Christian Nzinga Mbemba became king, taking the European name of Afonso I. His long period of rule is a study in frustration, since he seemed not only to believe in the superiority of Western technology and political systems but also at first trusted the Portuguese implicitly. He remodeled his court, creating dukes and counts, and required these newly renamed nobles to wear Western clothes wherever possible. Afonso sponsored the education in Portugal of many sons of the nobility. One of his sons, Henry, spent thirteen years there and returned as the bishop of Utica, the first and last black bishop of the area.

In conjunction with the missionaries Afonso sponsored building programs, particularly at the capital, which he had renamed São Salvador. A cathedral, palace, and service buildings were erected there. One Portuguese visitor reported in 1588 with obvious exaggeration that the population of this chief city was 100,000. Afonso could read and write Portuguese and carried on an extensive correspondence with his fellow-monarch in Lisbon. In the latter part of his reign these letters reflected his disappointment with the actions of the Portuguese and his disenchantment with them for not living up to their ideals.

Many missionaries as early as 1508 seemed more concerned with trade and profits than with spreading Christianity. The real damage to Kongo was done by merchants and proprietors from São Thomé. Sugar had been introduced to this island and its production required slaves. The traders operated openly from São Salvador, purchasing slaves or conducting their own raids within the manikongo's domains. Afonso's complaints were virtually ignored by the Portuguese crown and his messengers sent to complain of the abuses were turned aside at São Thomé. Christianity had created great divisions in the state and the slave raiding of the Portuguese caused more. Afonso's power was undercut throughout the kingdom by the time of his death in 1543.

Due partly to the method of choosing a manikongo, but also because of the anti-Portuguese feelings, the choice of a successor to Afonso brought on civil war. Eventually Afonso's nephew Diogo became king, but by then the few Portuguese resident in Kongo had the upper hand and slave raiding and trading was unchecked. A brief renaissance was felt after 1548 with the arrival of a new Jesuit mission. After some initial success, however, the missionaries admitted failure in reorienting the kingdom. A second Jesuit mission had no more lasting results. In 1556 Diogo's armies were defeated by the ruler of the tributary state of Ndongo and after this the manikongo's authority south of the Mbrige River was minimal.

At the death of Diogo in 1561 Kongo underwent an even bloodier civil war than that of the 1540s. The disturbances were so devastating that the Portuguese diverted their ships away from the Congo River. Thereafter Portuguese trading activities became focused upon the Ndongo kingdom to the south and were never to return in the same numbers to Kongo. By this time Portuguese missionary ardor had also cooled, and with the merchants focusing their attention elsewhere the kingdom of Kongo slowly expired.

The invasion of the Jagas no doubt helped the slavers to decide to invest their funds elsewhere. The Jagas appear to have been warlike groups of Bantu from the interior, possibly with some connections with the Luba-Lunda. They owed their power to their military organization. All other facets of society were subordinated to it. The Jaga traveled fast in small groups, utilized surprise attacks, and gave no quarter to their enemies. Perhaps even more potent than their savagery in battle was the terror they inspired in their enemies because they were cannibals. The Jagas terrorized all the coastal kingdoms through the midseventeenth century and were responsible in part for creating the new states of Yaka, the Ovimbundu kingdoms, and Kasanje before dissipating their strength east and southeast of the Kwango. These were the people who broke the power of the manikongo in 1568, driving him and his court to an island in the Congo River. In 1570 a contingent of Portuguese troops drove the Jagas away and restored the manikongo to São Salvador.

The latter part of the sixteenth century was a period of reconstruction for the Kongo. It appears that its two kings, Alvare I (1567–1583) and Alvare II (1583–1617), were among the most able to rule the kingdom. They resisted Portuguese pressure for more concessions and refused Portuguese demands to be allowed to build more forts. Although they could not stop the slave trade completely, they did manage to regulate it. The arrival of Dutch traders at Mpinde gave the manikongo another European group to play against the Portuguese. The last quarter of the sixteenth century witnessed a decided shift away from the Portuguese, and the manikongo tried to establish firmer relations with the Vatican. In 1613 a permanent ambassador of Kongo was resident in Rome. The Spanish king, the ruler of Portugal between 1580 and 1640, took an equally hostile position toward the Kongo, expressing the Spanish attitude that no aid should be sent to the Kongo which would strengthen the power of the manikongo.

The colony of Angola on the flanks of the kingdom of Kongo gave the Portuguese great powers of interference in the internal affairs of the kingdom. Their activities became crucial after the death of Alvare II in 1614. Succession, always complex for the Kongo, was not finally settled until 1641 and the country was wracked by dissension. In a period of slightly over twenty-five years there were six different kings. The provinces of Mbanda, Nsundi, and Soyo were in periodic revolt. Internal decay was on the surface arrested during the twenty-year reign of Garcia II (1641–1661) who allied Kongo with the Dutch after they took Luanda from the Portuguese in 1641. Arrival of new forces from Brazil seven years later caused the Dutch to capitulate. Had the governor of Luanda had more troops at his disposal, the Kongo would have lost its independence then. Continuing trouble with the kingdoms of Matamba and Kasanje prevented this result.

In 1645 Italian Capuchin friars arrived in the Kongo to begin missionary work in the provinces. By midcentury thirty priests were in the area and their efforts were at first welcomed by Garcia II. In the times of trouble that had preceded the coming of the Capuchins few priests or teachers had come to São Salvador, and almost all Portuguese residents had fled the kingdom. Under the pressure of civil war, slave trading, and lack of contact with Europe Christianity, never strong in the kingdom, had become in places only a memory. The Capuchins after some initial success gained the enmity of the manikongos, and although they continued to work until the close of the century, their impact on the Kongo was minimal.

Famines, locusts, and pestilence added to the distress of Kongo, and after 1667 the kingdom disintegrated into anarchy. The provinces of Mbamba and Mpongu each supported a claimant to the throne. In 1687 São Salvador was completely destroyed. The decay in the authority structure spread to the provinces, where the lesser chiefs and the people turned on the nobility. In 1710 when the kingship was restored the manikongo had no real power. Vansina says of this period that local chiefdoms "recognized a far away and impotent ruler which at the same time kept alive the dream of a wide-flung kingdom as it had once been." The noble experiment launched by Afonso I with Portuguese encouragement was destroyed even before the monarch's death by the demands of the slave trade. The last century and a half of the unified Kongo kingdom was a story of abandonment by the Portuguese. Except in rare instances they concerned themselves with that kingdom only when its policies impinged on their economically more important territories in the hinterland of Luanda.

The Portuguese and Angola

Responding to the request for missionaries by the Ngola, the Portuguese sent four priests to Ndongo under the guidance of a young nobleman, Paulo Dias de Novais, in 1560. Soon after their arrival the new ngola's attitude changed and the Portuguese became virtual prisoners. Dias was released in 1565 only because Ndongo was being threatened by civil war and the king believed Dias could bring him military aid. Dias returned to Ndongo in 1566 and conceived the idea of establishing a Portuguese colony in the territory. Although Dias was interested in furthering Christianity, his concern was also motivated by the belief that there were rich mines in the interior. In 1571 the Portuguese crown granted Dias permission to establish at his own expense a colony. He became its first governor and received a grant to the southern part of the territory in recompense for his expense and trouble. Four years later Dias and 400 men landed on the island of Luanda and in the following year began to build the town of Luanda on the mainland opposite the island.

Internal diffculties in both the kingdoms of Kongo and Ndongo enabled the Portuguese to establish their colony without native opposition. However, war with the Ngola began in 1579, and conflict in some form between the Portuguese and their neighbors lasted for over a century. In the southern portion of Dias' land a new town, Benguela Velha, was constructed, and by the mid-1580s the Portuguese military were established at the juncture of the Lukala and Cuanza rivers. At times in the early stages of these wars of conquest the Portuguese could not follow up their natural advantages because of lack of support

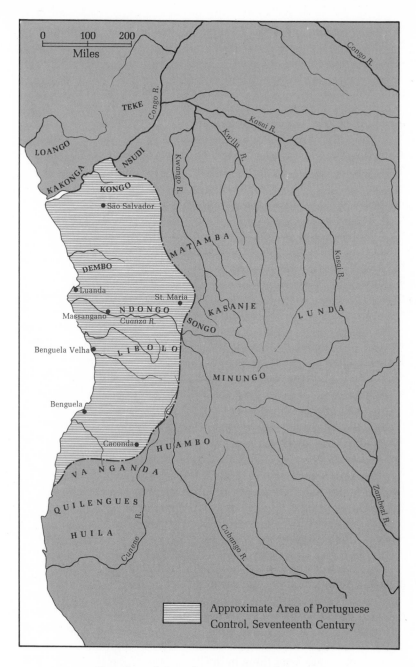

Peoples of Angola, Seventeenth Century

163

from Spanish authorities, who ruled Portugal from 1580 to 1640. Nevertheless, the wars dragged on, fed partially by the increased demand for slaves. Conquered territory was organized into military districts. Captains in charge of districts were not paid and became closely associated with the slave trade. In many cases conflict with the Africans was begun by the rapacious attitude of these commanders.

The war with Ndongo after 1600 was particularly savage. At times the Portuguese allied themselves with Jaga groups. The ngola's forces were constantly defeated and at times most of the Ndongo territory was lost. Famine became widespread, markets closed, and trade routes were blocked before peace was concluded in 1622. The ngola recognized the Portuguese right to build and man a fort deep in the heart of his kingdom. In return the Portuguese promised help against the new, powerful kingdom of Kasanje located on Ndongo's eastern borders. The Kasanje were Lunda emigrants who in the early seventeenth century, with the help of the Imbangala or Jaga, created a militarily more powerful kingdom than the Ndongo.

Disturbances within the Ndongo political structure prevented the terms of the treaty from being carried out. The young ngola died in 1623 and his sister Anna Nzinga, who had negotiated the treaty of 1622, seized power. For over thirty years she was the dominant figure in opposition to Portuguese expansion. She rebuilt the Ndongo army, using Portuguese-trained Africans as a nucleus, and also entered into alliances with the Jagas. Nevertheless, despite the weakness of Portuguese forces and the growing influence of the Dutch traders, Nzinga and her followers were driven out of Ndongo territory. By installing a puppet ngola the Portuguese effectively ended the Ndongo kingdom. Nzinga, with Jaga help, however, conquered the kingdom of Matamba in the east and continued to oppose the Portuguese from this more removed and stronger kingdom.

Meanwhile the Portuguese had established in 1617 another coastal town, Benguela, on Lobito Bay. The penetration of the interior of central Angola was more peaceful than in the north, partially because the slave trade was not as important a factor in the south. The settlers at Benguela were farmers rather than traders. Another reason for activities in the highland areas by some Portuguese was their belief that vast mineral wealth was to be found there. Many Portuguese moved into the hinterland

and intermarried with the Africans. The tribesmen there were the Ovimbundu, whose population was akin to the southwestern Bantu. Jaga groups in the seventeenth and eighteenth centuries were responsible for the creation of a series of separate although culturally related states. By the end of the eighteenth century all of the Ovimbundu kingdoms such as Kakonda, Bihe, and Wambu were in existence.

In late 1641 the Dutch captured Luanda and Benguela, the Portuguese in the north retreating to the interior station of Massangano. Only the puppet ngola remained loyal to them. Most of the lesser chiefdoms and the kingdoms of Kongo, Matamba, and Kasanje supported the Dutch. Nevertheless, the Portuguese held on for seven years against these combined forces. Dutch occupation of Angola seriously interfered with the Brazilian economy by reducing the number of available slaves. In 1648 Governor Salvador de Sá, with a force of approximately 1,500 men from Brazil, recaptured Luanda and Benguela. Coastal Africans who had supported the Dutch were slaughtered or sold into slavery, and within two years all states hostile to Portugal had been negated. Kasanje and Matamba entered into long, drawn-out peace negotiations. Nzinga, by then an old woman, finally signed a treaty with the Portuguese in 1656. Matamba lost all of its land west of the Lukola River, but it escaped being made a vassal state to Portugal. Although there were sporadic outbreaks, peaceful relations between Matamba and Kasanje and the Portuguese became the policy of all parties. The Portuguese had discovered that these two states, acting as mediators in the interior slave trade, were far more valuable than the old decimated kingdom of Ndongo had ever been. A new peace treaty was signed in 1684, and this one was respected until 1744.

New towns were established by the Portuguese in the immediate hinterland such as Caconda Velha, and the surrounding territories were thoroughly searched but no mining potential was found. The Portuguese were thus left in Angola with only one product of value — slaves. The wealth of Portuguese residents and the European charm of eighteenth-century Luanda depended almost entirely on the export of this commodity. Brazil seemed insatiable in its demands for a labor force. Because of this economic link Angola became in the eighteenth century, with the full knowledge of the Lisbon government, almost a dependency of Brazil.

The political organization of the colony was both a result of the pressures of slave raiding and a causative factor in the continuance of the trade. The governor was in charge of the colony and ruled within the context of his instructions received from Portugal. In the eighteenth century many of the governors were Brazilians. The governor was not a completely free agent in Angola, since he had to consult with the bishop, the chief justice, the commander of the army, and also the powerful council of Luanda. The entire area under Portuguese control was divided into military districts, or presidios, under the command of captains. These men were almost absolute in their districts. There were three towns, Luanda, Massangano, and Benguela, with their own councils. These councils were very powerful, particularly in Luanda, and aligned against a new, untried governor could very often dominate the central government.

Each presidio was further divided into chiefdoms, whose native rulers were supposed to continue their traditional political functions and also carry out the orders of the captains. Not until 1730 when the governors were given a definite stipend did any of the officials receive a salary. The captains of the military districts were allowed to keep a portion of the tribute collected, and they also engaged in trade. It was therefore to their advantage to get as much as possible from the chiefs in their territories short of causing a general uprising. A state so organized and heavily dependent upon the slave trade was constantly seeking to expand the area of its slave recruitment. It was also a polity that was almost impossible to reform.

The constant wars of the sixteenth and early seventeenth centuries provided large numbers of captives for the slave ships. These wars combined with normal trading activities drastically reduced the population of the coastal region by the year 1700. The bulk of slaves transported in the eighteenth century came from the deep hinterland. Some of these were the results of raids, but most were acquired by trade. Private traders and captains of presidios were not averse to starting a localized war for their advantage. The Portuguese government licensed corporations to obtain certain quotas of slaves. The slave contractor of the corporation would function through local merchants and native traders. The local entrepreneur or contractor would fit out caravans for African and Portuguese traders who would penetrate the interior, staying at times for over a year. The most fruitful areas for purchasing slaves were in Matamba and Kasanje. There slaves purchased or captured deep in the Congo basin were presented for sale. Another good area for recruitment was the Ovimbundu territories in the southern highlands. The basic trade goods were similar to those utilized elsewhere in West Africa — cloth, iron bars, and manufactured items. Because of the obvious dangers, the Portuguese until 1760 banned trading firearms to the Africans. This ban, however, placed the Portuguese at a disadvantage, since slavers of other nationalities had no such delicate scruples.

When the trade goods were exhausted the slaves were marched to one of the main ports. There they were held in baracoons awaiting shipment. Some attempts were made to revive the health of the slaves, who had been forced to march for hundreds of miles under the worst of conditions. Once transferred to Portuguese ships, their lot was perhaps worse than that of slaves who were transported by other European carriers. Portuguese ships were generally smaller and overcrowding was a commonplace practice. The four- to five-week voyage to Brazil was an ordeal which as a general rule one slave in five did not survive.

No one knows the numbers of slaves taken from Angola. Some estimates run as high as four million transported between the sixteenth century and 1836. Brazil certainly absorbed over fifty percent of the total number exported. Some other statistics will hint at the magnitude of the trade. In 1798 Liverpool, the largest of the British slave ports, had approximately 150 slave ships engaged in the trade. Of these, 69 were actively involved in Angola. One historian, David Birmingham, estimates the average annual number shipped in the mid-seventeenth century to be 10,000 persons. In the early eighteenth century the annual export dropped considerably to an average of about 6,000. After 1730, however, the numbers increased to more than the seventeenth-century levels.

By 1800 the eastern frontiers of Angola had become relatively stabilized. The slave trade continued to flourish, although more Portuguese were critical of the entire system. The reform governor, Sousa Couthino, in the 1770s introduced some local industry to Angola, but the colony still depended almost exclusively upon its exports of slaves. Luanda, a European-type city with churches, mansions, and gardens, was controlled by an inbred, stagnant society which had forgotten the pioneering activities of its founders. Relaxation of the Portuguese drive to annex territory meant relative security for the Ovimbundu kingdoms of the southern and eastern territories of Kasanje and Matamba. This balance between the interior states and the Portuguese continued until the scramble for Africa in the latter nineteenth century forced Portugal once again to expand its territory.

The Portuguese and Mozambique

Early Portuguese activities between the Zambesi River and Cape Delgado are in reality a part of the history of East Africa. The Swahili towns of Mozambique and Sofala before the Portuguese were merely less profitable counterparts of those city-states further north. To a great extent, particularly in the sixteenth century, the importance of Mozambique depended upon non-African factors, especially the supremacy exercised by Portugal over the entire Indian Ocean. Portuguese activities on Mozambique Island and in the interior in the seventeenth century were freed from such dependence, since Portugal lost her hegemony over the Indian Ocean and the Zenj states regained their freedom.

The Portuguese were introduced to Mozambique in March 1498 when ships of Vasco da Gama put into the harbor. In 1505 the fleet of Viceroy Francisco de Almeida landed troops and supplies at Sofala with instructions to build a fort. The Portuguese soon dislodged the Arab sheikh and even before their mud fort was completed controlled the town. Sofala was important for the Portuguese because it was considered the gateway to the supposed fabulous gold mines of the interior. The interior trade from Sofala was controlled by a factor, and very shortly another factory was established at Quelimane.

The most important Portuguese station on this section of the coast soon became the island town of Mozambique. Construction there began in 1507 on administrative buildings, a hospital, and a fort. Largely because of its location midway between the northern Portuguese stations and Sofala and because of its harbor Mozambique became the administrative center for the Zambesi territory. Its prosperity in the sixteenth century did not depend upon African trade but was due to its location as an important way stop for ships bound to and from India. In the middle of the sixteenth century construction was begun on a great fort which continued for forty years. The soundness of the fort was proved in 1607 when it withstood a Dutch invasion fleet. The population of Mozambique in 1600 has been estimated at 400 European men.

The administrative chief of the Portuguese settlements to the south was the captian of the fort at Mozambique, a position that was normally given as a reward for long, excellent service to the empire. The perquisites of the office meant that each captain ended his three-year period of duty a relatively wealthy man. Later he was given the sole right to trade in certain products in areas not previously reserved for the crown. These privileges were later extended to include the rights to the entire Zambesi trade. In return, the captain paid a large sum before attaining the office and was responsible for the upkeep of the administration and the military. The captain's autocracy was limited by certain factors. He was constrained to follow the regulations issued from Lisbon and had to submit reports directly to his superior, the viceroy of India. Later distance and weakness of his forces compared to those of some of the interior Portuguese were even more effective checks on his authority.

In 1509 António Fernandes began the first of three exploratory trips into the interior from Sofala. He visited the mines of Manica and made contact with the lesser chieftains and finally the Monomotapa. Fernandes' reports of the wealth available whetted the appetites of Portuguese officials. In 1531 the Portuguese established a trade fair at Sena, and from that time forward the town became an important port on the Zambesi. Some time later Portuguese traders moved into Tete, located almost 250 miles from the sea. They also established smaller stations such as Massapa on the Mazoe River and had many smaller transitory stations in Vakaranga territory. One Portuguese trader, Antonio Caiado, at midcentury became an adviser to the monomotapa and resided permanently at his capital. Portuguese administrators honored Caiado with the title captain of the gates, reflecting their wish to open the gates of the fabulous wealth of the Monomotapas.

Despite all such activity the products of the interior trickled coastward only to Sofala, Quelimane, and Mozambique. There were many reasons for this lack of trading activity. One was the hostility of the Swahili merchants toward the

Portuguese interlopers. These men worked actively against Portuguese traders and developed new routes of trade which bypassed Portuguese towns. Another more fundamental reason was that the richness of the interior mines existed only in the minds of the Portuguese. Later reports by officials such as Vasco Homen, who viewed the gold mines of Manicaland and also the silver area of Chicoa, confirmed the small yield of these mines. Homen reported that a much more regimented labor force and expensive, complex machinery would be necessary to raise the production figures substantially.

In 1568 the young Portuguese king Sebastião, influenced by a rumor of wealth in the Zambesi region and wishing to avenge the death of the Jesuit missionary da Silveira, decided upon conquest. To accomplish this purpose Francisco Barreto, outfitted with an army of over 1,000 men, left Belem in 1569. The entire expedition was a disaster. Not until 1571 did Barreto reach Sena, from which point he carried on continuous and ineffective campaigns against African chiefdoms. By 1573 when the troops were withdrawn Barreto was dead of fever and only 200 men were left of the original number. Barreto's lieutenant, Vasco Homen, was more successful. Recruiting an army of approximately 400, Homen left Sofala in 1574, reached Manicaland, explored above Tete, and investigated the legendary silver area of Chicoa. Over half of the men were lost to the climate, disease, and African attacks. Homen's negative report on the mines and the loss of life attendant on the two expeditions changed Lisbon's attitude toward conquest.

Thirty years later the schemes of direct exploitation were revived. Despite Homen's report, the Portuguese crown was determined to gain direct control of the silver mines. To accomplish this objective a captain-general was appointed whose authority exceeded that of the captain at Mozambique. Portuguese merchants, who did not relish having their trade undercut by the new establishment, refused to cooperate. The captains of Mozambique did not aid the new officials in their schemes. Disease, African hostility, and the minimal value of the interior territory itself once again defeated the Portuguese plan and it was abandoned after ten years.

By 1700 the Portuguese had lost control of the cities north of Cape Delgado and had been driven out of the largest share of the East Indian trade. This decline was reflected in a slowing down of the economy at Mozambique, which was greatly dependent upon the seaborne traffic. Sofala and Quelimane had lost the importance as stations for the interior gold trade that they held a century before. It has been estimated that there were over 1,000 Portuguese in the area from Mozambique in the north to Delagoa Bay in the south. Of these the greater number were in the vicinity of Mozambique Island. There were approximately fifty Portuguese at Sena and an equal number in the vicinity of Tete.

Portuguese hopes of conquering the interior had proved fruitless, and, in addition, had played an important but not primary role in undermining the authority of the monomotapas. The Vakaranga kingdom succumbed more to internal pressures inherent within the institutional framework of the kingdom than from Portuguese attacks. The major outside element in leveling the Vakaranga was the incessant pressure upon the southern borders of the territory by the kindred Rozwi kingdom of the Changamire. The breakup of the Monomotapa empire did not work to any immediate advantage for the Portuguese. They never controlled any of the mines directly, although with the mines of Manicaland falling to the Rozwi it was more difficult for the minerals to find their way to the Portuguese coastal towns.

Two factors in the Portuguese occupation have yet to be mentioned. These are the spread of Christianity and the slave trade. As noted previously, one reason behind the Portuguese explorations of the fifteenth century was the desire to Christianize heathen peoples. Thus from the very beginning of Portuguese Mozambique there were priests and missionaries present. The Jesuit order sent large numbers in the latter sixteenth century, as did the Dominicans. The missionaries followed the traders into the interior and in some cases, as with da Silveira, were ahead of them. In all of the permanent interior stations there was a church, and individual missionaries did heroic work. There were a few examples of mass conversion. Just before he was killed by the monomotapa da Silveira had baptized that monarch, his wife, and many of the nobles of the court. Hostility evinced toward all Portuguese, abetted in the earlier period by Swahili merchants, however, kept the numbers of African converts at a minimum.

In the seventeenth century the Jesuits worked near Mozambique Island while the Dominicans lived within the separate interior chiefdoms of the Vakaranga. The latter concentrated their efforts on the youth and sent many promising young men to India to be trained for the priesthood. Apathy, neglect, disease, and the climate took a frightful toll of the missionaries. Not only did they pay with their lives but their zeal wasted away. In the eighteenth century the orders became a part of the prazo system, which demanded that they deal in slaves. By 1800 there were only a few priests, and after almost 300 years Church influence did not extend far beyond the boundaries of the towns.

Slaves had been an item in the East African trade for centuries before the arrival of the Portuguese. Only hints are available as to the volume of this trade, but it was obviously quite small. The establishment of Portuguese hegemony on the coast seems not to have altered the trade very much. It remained relatively unimportant until the beginning of the nineteenth century. The market for slaves was the Indian Ocean area. Mozambique was too far away and the Cape passage too dangerous for the Atlantic trade to have much effect upon its economy. The Portuguese, therefore, did not attempt any systematic exploitation as they were doing in Angola, although the prazo system, which was developed in Mozambique, depended for its operations upon slaves.

The unique and most typical institution in the territories controlled by the Portuguese in the eighteenth century was the prazo system, which started in the sixteenth century when individual Portuguese moved into the interior. Some, by giving assistance to local chiefs or monomotapas, were rewarded by gifts of land. These grants, much as their medieval European counterparts, included the African inhabitants. The favored Portuguese adventurers took African wives, lived on the land, and built up their own private armies. When Portuguese authority was effectively extended past Sena the government had to recognize the grants. In fact, it went further and expanded the system by assuming the right to award land to some of its servants. These crown grants originally were to be no larger than three leagues square. Grantees also promised to reside on the grant, cultivate the land, and marry only Europeans. These conditions were unenforceable, and the prazeros extended their holdings as much as local situations would permit. Most of the grants were so large that to bring all the area under some type of cultivation was an impossibility.

The prazero was his own law over the people who lived on

his land. Technically there was a difference between a colono who resided on a prazo and a slave. In actual fact the colonos' freedom was only theoretical and in practical terms he was treated as a slave. The prazero set the level of tribute money to be collected by the native authorities on his land and also established the method of payment. Their private armies made the prazeros collectively the strongest force in the colony. By the eighteenth century there were few pure Portuguese prazeros; most were mixtures of Portuguese, African, and Indian. Some of these landlords lived in great luxury, although reports of the latter eighteenth century indicate that the economic high point of the system had long passed. The Lisbon government from time to time tried to modify the system and check its barbarity toward Africans, although the will and the means to enforce any regulations concerning the prazos were lacking. The system was finally abolished in 1832, but it continued to exist until the latter nineteenth century.

SIX
South Africa

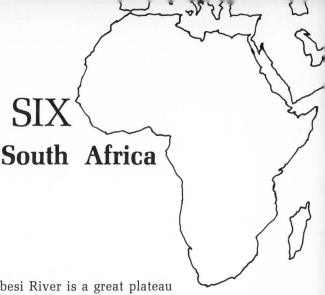

Geographic setting

Africa south of the Zambesi River is a great plateau with an elevation of between three and four thousand feet. The land, which is higher in the eastern portion and falls away to the west, is cut through by three great river valleys — the Zambesi, Limpopo, and Orange. The Zambesi and Limpopo rivers flow from west to east while the Orange River rises in the Basuto highlands and flows east. The plateau falls toward the coast in a series of terraces, which are most noticeable in the extreme south in the Great and Little Karroo. The Drakensberg chain of mountains separate the inland high plateau from the coastal belt of subtropic vegetation and Mediterranean climate. South of present-day Mozambique this coastal strip is quite narrow. In the area of present-day Swaziland and Natal the belt is cut by many streams. The valleys are wooded and the palm belt extends far south. The southern portion forms the productive Mediterranean farm land of Cape Colony while in the far west the most obvious feature is the Namib Desert.

Southeast trade winds blow throughout most of the year, bringing regular rains in the summer (December–February) in much of southern Africa. In the western areas, the winds take up more moisture than they deposit and the land therefore becomes drier in the western Transvaal and Bechuanaland region. A large portion of western Bechuanaland and southwest Africa is made up of the arid Kalahari and Namib deserts.

East of longitude 25 degrees east are the subtropical grasslands with their many rounded, well-grassed hills and well-watered valleys. The soil is fertile and there are many stands of excellent timber. Much of this area yields good harvests to hoe-type agriculturists such as the Nguni. From the eastern coast the land rises westward to the high veld grasslands. In the Transvaal and Lesotho is much rich cattle country, but the land will also support farming. Forest lands decrease as one moves from east to west. The low veld follows the Limpopo and Komati rivers southwest between the highland areas and the eastern Kalahari. This low veld in the past provided a migration route for many Bantu people.

The highland nature of much of southern Africa has provided protection against many of the debilitating African diseases, although malaria is prevalent everywhere north of latitude 25 degrees south. Sleeping sickness is of the cattle variety and is present in tropical areas below 4,000 feet. The tsetse fly, however, needs the humidity of river banks and cannot survive in areas of much light. Southern African cattle keepers could avoid the worst of the disease by confining their stock to the high grasslands. In areas where the fly was dominant settlers were forced almost entirely into farming.

The eastern and southern portion of the coastal strip is very fertile and can support intensive farming as well as cattle-tending activities. The high grasslands are perfect range country. Only in the north in parts of the Limpopo Valley, in the far west in the Okavango marshes, and in the Kalahari and Namib deserts is life particularly hazardous. The Kalahari is not a true desert, being composed of red desert sands, stone outcroppings, and white tufu. It is crisscrossed by old river beds. In the northeastern section a portion of the Okavango River is flooded, creating a hundred-mile-long strip of marshland. When the dry season returns many large salt pans are exposed in this area. Even in the driest part of the Kalahari there are many leguminous plants which can provide food and liquid. Particularly important for the Bushmen is the tsuma melon.

There are four good invasion routes from the north. One is the coastal strip lying eastward from the Drakensberg mountains. Another is the high plateau, which is merely an extension of the highlands of Rhodesia. A third route is that of the low veld, which extends into Botswana. The last and probably least used is the westernmost section, which is a continuation of the low plateau of modern-day Angola.

The Bushmen and Hottentots

Although the majority of the natives of southern Africa speak either Bantu or Khoisan languages, the area is a racial melting pot. The mixing of Negro, Bushmen, and Hottentots both north of the Limpopo and in their present location for a thousand years created a variety of subracial types. This variation, although noticeable among the Bantu, is more striking among Khoisan speakers.

A brief survey of what is known of the Bushmen and Hottentots will indicate how such mixtures came about. Bushman and Hottentot origins are still a mystery, although several different theories have been proposed to explain them. As noted earlier, a Bushmanoid type at one time inhabited a large part of Africa. Confronted by superior cultures, these hunters were either eliminated, assimilated, or pushed further to the south. There is evidence that variations of these people lived in harmony with the early Bantu invaders of central and eastern Africa. Excavations of living sites of some of the people of southern Rhodesia in the period before the Shona kingdom have brought to light great variations in skeletal configurations. Some specimens are tall and others quite short, indicating a considerable amount of intermarriage between Bantu and Bushmanoid long before the major Bantu invasions of southern Africa.

The basic physical type prevalent in southern Africa before the year 1000 is not known. One theory holds that the dominant Bushmanoid or Capoid was larger than the modern Bushman and that the present-day Khoisan speakers are variants of this original type. Whether this assumption is correct or not, the one definitely established fact is the long history of Bushmanoid residence in southern Africa. Hundreds of cave and rock paintings have been discovered to indicate the long occupation of these people, who were hunters and gatherers with many of the same ways as their descendants of the Kalahari.

The languages of both the Bushmen and Hottentots belong to the Khoisan family. Both languages utilize a simple syntax with few subordinate clauses. Nouns are expressed in three different cases and verb usage is not complex. The Khoisan languages are difficult because each word has its own special tonal inflection and clicking sounds predominate. Bushmen have as many as six different clicks while the Hottentots have four such sounds. The languages of the two peoples were so different from other African languages that all early European visitors made note of it. John Davys, writing in 1600, stated of the Hottentots that "their words are for the most part in-articulate, and, in speaking they clocke with the tongue like a brood-hen, which clocking and the words are both pronounced together, verie strangely." So complex was Bushman speech that nineteenth-century missionaries lived for years with these people without ever mastering their language.

There are two major divisions of the Khoisan speakers of southern Africa which have been extant since the early days of European contact. The Bushmen proper, divided into a number of different sections, who today live in certain parts of Botswana and southwest Africa, inhabited a much larger area in the sixteenth and seventeenth centuries. They are noted for their small stature, delicate bone structure, light skin hue, lack of body hair, peppercorn head hair, and a tendency to accumulate fat around the buttocks, a characteristic called *steatophygia*.

The political and social structure of the Bushmen is very simple, with no chiefs or headmen. The head of a family group is normally the highest element of control. They are hunters who today are experts in the use of the small bow and poison-tipped arrows. Some records indicate that many Bushmen in the eighteenth century were mainly food gatherers and had not developed hunting techniques to any extent. Forced into an inhospitable environment, they survive, even today, by gathering wild vegetables, melons, grubs, snakes, and mice. They build temporary houses of grass which are designed to blend into the countryside. Some wandering bands are content to construct only lean-to structures and sleep in scooped-out holes in the ground.

The Bushmen of today have a number of subdivisions. The Saan, who live in parts of the Namib Desert and in the mountains of Namaland, have adopted the language and much of the religion, law, and customs of their immediate neighbors, the Hottentot Nama. The Heikum, Kung, and Auen Bushmen of the Kalahari are smaller and retain more of their own customs than do the Saan. They are normally smaller, measuring five feet tall or less, and their skin coloration is light yellow.

A number of Dutch records survive from the eighteenth century concerning the Bushmen. Long before that period cattle-tending Hottentots had forced the Bushmen into the interior areas of southern Africa. The accounts note areas where the Bushman roamed and Dutch attitudes toward these people. Otherwise the records do not tell much of the Bushmen. We do not know whether the Cape Bushmen resembled the present people of the Kalahari or those of Namaland. Visits of early nineteenth-century European explorers such as Henry Lichtenstein and Colonel John Collins indicate that there was a great variation in the stature of Bushmen even in a single living group. We do not know definitely whether the social and political system of these early people was more organized than the present observable structures, although this is improbable.

In the latter eighteenth century there were large numbers of Bushmen in the northern areas of Cape Colony who were a constant threat to the cattle of both the Hottentots and Boer frontiersmen. The Boers, aided by Hottentot trackers, conducted virtual wars of extermination against the Bushmen. In fact, Colonel Collins reported that in a six-year period in the northern areas over 2,500 Bushmen had been killed by armed bands of farmers. Diseases such as smallpox, which took a frightful toll of the Hottentots, also wrought havoc among the Bushmen. By the opening of the nineteenth century the Bushmen had ceased to be a threat to white settlers except for sporadic cattle raids upon farms on the extreme frontier.

The second major grouping of Khoisan speakers in southern Africa are the Hottentots. Older theories which made the Hottentots products of intermarriage between Bushmen and invading Hamites have largely been discounted. The linguist Joseph Greenberg's statement that the Hottentots were probably of the same racial stock as the Bushmen and simply developed differently due to better diet and different gene pools is probably accurate. They spoke a similar type of language which used clicking sounds and exhibited many of the same racial characteristics as the Bushmen. The Hottentots were slightly taller than the Bushmen, had a yellowish complexion, peppercorn hair, and *steatophygia*. They differed from the Bushmen mainly in a cultural sense. The Bushmen were gatherers and hunters while the Hottentots were stock keepers.

The southerly progress of the cattle-keeping culture from northeastern Africa through eastern Africa is imperfectly known. It appears, however, that one people, probably the Nilotes, were responsible for the spread of cattle from the north before the arrival of the Bantu in eastern Africa. Residual Hottentot populations, such as the Sandwe present today in East Africa, indicate that there were larger numbers of Hottentots present in this area when cattle tending was introduced. Presumably the Hottentots learned their skills from these people and not from the Bantu. This knowledge was then disseminated to groups who were living in the southern areas or was carried there by migrating bands who had been forced to move by the Bantu invasions. Hottentot stock keepers were present in the extreme southern part of the continent by the fifteenth century. In all probability Diogo Cão in 1484 encountered groups of Hottentots in what is today southwest Africa, and two years later Dias certainly made contact with them further south in regions of the Cape.

Sixteenth-century Portuguese explorers reported in some detail the habits of the Hottentots they observed. So similar are the descriptions that they could have been written by Dutch settlers a century and a half later. All noted the Hottentots' small stature, skin coloration, and pastoral pursuits. In several accounts Europeans commented upon the curious sounds emitted by the Hottentots, and one observer noted that he did not believe a European could ever come to understand the language. All of the Portuguese who stopped in southern Africa traded with the Hottentots. They described the fine cattle and sheep owned by the wandering people. Few Europeans reported encountering large numbers of Hottentots even though they could observe signal fires burning at night in many places. Contrary to their later activities, the Hottentots were viewed by the Portuguese as fierce, dangerous people. Dias had trouble with a few Hottentots he dealt with, de Gama's men fought with them, de Saldanha lost men in action against them and was himself wounded, and d'Almeida, the viceroy at Gao, with sixty men was killed by the Hottentots.

Hottentot social and political organization remained relatively static until a permanent European base was established in southern Africa in 1652. The basic Hottentot political unit was the clan, which was normally a small unit ruled by a chief whose authority within the band was considerable. Little is known of

Hottentot concepts of property and utilization of land. Obviously the ever-increasing herds of cattle and flocks of sheep created localized grazing problems. There were a few cases in which such conflicts between clans were resolved by the creation of larger political units. Kouben Hottentots moving into Namaland in southwest Africa, for example, created a coalition of different peoples ruled over by a Hottentot chief. The typical pattern, however, remained the clan organization, and conflicts between clans were settled by warfare. The inability of the Hottentots in the Cape area to cooperate with one another against a common enemy was one major reason for the quick success of the Dutch in dominating the immediate hinterland.

Hottentots knew how to work in metals, particularly iron and copper. Dutch settlers quickly discovered that Hottentots prized copper wire and sheet above all other trading goods. The Hottentots were primarily herdsmen, however, who placed a high value on their sheep and cattle. Dietary customs varied among different Hottentot groups, but most did not kill their cows unless the animal was very old. Some, such as the Namas, did slaughter animals regularly. All Hottentots milked their cattle, some drinking the fresh milk while others allowed it to ferment. The Hottentots built beehive-style mat huts of a more substantial type than the Bushmen, but their werfs were not permanent establishments. When the season or the grazing demanded they would move to new locations with their animals.

Jan Van Riebeeck was sent by the Dutch East Indies Company in 1652 to establish at the Cape a revictualing station for ships engaged in the East Indies trade. He was expressly ordered to avoid hostilities with the Hottentots and to establish good trade relations with them in order to obtain the cattle and sheep necessary to make his enterprise a success. The fort he constructed helped to minimize the danger from the Hottentots which had so marked other European experiences with them. The Dutch dealt primarily with two groups of Hottentot clans, the Saldanhars, who lived in the immediate vicinity, and the Strandloopers, or Waterman Hottentots.

Trade at first was brisk and there were few problems. The Hottentots were happy to trade their stock for pieces of copper and tobacco. Van Riebeeck's *Journal* is packed with details of such transactions. He recorded at the beginning how he was able to obtain a sheep for a few pieces of copper and one fourth of an ell of tobacco. A cow was worth about two and a half guilders worth of the same trade goods. Inevitably the price went up, but in a short period he had accumulated a large herd of cattle and sheep. Another facet of the Hottentots became apparent very soon. They did not have the European respect for private property and would take anything they could. Early in 1653 the entire cattle herd of the fort was stolen by the Strand-loopers with the help of one of the Hottentots employed by Van Riebeeck.

It soon became obvious that the needs of the company could not be met by trading with the Hottentots. In 1657 the first free Dutch burghers were allowed to settle in the Cape. By 1688 the group numbered over 600, and in that year 200 Hugue-nots arrived in southern Africa. Although such colonization did not solve the problems of the Dutch East Indies Company, it did spell disaster for the Hottentots. Land and cattle could be obtained only by trading for them or taking them from the natives. The better organization of the Europeans — and their guns — soon drove the Hottentots from land that had once been theirs. Although the company disapproved of the movement of the colonists into the interior, it was impossible to stop them. The two Van der Stels, whose governorship spanned the last twenty-five years of the seventeenth century, actively encour-aged exploration of the hinterland. The pattern of Dutch-Hottentot relations was set before 1700. Wherever the Dutch moved in any significant numbers into the interior they caused a rapid breakdown in the loose social and political organization of the Hottentots.

In the eighteenth century, with the continual advance of Dutch colonists into the interior, most of the coastal Hottentot clans lost all cohesion, becoming landless people with few if any cattle or sheep. The great smallpox epidemics of 1713 and 1751 killed thousands of Hottentots, who had little immunity against European diseases. Nor were the Europeans the only disruptive influence on the Hottentots. Bantu clans moving west and south had occupied lands that had previously been Hottentot grazing grounds. A large number of Hottentots lived as virtual prisoners among the Xosa east of the Great Fish River.

By 1800 three distinct Hottentot groupings could be dis-cerned in southern Africa. The first were the coastal Hottentots, who were landless, fragmented, and totally at the mercy of their more powerful Dutch and Bantu overlords. Miscegenation had begun very early, and many sedentary Hottentots bore the stamp of the Bantu and Dutch. The second grouping of Hottentots exhibited these racial traits to a certain degree, but they were more marked by their acceptance of some European culture patterns. Perhaps the best example of these groups were the Griquas, who before 1813 were known as the baastards. Many of them dressed in European clothes, practiced agriculture as well as cattle keeping, used guns, and had horses. In the nineteenth century they proved very receptive to Christianity and organized themselves in a series of republics under chosen captains. The last division of the Hottentots were those of the far interior, who had only minimal contact with the Dutch. These groups continued well into the nineteenth century to live in much the same manner as their ancestors before the arrival of the Europeans.

In the nineteenth century Hottentots of all three types were brought under either British or Boer control. Continued miscegenation, breakdown of the clans, and the growing urbanization of the Cape areas were the major factors that converted the Hottentots into the special mixed group known today as the Cape Coloreds.

The southern Bantu

Reconstruction of the Bantu past in southern Africa is almost impossible. The difficulties noted elsewhere of making valid generalizations concerning preliterate people also apply to the southern Bantu. A further and almost insurmountable problem is encountered in South Africa. In the early nineteenth century a series of revolutionary innovations by some of the Bantu led to the mfecane, or a decade of movement, warfare, and killing aptly defined as the time of crushing. Very few Bantu in southern Africa were unaffected by the mfecane; untold thousands of Bantu were killed, some clans disappeared, and many moved hundreds of miles from their original locations. From the carnage and chaos there emerged a number of strong nations such as the Zulu, Swazi, and Basuto. These were collections of many clans, a number of which had previously been hostile to one another. Separate political, social, and economic customs of the differing clans were rationalized within the context of the new nations. The many wars with the British along the eastern Cape frontier in the nineteenth century also served to coalesce the Xosa clans and cause new forms of social and political organization to develop among them. Few detailed accounts of Bantu life exist before the mfecane, but later writers assumed that the behavior patterns of a Bantu group within the nation had been the same before the revolutionary period. Although untrue, the assumption was not an obvious mistake, since even among the Bantu the memory of old ways tended to die out. Thus any generalizations concerning the southern Bantu prior to 1800 are more questionable than similar comments applied to the Bantu in Central and East Africa.

The Bantu of southern Africa can today be divided linguistically into three separate groups. The western Bantu, who live north and south of the Okavango River, presumably arrived at their present locations by a different, shorter, more western route than the other southern Bantu. Major tribes of the western group are the Ambo, Herero, and Mbundu of Angola. The south-central Bantu are the various Shona groups of southern Rhodesia. The southeastern group, which includes the majority of the people of South Africa, has four linguistic subdivisions — the Nguni, Shangan-Tonga, Sotho, and Venda. The major Nguni people are the Xosa, Zulu, and Swazi. The Sotho are represented by the southern and northern Basuto and the Tswana. We know from present groupings that there were a number of different southerly migrations by a least four separate subgroups of the southeastern Bantu.

The ancestors of the Sotho were probably those pre-Shona Bantu who were skilled in mining and ironworking in Rhodesia. Some had probably moved south of the Limpopo River before the arrival of the Shona. Greater numbers of Sotho migrated after the establishment of Shona hegemony, particularly after the development of the Karanga empire. There is considerable evidence that these early Bantu had lived harmoniously with the Bushmen and Hottentots. Thus the association that resulted in racial and linguistic changes among the Bantu is very old. Some Bantu established a series of fortified outcrops in the northern Transvaal area and manned these until the fifteenth century. The major rock fortress of these people was the Mapungubwe. The people who lived in or near these forts were skilled artisans in iron and gold and evidence suggests that they could have been Sotho.

Groups of migrating Sotho and Nguni Bantu later disrupted the Karanga empire in the late sixteenth century. These

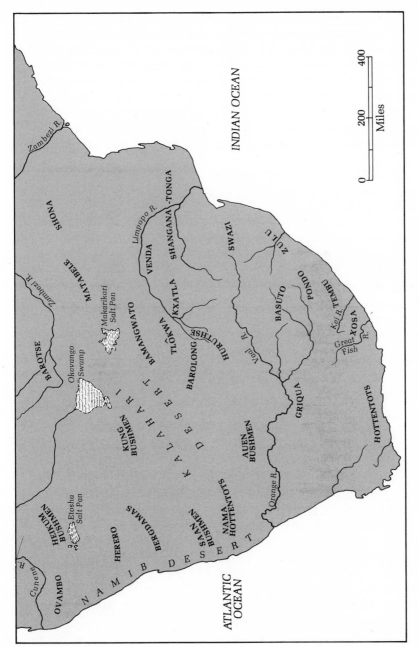

Peoples of South Africa

185

wanderers played an important role in conjunction with the Changamire and Portuguese in undermining the authority of the Monomotapas. Some Sotho groups obviously passed through the lands of the powerful Changamire kings, although most of the Nguni probably bypassed that state. The bulk of the Nguni probably moved south through what is today Mozambique, following a route parallel to the coast. The Nguni tended to settle in the fertile lands of the coastal plain between the Drakensberg mountains and the sea. The new Sotho invaders tended to join those already present on the high plateaus behind the Drakensberg Mountains.

One large group of the Sotho, today called the western Sotho, moved southwestward, skirting the eastern fringes of the Kalahari Desert. These western Sotho comprise all of the Tswana people together with small groups still residing in the Western Transvaal. The Tswana are today divided into a number of different segments. The most important of these are the Barolong, Bahuruthse, Bamangwato, and Bakwena. Eastward in the Transvaal one encounters the eastern Sotho. The most important of this Sotho group are the Bapedi and those people such as the Kwena and Koni who have long been under Pedi influence. In the area of LeSotho live the southern Sotho. Before 1822 two separate kinds of southern Sotho could be identified on the basis of their migration patterns. There were those groups that had migrated there from the west, such as the Sia, Tlokwa, and Phuting, who were related to the Tswana, and those from the east such as the Phuthi, who perhaps had been a part of the old Sotho population of the Swaziland area.

Nguni settlement patterns before 1800 are even more difficult to reconstruct than are those of the Sotho because of the effect of Zulu activities. Hardly any coastal people escaped the disruption associated with the growth of the Zulu nation. Some, like the Lala people, were almost totally destroyed. One can, however, attempt a very generalized statement of the eighteenth-century living areas of various groups. The Xosa and related groups, such as the Ndlambe and Dushane, were in the extreme eastward portion of Cape Colony by the opening of the eighteenth century. East and northeast of the Xosa lived the Tembu and their offshoots, such as the Hala and Jumba. These people have traditions of movement to those locations from the Natal area. In Natal there were a number of separate Bantu groups, some of whom were not Nguni. The Lala and Mbo might have had a Shona origin. However, the bulk of the population in this area by the eighteenth century belonged to a large number of Nguni clans which extended northward into present-day Swaziland. The northern and central portions of Swaziland were peopled by a variety of Sotho clans. The Swazi nation of today is the result of nation building which occurred under two nineteenth-century rulers, Sobhuza and Mswazi.

As noted previously, the southern Bantu were differentially affected by close proximity to Khoisan-speaking people. Analysis of skeletal and facial characteristics has indicated that certain Bantu groups such as the Tswana, Fingo, and Mpondo had been most affected by intermarriage with Bush stock while the Shangana, Tonga, and Zulu showed fewer Khoisan characteristics. Skin coloration has also been examined as a possible indication of mixing. In general, these investigations of present-day Bantu confirm the conclusions reached by the study of skeletal characteristics. A possible discrepancy in this evidence of Bushmen influence on the different Bantu arises when linguistic measurements are used. The Xosa, Swazi, and Zulu, who show by physical measurements only a slight amount of Bushman influence, have absorbed many clicking sounds into their language. One would expect from physical evidence that the Tswana would also have adopted certain aspects of the Khoisan languages, and this is not true. The ultimate explanation for this seeming inconsistency could be that cultural and linguistic borrowing does not depend upon intermarriage between groups.

If one presumes that Khoisan groups possessed cattle before the arrival of large numbers of Bantu in eastern and southern Africa, then perhaps the Bantu learned their cattle-herding skills from the Hottentots. This suggestion, however, is speculation. All that can be said is that certain southern Bantu had adopted animal husbandry as an integral part of their economies before the arrival of the Europeans. The Nguni were particularly attached to cattle, valuing it as a source of food, as a status symbol, and for use in religious and social ceremonies. Some portions of Bantu territory are infested by sleeping sickness and therefore the cattle herds are small. Nevertheless, the people living in these areas, such as the Shangana-Tonga and the Venda, still keep cattle wherever possible. Most of the Bantu also had herds of goats and sheep and kept hybrid chickens. All the Bantu groups depend upon farming. The Sotho groups depend to a larger extent upon agriculture than did the Nguni.

Kaffir corn (*Sorghum vulgare*) was the most common crop cultivated, although maize was also grown by most farmers. Cane, melons, beans, and sweet potatoes were also raised.

In southern Africa there developed Bantu societies which differed widely from one another in many ways. They were, however, sufficiently homogeneous to permit some generalizations concerning social and political organizations. The most characteristic common feature of the Bantu in the eighteenth century was the clan, in theory a body of kinsmen who either were or believed they were descended from a common ancestor. Actual kinship relations to an ancestor were much more true before the mfecane. Even in the eighteenth century, however, the larger clans had grown by absorbing nonrelated people. The size of a clan, depending upon a number of variables, could be as small as ten families or could comprise thousands of people. The Xosa, Tswana, and Zulu tended to have very large calns.

Each clan was normally governed by an hereditary chieftain. Among most Nguni and Sotho clans this position passed automatically to the eldest son of the former chief's "great wife." Only a few groups such as the Shangana-Tonga chose their chiefs from among the brothers of the deceased ruler. Some of the smaller northern Sotho were governed by a woman, who was considered a male and had married "wives." Heirs in these cases were assured by male relatives of the chief. The eldest daughter of the first wife would be the heir apparent. However, this practice was an exception to normal procedures. In theory the totality of government was concentrated in the hands of the chief. In actual practice he delegated authority to many individuals and institutions within the clan. All chiefs had confidential advisers, generally close relatives, whom they consulted before making major decisions. The most important official was called the induna by the Nguni. He carried out the chief's orders, screened law cases for the chief, helped in ritual ceremonies, and aided in planning for war. Some of the larger clans had many specialized aids to the chief, such as the master of the household, legal adviser, and assessors.

Chiefs could, if necessary, also refer important matters to a much larger council. The composition of this council varied from clan to clan. Among the Nguni, Tonga, and Venda this council evolved in the nineteenth century as the main governing body of the larger clan agglomerations. Among the Sotho after the mfecane the general assembly of all initiated men (the pitso) came to serve this purpose. Larger clans were divided for administrative purposes into smaller subdivisions governed by subchiefs and headmen. There were also age sets, designed to aid the chief, but which could also act as a check upon the ruler's theoretical powers.

The eastern Nguni, from the Xosa on the Fish River to the Tonga groups on the Pongola River, played the largest role in the history of South Africa. Of these the group later called the Zulu would have the most prominent role. In all Nguni areas continual grouping and regrouping of clans took place, depending to a large extent on the capabilities of individual chiefs to dominate neighboring clans. If the chief was a strong ruler, he could assimilate weaker neighboring clans. For the lifespan of an individual chief it was possible for something akin to a nation to emerge, with various different clans paying homage to a paramount chief. However, these structures did not outlive the chief. Upon the collapse of one such polity others would begin to form and the center of power would shift. This type of political amalgamation and the practice of exogamy insured the preservation of some cultural homogeneity over vast areas of southern Africa.

By the middle of the eighteenth century the coastal strip was completely filled by Nguni groups. Boer farmers in the extreme south near the Great Fish River blocked further expansion southward. Over 1,500 years of wandering by the Bantu had thus come to an end. Always before there had been open land, lightly defended, to absorb an excess human or cattle population. After midcentury any relief from overcrowding had to be obtained at the expense of other clans or the thinly populated white settlement of the eastern Cape. Tensions rose slowly in the Nguni areas, and it was not until after the turn of the century that major reorganization of the political and military structures began to take place, a reform that would eventually change all Bantu life in southern Africa.

Warfare among the Nguni was an extension of the hunt. All adult males in a clan were considered warriors and they were grouped in an unorganized fashion in a unit called an impi. The basic offensive weapon was a six-foot, iron-tipped spear which could be thrown over 150 feet with some degree of accuracy. For defense a club with a knobbed end called a knob-kerrie was utilized. Each warrior carried a large oval-shaped cowhide shield. Since the clans were all similarly equipped and there was little organization to the impis, a battle was usually settled by weight of numbers. Many wars were decided by the armies of opposing clans meeting at a prearranged point. The opposing impis would, after a preliminary period of hurling insults to one another, close and the battle would begin. The losers lost cattle, land, and people, but the actual loss of life was normally minimal.

It is beyond the scope of this work to discuss in detail the careers of Dingiswayo of the Metetwa clan and Shaka of the Zulu which led in the early nineteenth century to the bloody upheaval of the mfecane. The reforms they instituted, however, were superficially simple. A minor change was made in weaponry. The long spear gave way to the short-hafted, heavy-pointed stabbing assegai. Impis were reorganized and a rigid discipline was imposed on the warriors. An effective command structure was evolved and there developed the tactic of the oxhead movement, a battle plan designed to envelop an enemy force and totally destroy it. Discipline and new tactics ushered in a period of warfare in which the objective was to defeat utterly an opposing force and to absorb the remnants within a new state structure in which the institution of the paramount chief would outlive any individual chief. By 1820 these innovations had allowed Shaka to create from scattered clans the mighty Zulu nation. Some chiefs by adopting similar innovations were able to protect their lands and thus create different Bantu nations. Other clans, fleeing from the Zulu, cut into the territory of their neighbors, beginning a domino effect that embroiled the vast Sotho areas for fifteen years in a devastating series of wars.

Europeans in southern Africa

Portuguese expeditions had reached southern Africa before the close of the fifteenth century. Diogo Cão, leading a coastal exploring expedition in 1484, landed on the coast of southwest Africa north of present-day Swakopmund. Two years later two ships under the command of Bartolomeu Dias rounded the Cape of Good Hope and followed the coast as far east as the Great Fish River before being forced by his crew to turn back. Vasco da Gama arrived at False Bay on November 22, 1497, on his voyage to India. Each of these exploring ventures was aimed primarily at extending Portuguese knowledge of the coast so that advantage could be taken of any profitable areas discovered. The early expeditions reported little to be gained in trade by permanent establishments in southern Africa. The Hottentots were considered to be hostile and treacherous. Even simple barter between the ships' crews and the natives for cattle and sheep was very dangerous. Antonio de Saldanha in 1503 was wounded by natives encountered at Table Bay and, as mentioned earlier, seven years later Viceroy d'Almeida with his sixty men were killed by the Hottentots.

In the sixteenth century the Portuguese in an attempt to dominate the Indian Ocean trade stretched their resources of men and ships so thin that they abandoned many areas in Africa previously considered important. They could ill afford to spend money and men to establish a new base in southern Africa. Their possessions on the Gold Coast, in the Congo, and at Mozambique provided revictualing and refitting bases for their ships en route to India and the Far East. To these practical reasons for avoiding the area the Portuguese added superstition and suspicion. To them the Cape was known as the Cape of Adamastor, the vengeful spirit of storms. It was a place to be avoided.

Sixteenth-century Europe was torn by dynastic and religious wars with the Spanish kings Charles V and Philip II attempting to secure Spanish hegemony and Catholic orthodoxy. One result of these conflicts was the revolt of the northern portion of the Spanish Netherlands. The citizens of this new Dutch Republic were merchants and seamen who struck against Spain on the oceans as well as on land. For the Portuguese the sixty years of Spanish rule which began in 1580 was a disaster because the Dutch soon discovered that the eastern areas were the weakest parts of the combined empire. In 1595 Cornelius Houtman sailed around the Cape and discovered how rich was the Indian Ocean trade and how weak were the Portuguese defenses. Within ten years of the creation of the Dutch East Indies Company in 1602 the Portuguese had been stripped of their monopoly of the Eastern trade. In 1623 the Dutch thwarted English attempts to share the trade of Amboyna, in 1641 the Dutch took Malacca, and in 1658 they captured Ceylon. The Portuguese still maintained a foothold in the eastern trade, and the English had begun their drive for domination of India. In the seventeenth century, however, the infant Dutch nation became dominant in the world's carrying trade, and its newly won trading spheres in the East proved profitable beyond the imaginations of the founders of the empire.

In exploiting the opportunities of the Indian Ocean the Dutch in 1611 had discovered a new, easier route to the East Indies. Instead of sailing along the eastern coast through the Mozambique channel Dutch mariners after rounding the Cape sailed almost due eastward to the Indies. This long sea voyage made it imperative to have a station located in the vicinity of southern Africa, and therefore Jan van Riebeeck was dispatched to the Cape by the company in 1652 to establish such a post. His instructions were explicit; he was to construct a fort and make friends with the Hottentots in order to obtain the food to supply the passing ships. The task, however, proved more difficult than was at first imagined and the company authorized a new approach to the supply problem. In 1657 the company agreed to the suggestion that nine of the company's servants become free burghers with small leaseholds of thirteen and a third acres. The responsibility of these first farmers and those who followed them was to raise food and to sell it to the company at fixed prices. Neither at this juncture nor later did the company contemplate establishing a colony which would dominate the hinterland. By 1688 the number of colonists at the Cape numbered almost 600, and in the next year they were joined by 200 refugee Huguenots who had fled from France after the revocation of the Edict of Nantes. The new arrivals were skilled artisans, merchants, and farmers who within a generation had melded into the predominantly Dutch population. Simon van der Stel, who was governor from 1679 to 1699, introduced advanced farming techniques and encouraged the exploration of the hinterland areas. Despite all such changes, the colony at the turn of the century was not able to satisfy the needs of the ships and was carried as a deficit upon the books of the administrators in Batavia.

From the beginning the company had attempted to restrict contacts between settlers and Hottentots and to prevent Europeans from moving into the interior. This policy could not be maintained in the face of an open frontier and the harsh monopolistic practices of the company. The sale of meat, wheat, wine, and other crops had to be to the company at fixed prices. Retail licenses were required of all merchants, a requirement that, in effect, placed a tax upon all imported products. The company's land policy was one better geared to Europe than to southern Africa. Restrictions on the amount of land occupied, although not appreciated by the farmers of the western Cape, were not disastrous. In the eighteenth century, however, such limits when applied to poorer land or to cattle farmers were ridiculous. By 1700 many farmers had given up raising crops for cash and were concentrating on self-sufficiency. With land difficult to obtain legally, many younger men became stock farmers, running their herds beyond the legal boundaries of the Cape. As previously noted, the Hottentots with their weak political structure did not offer much resistance to the frontier Boers.

From the beginning of the colony supreme decision-making was vested in the chamber of seventeen in Holland. This chamber represented the shareholders of the company and also the six provinces of the Dutch republic. It made the important policy decisions for each territory in which the company operated. Administration of this policy was devolved upon a governor general and his council located in Batavia. The Cape governor and his council of policy had thus to satisfy an administrator located far away in the East Indies as well as the chamber of seventeen situated in Holland. The administration of Cape Town was always small and the company did not provide the governor with an adequate military force. As noted previously, the Cape administration was highly centralized. Regulation of local activities was handled by means of ordinances issued by the governor. The judiciary included a court of commissioners for petty cases, a matrimonial court, and an orphan court. The chief judicial body was the council of justice, composed of members of the governor's council and three Cape Town burghers. All of these were appointive agencies and were directly amenable to control by the governor. There were no courts for the inland area until the circuit court was established by the British in 1811. Thus all litigation involving western Cape farmers or frontier Boers had to be adjudicated in Cape Town.

Although the official policy was to prevent unrestricted movements into the interior, settlement of the western Cape area had proceeded so far by 1685 that the company was forced to establish a system of local government. The company defined a local government area, called a drotsdy. The chief administrative officer of the drotsdy was the landdrost, who was a company appointee, who could refer certain matters to a council of local farmers called the heemraaden. The company by creating the first drotsdy of Stellenbosch in 1685 thus believed it had solved the problem of controlling the interior farmers. In fact, it encouraged a more independent attitude on the part of these farmers. The landdrosts throughout the century were either farmers in the district or soon became so and their administrations tended to reflect the desires of the farmers rather than the company. As interior settlement progressed two other drotsdys were created, Zwellendam in 1746 and Graaf Reinet in 1786. The establishment of these units of local government are eloquent testimony of the failure of the company to halt interior settlement.

The possession of land was theoretically controlled by the government. Although not the only form of capital available, land was by far the most plentiful. Adventuresome young farmers could turn their backs on the more settled areas and attempt to carve out a new life on the frontiers. The company in the eighteenth century ceased to grant freehold land but instead tried to control landholding by requiring a quit-rent fee for occupation. This fee, however, was normally only five pounds for a 6,000-acre farm. As should have been obvious, this device did not prevent the Boers from trekking. The company also drew many lines in the interior beyond which company servants and free burghers were not to pass. The restlessness of the veld Boers increased during the century as the power and prestige of the company waned. Even had the company not been growing bankrupt it could not have enforced its many rules upon the veld Boers.

Three types of Boer settlers were discernible by the opening of the eighteenth century. The first group comprised the urban society of Cape Town. Most of its inhabitants were involved in trade, business, or government. The richer burghers built stately houses and raised large families in an atmosphere similar to that of Europe. Cape Town was the cultural center of southern Africa. There were schools and churches. The stringencies of isolation were modified in Cape Town by continued contact with eighteenth-century Europe.

The second Boer type was the settled farmer of the western Cape; Stellenbosch rather than Cape Town was the chief town for this group. Although these farmers also became stockmen, first with cattle and later with sheep, they also specialized in cereal crops and grape culture. Their farms, small by South African standards, were almost self-sufficient units, averaging slightly over 160 acres per holding. Grain and wine surpluses from these farms could be sold in Cape Town to provide the

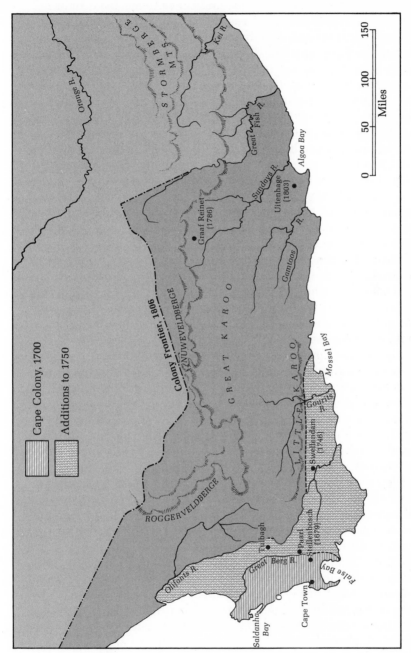

Expansion of Cape Frontiers

Cape Colony, 1700

Additions to 1750

Colony Frontier, 1806

Orange R.

STORMBERGE

Kei R.

Great Fish R.

Sundays R.

Algoa Bay

Graaf Reinet (1786)

Uitenhage (1803)

Gamtoos R.

NUWEVELDBERGE

GREAT KAROO

LITTLE KAROO

Mossel Bay

Gourits R.

Swellendam (1746)

ROGGERVELDBERGE

Tulbagh

Paarl

Stellenbosch (1679)

Great Berg R.

Olifants R.

Saldanha Bay

Cape Town

False Bay

0   50   100   150

Miles

spices, clothes, furniture, guns, and other items that could not be produced on the farm. These farmers were the landed gentry of the settlement and they tended to look down on their urban cousins as being unstable. The life of such a Boer and his large family was the typical routine of farming broken by visits of neighbors, trips to Stellenbosch or Cape Town, and frequently such social occasions as funerals, weddings, and auctions. These settled Boers were conservative, moral Calvinists, and through their very existence they posed a continual problem for the company administrators. However different were the inhabitants of Cape Town and the rural Boers, together they formed a commercial, social, and economic community.

The third class of Boer was the veld Boer, who because of economic and social pressures fled the confines of the western Cape for the freedom of the frontier. The large farms of 6,000 acres loaned by the company to this group were used primarily for the grazing of cattle. These locations were easy to obtain and were abandoned whenever the mood overtook the farmer. All the family possessions would be loaded in the ox wagon, the livestock collected, and the family and their Hottentot servants would trek to a new location. The general route of movement was at first past Stellenbosch and Tulbagh, thence to the north and northeast. The veld Boers, like their frontier counterparts everywhere, established themselves far from any settled location, with a mode of life in some instances scarcely higher than that of many of the aborigines who were their neighbors. They grew to despise any form of control exercised over them by the government. Acting as the advance guard of what they deemed civilization, they were a law unto themselves. Their religion, seventeenth-century Calvinism un-alloyed by contact with more liberal ideas, acted as a unifying force for the frontier Boers. Although Calvinism was a major cohesive force on the frontier, it was individualistic and the Boers tended to compare themselves with the chosen people of the Old Testament. Nor did the more settled burghers of the urban areas possess radically different convictions. The opportunity to exercise their freedom was simply more circumscribed. If town living became too controlled, they could always move away from the offending authority. This demand for freedom, not stilled even by village life and the willingness to move, was the Boers' ultimate answer to established government.

The first recorded contact between Boer and Bantu took

place in 1702. A Boer hunting party engaged in raiding Hottentot kraals encountered a small party of Bantu and a brief skir-
mish took place. In 1736 another Boer frontier party operating
over 300 miles east of Cape Town met with what obviously
were advance elements of the southward-moving Xosa. The
relatively uninhabited territory of the eastern Cape region
proved to be a great inducement for Boer settlement. In the
two decades after 1750 hundreds of Boer families settled in
the area up to the Great Fish River. Despite company rules
against it, they began to trade freely with the Xosa. In 1778
Governor van Plettenberg visited the eastern areas and was
gratified to see what apparently were harmonious relations
between the farmers and Xosa. He met with two Xosa chiefs
and entered into an agreement with them whereby the Fish
River would be the dividing line between white and black.

This agreement and many subsequent treaties betrayed a
profound ignorance of the Bantu. Europeans took for granted
that the Bantu had concepts of private property similar to those
of white farmers. Further, the Xosa chiefs were only clan chiefs,
with no power to make binding agreements for Xosa who did
not belong to their clans. A more basic misunderstanding had
to do with the economics of the frontier area. Both Boer and
Bantu were cattle herders, in competition with one another for
stock and grazing land. Each society had internal pressures that
demanded continual expansion in search of more land. The Fish
River was not a natural boundary, since it could be crossed
easily by both Bantu and Boer. Close proximity between such
competitive groups could only lead to violence. In the year following van Plettenberg's visit there were a series of reciprocal
cattle raids and a few minor skirmishes. The company government decided to help the farmers enforce the terms of the treaty
and sent a strong force to the frontier. This began the first
Kaffir War, which was a minor confrontation compared to later
conflicts. The Xosa were driven back across the Fish River and
5,000 head of cattle were taken as indemnity.

The company created a new drotsdy, Graaf Reinet, in 1786,
primarily to enable the landdrost to prevent violations of the
border and thus keep the peace. This was another impossible
task which the company undertook, since the landdrost was not
provided with troops or police. For these he had to depend
upon the local commandos, whose leaders wanted an aggressive
policy not favored by the company. Trading and raiding there-

fore continued unabated. In 1789 a Xosa chief, Ndlambi, led his followers across the river and drove some whites from their farms. Immediately a two-man investigation team was sent from Cape Town to arrive at new agreements with the Xosa. One of the members, H. C. Maynier, reported that much of the trouble was caused by the Boers. Their cattle traders were guilty of using violence against individual Xosa and some Boers were engaged in trading guns to the Bantu. The commissioners managed to arrive at an agreement based on the Xosa admission that the whites "owned" the land west of the Fish River. However, the reason for previous clashes was not removed by this settlement.

Maynier was named landdrost of Graaf Reinet. His past record and dedication to upholding company rule meant constant friction between himself and the Boers. A severe drought in 1791–1792 placed a premium on grazing lands and Boers began to drive their herds into Xosa territory. The situation was made worse by a brief coalition between some aggressive Boers and the Xosa leader Ndlambi to raid for cattle. In retaliation other Xosa clans attacked the Boers and the second Kaffir War began. Maynier called up a commando and it drove the Xosa forces back as far as the Buffalo River. Peace was then arranged, but not to the satisfaction of the Boers, since Maynier did not demand an indemnity in cattle to replace their losses.

In early 1795 the Boers, thoroughly disillusioned by the Cape government, rebelled against its representative, Maynier. Commandant van Jaarsveld and forty burghers expelled the landdrost and established a republican government. Swellendam drotsdy soon followed the lead of Graaf Reinet. The company, however, did not have to deal with the rebellion, for the British by invading the Cape inherited the problem. The rebels reluctantly gave up their republics in hope that the British would settle the Xosa question by force. The British commander, General Dundas, sent a new landdrost to Graaf Reinet along with a few troops. In 1799 van Jaarsveld was charged with forgery and was arrested by the landdrost. Another rebellion against the central government broke out, led by van Jaarsveld, Coenraad Buij, and Marthinus Prinsloo. The landdrost was expelled and Prinsloo became the head of a new government. The British, reacting quickly, dispatched troops and soon crushed the rebellion. Almost immediately a quarrel arose between two Xosa chiefs, Gaika and Ndlambi, and the

Xosa spilled across into what was considered white territory. Dundas and strong commando units eased the threat of invasion of this third Kaffir War and reinstalled the unpopular Maynier as landdrost. Maynier attempted to come to terms with the Xosa, forbade private commandos, and tried to protect Hottentots who worked for Boer farmers. The Boers did not appreciate these attitudes any better than they had in 1795, and the British were forced by the threat of another rebellion to recall him.

While these events held the attention of interior Boers, the company was fast losing its struggle against the changes of the eighteenth century. Disturbances in Holland and the decline of Dutch sea power contributed to weakening the company. Its huge staff and manifold responsibilities made it difficult to supervise, and its monopolistic practices were out of step with the economic policies of its European rivals. In 1792 the company paid its last dividend and by 1794 it was bankrupt. In the late 1780s the Cape, poorly administered though it was, cost the company more than its entire operation in the East Indies. Various reforms were attempted for the troublesome colony. The last series of reforms were put into effect by two commissioners who were sent out in 1792 to replace the governor. These measures were in the direction of higher taxes and decreased expenditure, which only alienated further the Boers, who were also demanding a more active role in their government.

The Cape was occupied by the British before the crisis within the company brought serious disturbances within the colony. The British occupation was an outgrowth of its war with revolutionary France. With the victory of the French over the Royal Dutch forces in early 1795 it appeared that the French might occupy the Cape and thus be able to cut British trade routes to the East. A British expedition commanded by General Dundas landed at Simons Bay late in 1795. After a few brief skirmishes the company commander surrendered and 143 years of company rule came to an end. The British inherited more than a strategic base. They became the temporary wards of 1,500 officials, 20,000 burghers, and over 25,000 slaves. They were also presented with a frontier problem, with thousands of disaffected Boers confronting the advanced clans of the Nguni.

The first British occupation lasted eight years. Except to make a few necessary changes in the central government, they did little to upset the previous system. They ended the many restrictions upon trading, thus gaining the support of the free burghers of the western Cape. However, their "liberal" attitudes toward Hottentots, slaves, and Bantu soon gained the enmity of the frontier Boers.

The eighteenth century ended with no valid settlement of the border difficulties between the Boers and Xosa along the eastern frontier. The British balked at attempting a war of extermination against the Xosa, a plan recommended by the more militant farmers of Graaf Reinet. Under such circumstances it was inevitable that there would be other Kaffir wars until the balance of power shifted decidedly in the direction of one side. A large portion of the history of South Africa in the first half of the nineteenth century was devoted to the overriding problem of the Bantu frontier near the Fish River. British administrators at the Cape in 1800 little imagined that in the nineteenth century it would be the responsibility of their government to attempt pacification not only of the Xosa but also of the Bantu in the unexplored interior.

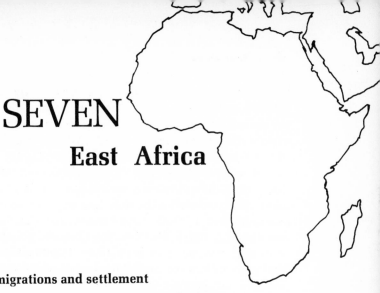

SEVEN
East Africa

Introduction to migrations and settlement

East Africa presents a more complex pattern of migration and interaction of native peoples than any other portion of the continent. In a period of over one thousand years Bushmanoid, Cushite, Bantu, Nilotes, Arab, and Nilo-Hamite peoples entered the territory from all directions. Early inhabitants could be driven out, absorbed completely, or continue to live next to the new invaders. A bewildering series of such invasions occurred after A.D. 1000. The serious study of the political, social, and economic structure of the inland peoples is less than a generation old. Oral tradition, linguistic evidence, and archeological discoveries provide certain high points for the period prior to the year 1800. Arab penetration of the interior and the arrival of more Europeans in the nineteenth century have provided the historian with written materials to supplement the relatively valid oral traditions of the Africans for this century. Many more investigations will have to be completed, however, before any cohesive picture of the history of East Africa prior to the year 1800 can be written. Materials presented for this earlier period must be viewed as extremely tentative. Therefore the following generalized account is but a synthesis, based on present evidence, of the main outlines of the movements and interrelations of the people of East Africa.

The absence of definite links between isolated events noticeable throughout Africa is particularly frustrating in East Africa. There is evidence of Stone

Age people living in western Kenya in the immediate post-Pleistocene period. Skeletal evidence also indicates a branching of these hunting peoples into at least one other type. This has been called Elementeitan type F_1, which could be proto-Hottentot or Bushmanoid. It is possible that this latter type became the dominant population in the settled portions of eastern Africa. Judging from excavations near Nakuru, this physical type could have persisted until well after the first incursions of the Bantu. Various sites in Kenya and Uganda have yielded artifacts that belonged to the Stone Age Bushmanoid whose dates overlap materials belonging to iron users. Presumably these more advanced people were Bantu. Remnants of the one-time dominant Bushmanoid peoples still exist in eastern Africa. Groups such as the Hadzapi Bushmen and the Sandawe Hottentots testify to the long life of these culturally less developed peoples forced to live in juxtaposition with strong Bantu and Nilotic neighbors.

One of the most crucial periods in East African history is the span between the fourth and twelfth centuries. This is the time when the first Bantu began to infiltrate the coasts and the central highlands. Certain inferences can be drawn from the few ancient descriptions of the coast. The *Periplus of the Erythrean Sea,* a Latin first-century sailors' guide, describes the coast as far south as Zanzibar. No mention is made of blacks. Three centuries later the *Geography* of Claudius Ptolemy mentioned blacks, but only in the far south, presumably near Cape Delgado. Al Masudi, who visited Zanzibar in the tenth century, discussed Negro people but indicated that they lived to the north, perhaps in the vicinity of the Juba River. The conclusion from these sources, partially borne out by investigations in Central Africa, is that the Bantu had reached the Mozambique coast by the fourth century. However, they were not yet in sufficient numbers along the coast of Kenya and Tanzania to be noted by an astute observer like Al Masudi.

There is considerable evidence gathered from sites in various places in Kenya, Uganda, and Tanzania of Bantu occupation after the twelfth century. Shards of dimple-based and channeled ware pottery, both associated with iron culture and the Bantu, are widespread. Linguistic evidence also indicates Bantu occupation of East Africa at approximately the time period suggested by archeology and the few written accounts. In a recent article Roland Oliver placed the Bantu dispersion into Urundi, Sukumaland, and Buganda at a later period than the Congo and Zambia. By utilizing Malcolm Guthrie's linguistic concept of general roots he assigned the migrations into these areas to what he called phase three of Bantu movements. This phase coincided with the general spread of East Asian foods such as the banana. Possession of such plants would have enabled Bantu groups to abandon their homes in the savannah and lightly wooded areas of the upper Congo basin for territories with higher rainfall. Unfortunately, our knowledge of these early Bantu is confined to such general statements. It is, nevertheless, definite that by the opening of the thirteenth century Bantu agriculturists were well settled in western and southern Uganda and in some of the more fertile parts of modern-day Kenya and Tanzania.

Some time after the year 1000 East Africa was first invaded by small groups of non-Bantu. These were the Bahima, Nilotic pastoralists from the southern Sudan. Any connection between these Nilotes and the iron culture of Meroë to the north is extremely speculative. It appears that they did not bring ironworking techniques with them. The route taken by iron after the fall of Meroë seems to have been westward toward Lake Chad, where it arrived long before it reached the pastoralists of the much nearer southern Sudan. The Nilotes probably found the Bantu using iron to exploit the relatively rich soils of Uganda and western Kenya. The Nilotes very likely brought two new factors to East Africa — cattle tending and a more efficient type of state organization.

The Nilotes were a minority within the population, although their better organization and more warlike character made them rulers of the Bantu majority. Oral legend refers to the Bacwezi, or tall men, having ruled prior to the establishment of the Luo in the interlacustrine region. This term could be a poetic reference to the Bahima or merely a reference to its ruling caste. The fusion of the Bahima with the Bantu resulted in the creation of larger states with more advanced cultures. Remnants of graded roads, cultivation terraces similar to those in Rhodesia, irrigation canals, and dams date to this period. Presumably the Bantu continued as agriculturists whose major responsibility was to provide food for their Nilotic overlords. The fondness of the Bahima for cattle, which would be duplicated by later Nilotic invaders, became a part of Bantu life as well. It is probable at this juncture that cattle culture passed not only to the Bantu but also to the Bushmanoid or Hottentot people who helped spread the practice further south.

Early movements into Uganda

Beginning in the early thirteenth century a new series of Nilotic migrations began from the southern Sudan. One series of movements was directed northward to the Bahr-el-Ghazal area. These Nilotic pastoralists were the ancestors of the Shilluk, Dinka, and Nuer. Of more concern to East Africa were the southward migrations of the Luo. As already noted, the western and southern portions of Uganda were already well settled by Bantu agriculturists and their Bahima overlords. The Luo who reached these areas in about 1500 displaced the Bahima and established a series of centralized, composite states. Here in Bunyoro and Buganda the synthesizing process begun by the Bahima was continued by the new overlords. The Bahima ruling class withdrew southward before the invading Luo and established themselves in Ankole, Latagwe, and Ruanda.

The greatest of the Luo interlacustrine polities was that of Bunyoro. The Bito kings (bakama) of Bunyoro ruled initially over the largest portion of central Uganda. After forcing out the Bahima they established a Sudanic-type state where the minority Nilotes controlled the chief offices in the bureaucracy. The king exercised supreme secular authority, which was greatly increased by his divine ancestry and his function as the chief priest. Power was shared with subkings, who initially were related to the royal house. The most important of these were the rulers of Busoga and Buganda. The political hierarchy of Bunyoro compared to that of Buganda was not formalized. Chiefs did not have the elaborate system of court retainers and servants that were noticeable at all levels of the Buganda system. Nor was the system of law as institutionalized in Bunyoro. Until the eighteenth century the armies of Bunyoro enforced obedience to the mukama and the kingdom was larger than it had ever been. In the early 1700s Buganda began to assert its independence and to expand the areas under its control at the expense of Bunyoro. A series of peaceful rulers in Bunyoro toward the end of the century coincided with strong, militaristic kings (kabakas) in Buganda. Peripheral areas began to break with Bunyoro and attach themselves to Buganda. By the end of

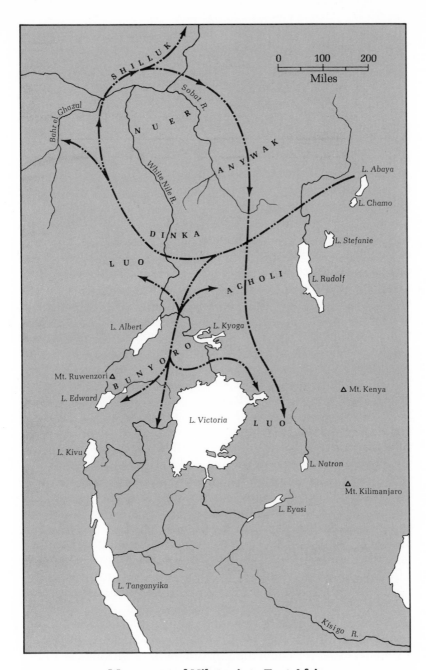

Movement of Nilotes into East Africa

the eighteenth century the kabaka controlled all of the western shore of Lake Victoria from Lake Kyoga south to the Kagera River. Bunyoro territory and influence was further lessened in the early nineteenth century when a son of the mukama established the kingdom of Toro independent of Bunyoro. It was also in this period that the Soga began to exercise more independence from Bunyoro. Busoga in the nineteenth century, although tributary to Buganda, began to develop its own peculiar institutions.

Eastern and northern Uganda were not heavily populated in the sixteenth century and in these territories the Luo invaders could not continue the centralizing forms they followed in Bunyoro. Instead they utilized minor Luo chiefs to rule over small numbers of non-Luo people. In Acholi, for example, the extended family became the basis of political and social organization. Scattered clans could be expected to come together in larger cooperative units only in times of war. This loose organizational pattern was transferred to new territories on either side of the Albert Nile north of Lake Kyoga in the seventeenth and eighteenth centuries. In the eighteenth century a portion of this territory was invaded by a new group of southward-moving peoples, the Lango, who also had their origins in the southern Sudan. They and the closely related Itseo had begun their migrations at least a century before. The Lango political organization was based on the village while the Itseo had developed clan-sized political units. Neither could be considered politically a tribe until much later. The Luo, who were displaced by these invaders, migrated eastward and eventually settled northeast of Lake Victoria. These Kenya Luo retained the name and also a political organization similar to that of their Uganda relatives in Acholi. They imposed their language and culture on the older Bantu residents and also forced other previously hostile clans of diverse people to unite in order to resist the Luo.

Certain general features of life in the northern interlacustrine area appear clearly by the close of the eighteenth century. From a complex pattern of invasions and wars there emerged societies of fusion. The pastoral Nilotic invaders had been absorbed racially by the Bantu in most areas where there was a significant Bantu population. Cattle culture introduced to all areas had profoundly changed the people's mode of life. In territories such as Acholi in the north and Ankole in the south, where the Bantu population was small and the geography favorable, the old system of cattle keeping remained relatively unchanged. This situation had political and social ramifications, since the ruling classes remained the cattle keepers. Elsewhere in Bunyoro, Busoga, and particularly Buganda the ruling classes had to compromise with the agricultural majority. Cattle owning remained a mark of status as well as affluence, but the rulers found it necessary to accept social and political forms more in keeping with the ideals of the Bantu farmers. The best example of such an accommodation is the kingdom of Buganda.

The kingdom of Buganda

In the eighteenth century a combination of factors worked together to make Buganda the most powerful of the interlacustrine kingdoms. With a more dense Bantu population Buganda could not be treated by its early Nilotic rulers in the same manner as Bunyoro. Bantu agricultural pursuits in time became the dominant mode of life of all the people. The clan system was incorporated directly into the centralized state built by the rulers (kabakas) of Buganda. While the Bukamas of Bunyoro were concerned with spreading and maintaining their influence over a vast area their vassals in Buganda were perfecting a model of centralized government. In the latter eighteenth century when Kabaka Kyabagu (died about 1780) began to challenge Bunyoro he had a much more effective government organization than any other East African state.

The kabaka was the key to the efficient operation of the government. In consultation with his council (lukiko) he made the important political and military decisions. All the major officers of the state owed their positions to appointment by the king. The kingdom was divided into districts and each district was placed under the jurisdiction of one of the nonhereditary great chiefs (bakungu). The bakungu received land and economic rights commensurate with their status, and they held their offices only at the pleasure of the kabaka. In each of these districts there were many subchiefs or heads of clans called bataka. The position of bataka was a remnant of the Bantu political system which predated their Nilotic overlords. As clan head the position of bataka was hereditary. The re-

sponsibilities of officials, however, did not affect the wider
sphere of Buganda government.

The primary function of chiefs was to maintain law and
order in their areas, to conduct certain public works such as
building roads and bridges, and to provide the necessary numbers of warriors to support the king in time of war. Chiefs on
both levels were empowered to try cases. A chief would hear
the arguments with his lukiko and render his decision. Both
defendant and plaintiff were required to pay court fees. On
most charges conviction meant payment of a fine to the court
as well as compensation to the injured party. Murder, thievery,
and adultery were crimes usually punished by death, although
mutilation could be ordered instead. Appeals from a decision
could theoretically be made to the court of a higher chief and
if necessary above this to the prime minister (katikkiro) and
finally to the kabaka. Since chiefs disliked appeals from their
decisions, in practice most cases were settled on the local level.

There were two other major classes in society — the peasants (bakopi) and the slaves (badu). The bulk of the population
belonged to the former group. The bakopi were fortunate in the
climate and soils of most of Buganda. The land, a high plateau
cut by erosion, has flat-topped hills with very fertile soil on the
sides. Rainfall is bimodal, with two definite rainy seasons,
although some rain falls every month. Much of the land can
support heavy cultivation. Agriculturists could settle one section of land and remain there, since there was little need for
shifting cultivation. The staple crops of Buganda were many
varieties of bananas. There were special kinds for cooking, for
roasting, and for making beer. Some banana gardens could
last for over twenty-five years. A farmstead also had cloth bark
trees and family gardens which provided sweet potatoes, millets, maize, and pumpkins. Wealthy men kept goats and cattle.
Although cattle keeping was of less importance in Buganda
than elsewhere, the owners took great pride in their herds.
Many herdsmen were Bahima who because of their skills enjoyed a special position within Ganda society. The kabaka had
the most cattle and they were divided into many different herds
which were grazed in various parts of the kingdom. Curdled
milk from these cattle was brought every day to the palace.

The kabaka's place of residence was the capital of the kingdom. The location of the palace, although changed a number

of times, was always in the vicinity of modern-day Kampala. Here the kabaka was surrounded by the large retinue necessary for his comfort and to aid him in administering the kingdom. The queen mother (namasole) and the queen sister (nalinnya) would live most of the year close to the kabaka. In the palace compound there would be quarters for the many wives of the king. It was normal for the kabaka to take wives from all parts of the kingdom so that each area would feel honored. The great officials of the kingdom were also required to be close to the person of the kabaka. The most important of these officials was the kitikkiro, who was responsible for conducting the everyday business of the kingdom and, in consultation with the kabaka, directing the bureaucracy. The governors of districts were also required to spend a portion of the year in residence near the king.

An active kabaka was able by personal contact to direct the energies of the kingdom. His appointive powers were normally sufficient to see that officials carried out their instructions. Certain other functions of the state were also reserved to the kabaka. It was he, in consultation with the lukiko, who decided whether the great drum signifying war should be beaten. Upon receipt of such knowledge the lesser chiefs would gather the able-bodied men from their villages and prepare for the military campaign. The kabaka also claimed the labor of all men in the kingdom. Thus he or his representatives could demand from the bakopi a certain amount of work on public projects such as road maintenance. Finally, the kabaka retained the power to tax. Collection of a tax was not a function of the chiefs but of a special group of officials appointed by the kabaka.

This brief survey indicates that Buganda was by far the best organized and most efficiently administered large state in East Africa. By the opening of the nineteenth century Ganda armies had overrun Busoga, forcing its king to pay tribute to the kabaka. The kingdoms of Buddu and Buwekula were dislodged from their allegiance to Bunyoro and came under the influence of Buganda. Chiefs of other tribes, many located as far away as Tanganyika, found it expedient to pay tribute to the kabaka. Buganda's supreme position throughout most of the interlacustrine area was not seriously challenged until the 1860s when the warlike Mukama Kaberega of Bunyoro briefly restored the fortunes of that state.

Movement of peoples and settlement in Kenya and Tanzania

The broad outlines of migration and settlement into modern-day Uganda are, if speculative, relatively simple to understand. There the Bantu agriculturists were subjected to a series of Nilotic invasions from the north. The newcomers formed a cattle-keeping aristocracy and in differing ways reached an accommodation, politically and socially, with the Bantu majority. Much of the history of the interlacustrine area is concerned with the construction of large polities. These centralizing tendencies have made easier the study of the area. The great kingdoms of Bunyoro, Buganda, Busoga, and Acholi became the focal point of interest. By contrast, the much larger territory of modern-day Kenya and Tanzania does not admit of such easy explanations. There were a bewildering series of invasions of Bantu, Nilotes, Nilo-Hamites, and Hamites which resulted in the present highly fragmented population and cultures of these areas. The invasions did not have a common point of origin; rather, groups of people moved into the territories from all directions. Although some of these migrations overlapped one another, very little is known of the interconnections between them. The invaders did not establish large centralized states but instead brought in diffuse political and social practices. Many of the most important later peoples did not have well-developed chief systems and some had only a clan organization. Of the more than one hundred recognized tribes in eastern Africa, over forty, most of them in Kenya and Tanganyika, have no chiefs.

Prior to the Bantu invasions most of Kenya and Tanzania was sparsely populated by hunting and gathering groups. Presumably most of these people, refusing to modify their practices, were killed or driven out after the Bantu arrived in significant numbers. Some survivors of this population, however, can still be found. The few hundred Hadzapi who live near Lake Eyasi in Tanzania are the last remnant of East African Bushmen. Further south are the Sandawe, who speak a language with clicking sounds which is related to that spoken by the Hottentots of southern Africa. There are also groups known as symbiotic hunters, of which the most important is the Dorobo. Traditions of many tribes indicate that the Dorobo were in control of much of the forest lands of Kenya when the Bantu first arrived. The Dorobo were much more flexible than the Bushmen and adopted the language and customs of their domi-

nant neighbors. All of the Dorobo of Kenya speak a form of
Nandi. This attitude at first preserved the Dorobo, but today
it is almost impossible to discern ethnic or linguistic differences
between them and the Bantu.

Dates of Bantu penetration are almost unknown, but on
primarily a cultural basis it appears that there were two separate main invasions. Most of the Bantu are presumed to have
migrated in a series of movements from west of Lake Victoria.
The bulk of these groups are patrilineal and show definite kinship with the Bantu of Uganda. Another Bantu type is resident
in southern Tanzania. Their institutions, particularly matrilineal organization, point to an origin in Central Africa west
of Lake Tanganyika. One reconstruction of the general movements of the northern Bantu has this population, after their
initial invasion, concentrated somewhere in the vicinity of
Mount Kilimanjaro. From this first dispersal area the Bantu
moved south and north parallel to the coast. Presumably the
southern groups formed the basis for the Chaga, Shambaa, and
other tribes of northeastern Tanzania.

The northern-moving groups could have migrated to an
area north of the Tana River, called Shungwaya by coastal
Bantu traditions. This area became the second zone of dispersal
for this type of Bantu. Perhaps under pressure from Galla
pastoralists, some time between the thirteenth and sixteenth
centuries groups broke away and migrated to the south and east.
Oral traditions of the present-day coastal Bantu support such
a conclusion. Some observers also trace the origins of the interior Kikuyu, Meru, Embu, and Kamba to this Shungwaya dispersal zone. H. E. Lambert has reconstructed the movements
of these people and arrived at approximate dates for their settlement in their present locations. These dates are Embu 1425,
Fort Hall 1545, Meru 1750, and Kiambu 1800. Lambert's thesis
has recently been attacked, largely because there is little oral
evidence among the Kikuyu and Embu to support such a conclusion. Thus the point of origin and dates of movement of the
most populous group of Kenya Bantu are still under dispute,
complicating even more the generalized picture of Bantu settlement in Kenya.

The Kikuyu and the nine closely related peoples form the
most important Bantu group in Kenya. Today they occupy a
large segment of the central highlands east of the rift valley.
The territory they have occupied for at least two centuries is

easily defended except in the northeast. The Aberdare Mountains in the west and a fairly continuous belt of forest land and dry plain on the periphery of the highlands afforded them protection. Even the warlike Masai soon came to understand that Kikuyu warriors with bows, sheltered by the forests, could not be swept aside as were the peoples of the plains. The Kikuyu were agriculturists, depending upon the cultivation of millets, beans, and sweet potatoes for their livelihood. They kept many goats, sheep, and some cattle, but were relatively unaffected by the cattle culture of their Nilo-Hamitic neighbors. They conducted a regular trade within Kikuyuland and also traded with their neighbors for such products as salt and cattle.

The Kikuyu had no chiefs. Their political and social system was constructed on institutions derivative of land and marriage and of groups that cut across these ties. The Kikuyu were organized into clans or muhiriga, which were mythical descent groups. Each of the nine major clans was defined not only by kinship but also by the lands they inhabited. The clans were spread throughout Kikuyuland and were divided into subgroups. At each level there were elders who administered the law, decided cases, and participated in religious ceremonies. Within a clan there were mbari, or descent groups, which jointly owned land. An official, the muramati, was in charge of matters pertaining to mbari lands. A combination of many mbari formed a district, or bwruri, which with the leadership of elders was the largest effective political unit among the Kikuyu. There seems to have been little effective formalized cooperation between districts. Cutting across the very complex clan and land system was the association of age and generation sets. A man or woman was a part of an age group and all others circumcised the same year were considered brothers. The age set system determined the composition of an organization for war and in many places determined the leadership of Kikuyu communities.

In the early eighteenth century the Kamba, a Bantu people closely related to the Kikuyu, moved eastward from the vicinity of present-day Ulu. Crossing the Athi River, they spread north to Kikuyuland and south to the Tsavo area. They were blocked to the southwest by the Masai, and in the northeast further expansion was restricted by the desert and Galla tribes. Kamba institutions were similar to those of the Kikuyu. They had no chiefs and their society was organized on a clan system not

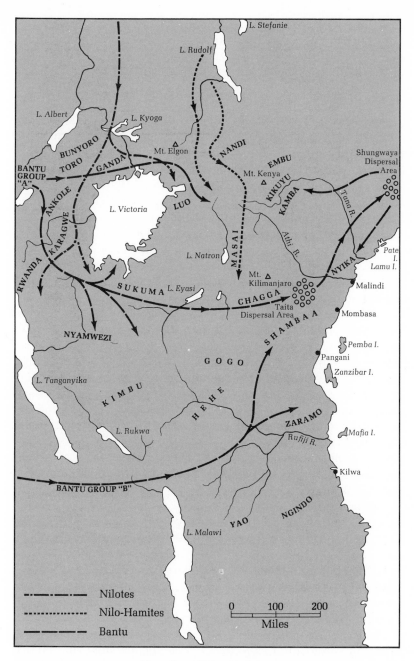

L. Stefanie

L. Rudolf

L. Albert

L. Kyoga

BUNYORO

TORO

GANDA

Mt. Elgon

NANDI

EMBU

Mt. Kenya

KIKUYU

Shungwaya
Dispersal
Area

BANTU
GROUP
"A"

ANKOLE

KARAGWE

L. Victoria

LUO

KAMBA

Tana R.

RWANDA

SUKUMA

L. Eyasi

L. Natron

MASAI

Athi R.

Pate
I.

Lamu I.

NYIKA

Malindi

NYAMWEZI

Mt.
Kilimanjaro

CHAGGA

Taita
Dispersal Area

SHAMBAA

Mombasa

L. Tanganyika

GOGO

Pemba I.

Pangani

Zanzibar I.

KIMBU

HEHE

ZARAMO

L. Rukwa

Rufiji R.

Mafia I.

Kilwa

BANTU GROUP "B"

YAO

NGINDO

L. Malawi

- · - · - · — Nilotes

·············· Nilo-Hamites

- - - - - - - Bantu

0   100   200

Miles

Peoples of East Africa

213

unlike the Kikuyu. Much of Kamba land was not fertile and the main settlements were concentrated near the rivers. The Kamba were agriculturists who practiced irrigation and grew mainly sorghums and millets. They kept more cattle than the Kikuyu, but were not particularly influenced by the cattle culture so dominant among the Masai. The Kamba, partially because of the marginal nature of much of their land, became famous as traders in ivory, grain, and slaves. Presumably this trade with the interior and with the Arab coastal cities was well developed before the close of the eighteenth century.

Eastward of the Kamba lived the coastal Bantu. These were small agricultural groups. The Pokomo, who lived along the Tana River, had no cattle and were greatly influenced by their Galla neighbors to the north. The Nyika, Digo, and Giriama were located south of the Tana River in the immediate coastal hinterland. Each of these agricultural people had a loosely organized political system with age set structures and tribal or clan councils but no chiefs.

Bantu groups in northeastern Tanzania show affinities to those immediately to the north in Kenya. The strongest of these groups, however, the Chaga, Shambaa, and Sagara, have developed a modified form of ritual chieftainship. It is speculated that this institution could have been introduced in the eighteenth century by the Nilotic Nyamwezi, who had by then become the dominant long-range traders of the interior. Presumably the Bantu groups near Mount Kilimanjaro derived from the hypothetical first dispersal area near Taita. This would also be true of the Bantu of western Tanzania, who also displayed patrilineal, rudimentary centralized polities under a semidivine chief.

In central and southern Tanzania were located Bantu who belonged to the group that had migrated from west of Lake Tanganyika. In the southern zone there were no large kingdoms because of the relative isolation from other Bantu or Nilotic and Nilo-Hamitic people. Clan leaders, or those called chiefs, ruled over only those territories that could be supervised personally. The most powerful of the central Tanzanian Bantu were the Hehe, Bena, and Gogo, who had probably moved north of the Rufiji River. All of these groups seem to be closely related and show affinities to the Ngonde, Namwanga, and Nyika people who live northeast of Lake Malawi. The northwest movement of the Gogo was halted by the southward movements of the Nyamwezi and the Masai.

This discussion of the peoples of Kenya and Tanzania has not so far mentioned the impact of the Nilotic, Nilo-Hamitic, and Hamitic invasions. Reference has already been made to the probable place of origin of the Nilotes, the Hima, and Luo invasions of Uganda and the effects of their overlordship over indigenous Bantu people. In Kenya the most important Nilotic group was the Kenya Luo, who were displaced from northern Acholi by the Lango and Itseo invasions of the eighteenth century. These Luo settled northeast of Lake Victoria and preserved a political and social system very closely akin to those of Acholi. Today they are the only Nilotic people in Kenya.

The Luo invasions of the interlacustrine area forced the previous Bahima rulers and their followers south into what is now southern Uganda. Here in time they formed the kingdom of Ankole and continued their cattle-oriented ways of life. The king of Ankole, the mugabe, divided his territory into districts and appointed subchiefs to administer these areas. The Hima exercised a monopoly of cattle and also of the high offices of the state. The resultant political system was quite loose, much more closely resembling the Bunyoro rather than the highly structured organization of Buganda. Land to the Hima aristocracy had little meaning except as pasturage for cattle. The Bantu agriculturists who lived under Hima rule were free to cultivate land wherever they wished as long as they carried out the duties assigned them by the cattle-owning aristocracy.

Bahima also migrated south of the Kagera River and established a number of separate petty states. The most important of these was the kingdom of Karagwe. In most of these Sukuma and Nyamwezi polities the Bahima did not introduce centralization in government, a feature that had been common with the Nilotes. Through intermarriage the Bahima aristocracy soon lost its racial exclusiveness and became like its Bantu subjects. It also lost its primary concern with cattle. The small states came to depend upon agriculture and later trade as their primary means of support. In the area immediately south of Lake Victoria are located the Sukuma chiefdoms while the territory around the present-day city of Tabora was occupied by the Nyamwezi. The Sukuma and Nyamwezi are very closely related linguistically and culturally. In both languages Sukuma simply means north. The Nyamwezi groups beginning in the latter eighteenth century became differentiated largely because of trade. They were the long distance interior traders and provided the bulk of the porters for European caravans in the nineteenth century. Because of their location near the main route from the interior to the coast the Nyamwezi and Sukuma provided many of the slaves sent to the Arab coastal states.

Another important set of invaders of Kenya and Tanzania were the Nilo-Hamites. It appears that their point of origin was somewhere near Lake Rudolf in the north. As their name indicates, they could be mixtures of Caucasian Hamites (Cushites) and Nilotic Negroes. The connections between the Nilo-Hamites and the Nilotes are still debatable, but the peoples are culturally and linguistically different. Nilo-Hamitic peoples of East Africa are the primitive, completely pastoral Karamajong of eastern Uganda, the Turkana and Nandi of Kenya, and the Masai, who live in both Kenya and Tanzania.

All the Nilo-Hamitic people are pastoralists. The Nandi groups and the Masai used the same invasion path into Kenya, the broad band of dry grassland stretching from the northern desert into Tanzania. Here the Nandi and Masai found pasturage for their herds and much game for hunting. All of the Nandi tribes such as the Sapei, Suk, Keyo, and Nandi proper were already in roughly their present location in western Kenya in the early seventeenth century. The Masai passed to the east of the Nandi and established themselves as the dominant force in central Kenya. Masailand extended from the Uasin Gishu plateau southward to Lake Naivisha and beyond to Arusha and Mount Kilimanjaro. No other people successfully competed with them for the open plains and plateaus.

The Masai were a nation only because of a common language and body of customs and beliefs. Their political structure was extremely loose and warped in the direction of the military. After arriving at the Uasin Gishu plateau, probably in the early seventeenth century, the Masai divided into subtribes, which in turn were linked together by common initiation ceremonies and age set patterns. The Masai economy was based on the possession of cattle. They believed that all cattle in the world by divine dispensation belonged to them. To protect their large herds and to acquire more by raiding Masai society depended upon its warriors. Every Masai went through six distinct phases in his life. Of these the fourth (ilbarnot) and the fifth (ilmorijo) were the most significant. Covering between ten and twelve years, these were the phases when the young Masai was a warrior (muran). In both phases he lived with other warriors of his age set, apart from the people. As an ilmorijo he could marry, but he continued to live separately from his wife in the warriors' village. In his final phase as an elder he made way for younger men in the warriors' village and returned to his wife's village.

The failure of the Masai to turn their warlike potential into larger, more viable political units was due to many factors. First there was the pastoralists' contempt for land other than as a place to graze cattle. Second was the unabashed feeling of superiority over all non-Masai. No attempts were ever made to bring non-Masai within the political sphere of the Masai. Probably most important, however, was the relegation of the elders to positions of secondary importance. Elders held a certain amount of judicial power, especially in matters having to do with women, children, and cattle. The murans, whose whole life was bound to warfare and cattle raiding, were the most important segment of Masai life. No firm, centralized political system could grow out of the military organization of the Masai.

While the Masai held the grasslands they were never able to make deep inroads into the lands of their more populous neighbors. The Kikuyu, Kamba, and Nandi were protected by natural defensive barriers and they outnumbered the Masai. Masai warriors probably did not number over 10,000 and they did not operate as a single unit as did the Zulu. Thus protected by forests, rivers, and hills and armed with bows and arrows the enemies of the Masai maintained their independence. In the early nineteenth century the southern thrust of the Masai was stopped by the Gogo in Tanzania. After these initial defeats the Masai never seriously threatened the Gogo, Hehe, or other central Tanzanian tribes again.

The Zenj states through 1500

The East African coast has been a part of the large Indian Ocean trading complex throughout the Christian era. Trading centers along the Red Sea and on the islands and mainland between Somalia and Mozambique have a long complex history. The *Periplus of the Erythrean Sea*, which dates from the late first or early second century, describes a significant trade between Rome and western India. In this trade some port cities of the Red Sea and the eastern African area became collecting points for the exchange of goods. The most important town on the East African coast mentioned by the sailors' guide was called Rhapta. The exact location of the town is unknown, but it is believed to have been in the area of northern Tanzania. The author of the *Periplus* mentioned that the trade there was regulated and the town was controlled by a ruler located in southern Arabia. The trading area north of Rhapta was less well organized. The town of Nikon, which was probably located near modern-day Port Durnford, was mentioned but not considered a competitor to Rhapta. By the time of the revision of Ptolemy's *Geography* (fourth century) the trading stations had become more important. Nikon was reported to be a major entrepot and Rhapta a metropolis. There has been confirmation of the veracity of these reports only by finds of Roman coins in locations reported by the *Periplus* and by Ptolemy.

Considering Rome's far-flung land and trading empire it would be strange had the Red Sea and Indian Ocean routes not been exploited. However important this trade was, it had almost ceased by the fifth century because of internal trouble within the Roman Empire, the rise of Sassanid Persia as an Indian Ocean power, and the importance of Axum in the Red Sea area. No evidence is presently available to indicate direct Persian or Axumite control of the East African coast. If the towns mentioned earlier by the Romans were important, there is no reason to believe that trade between them and Axum and Persia did not continue. Certain stelae near Port Durnford are reminiscent of those in Ethiopia. At this period Negro slaves are known to have been an important part of the military in Persia. Their probable point of origin was East Africa. There are also Chinese stories relating trade with Africa in this period. However, there exists no good proof that Chinese mariners ever arrived on the East African coast. African materials more likely arrived in China by a series of trading operations rather than by direct voyages.

A number of Islamic sources place the settlement in East Africa by Muslims as early as the seventh century. Such works as the *Kitab al Zunuj* and the *Chronicles of Lamu* are very questionable, since they are twentieth-century collections of earlier writings on oral tradition. Far more valuable is the *Chronicle of Kilwa*, which was written in the sixteenth century.

Much of its material after the thirteenth century has been checked by archeology and found accurate. The stories of conquest and movements of large numbers of colonists have not been confirmed by archeological discoveries, and there have been few finds of value that predate the twelfth century. This does not mean that many of these Arabic accounts are worthless, only that they indicate general movements and that their chronology is highly suspect. Obviously there was trade between the Red Sea and the East African coast in this early period. The Arab traders, however, were probably few and left behind no permanent buildings to mark their activities.

Arab geographers of the medieval period recorded contemporary accounts of the East African towns. Al Masudi visited Zanzibar in the tenth century and wrote of the trade in iron, ivory, tortoise shells, cloth, and slaves. He reported that most of the population of the coastal towns was Negro and that the people had been little affected by Islam. Ibn Hawqal, writing at the same period, confirmed these observations. By Idrisi's time in the twelfth century the trading centers were larger, particularly Mogadishu and Kîlwa. Idrisi also wrote that the bulk of the population of the towns was black and pagan. There is no indication of the height of civilization there or of the standard of living of the Arab traders. Neither is it possible to know in any detail the relations between the Arabs and majority black population of the towns and the immediate hinterland. The development of Swahili must have begun by this time, however, and Islam certainly had gained many converts among the Bantu of the coast.

The thirteenth and fourteenth centuries were a period when great Islamic kingdoms were being created in India, Iran, and Iraq, and Islam was being carried to Indonesia and the Pacific area. These powerful Islamic states all had maritime interests in the Indian Ocean. This expansion of Islamic commercial interests obviously extended to the East African coast. Ibn Battuta, who visited the area in the fourteenth century, does not mention a large pagan population. His descriptions of some of the East African towns are almost duplicates of his observations of the Western Sudanic states. It is reasonable to assume that the majority of the townspeople were blacks who had accepted Islam. By the fifteenth century a blend of Bantu and Arabic had probably been developed and accepted by most townsmen. This forerunner of present-day Swahili would have been the normal early language. The official written language, however, remained Arabic.

Exact information is lacking concerning interior trade in the period prior to the year 1500. There is no knowledge of the displacement of coastal people by the expansion of the populations of the towns. Effects on the coastal towns of Bantu and Nilo-Hamitic migrations are also unknown. Certain reasonable speculations, however, can be made. The very early interior trade was probably conducted by Africans and was small in volume. Certain luxury items such as ivory, tortoise shells, and a few slaves were brought to the coast by entrepreneurs who knew of the Arab market for such items. There is no evidence of Arab penetration into the territories of the Vakaranga where there were gold mines until the fourteenth century. Gold and copper probably were brought in small quantities to such trading areas as Sofala. Such occasional trade might have sufficed to support a few traders in the time of Idrisi but would not have been adequate to maintain the large, prosperous states of the fifteenth century.

The Africanist Gervase Mathew has stated that there were in the fifteenth century thirty-seven towns on the coast between Kilwa and Mogadishu. Of these Kilwa was the most important. Kilwa merchants appear to have established a regular trade route via Sofala in the south into the deep interior. Individual Arab merchants were present in great numbers in the Vakaranga kingdom. There they traded for gold from the mines of Manicaland and those further south and copper from the Congo. Ivory was obtained from many hinterland sources and brought to the coast along a number of well-established routes. A few slaves were also collected for use in the towns and for export to the courts of Middle Eastern and Indian princes.

Mogadishu, Malindi, Mombasa, and Pate, although not as rich as Kilwa, were also important terminal points for African trade. In the fourteenth century Mombasa appears to have been relatively insignificant. Within less than two centuries it had become as important as Kilwa and was described by the Portuguese as a substantial town of stone buildings, a mosque, and palace. The rulers of Pate Island very briefly in the fifteenth century conquered the towns of Lamu and Malindi and appeared to be challenging Kilwa for supremacy. In all the major towns this period of prosperity was reflected by building of stone mosques, public buildings, and complex and comfortable private houses.

Each of the towns was ruled in a similar fashion by Arab sultans supported by a trading oligarchy. Some of these rulers minted gold and silver coins, operated navies, and maintained considerable military forces. Despite the similarity of their political institutions and the fact that they were all Muslim, they never coalesced into larger, more viable states. Each trading oligarchy fiercly maintained its independence from its neighbors. Thus when the Portuguese arrived in the Indian Ocean area in force in the sixteenth century they found it relatively easy to conquer the towns one by one.

The Portuguese interlude

Portuguese contact with the city-states of the East African coast date from the first voyage of Vasco da Gama, who learned of the gold to be had in the hinterland from Sofala and the fact that Kilwa dominated the Indian Ocean trade in this commodity. Da Gama inaugurated the friendly relations with Malindi which lasted over 100 years by receiving an ambassador from that city who was later taken to Portugal. In 1502 da Gama on his second voyage captured Kilwa and forced its ruler to pay ransom and acknowledge the suzerainty of Portugal. In the following year Ruy Ravasco cruised along the coast, raiding, shipping, and taking tribute from the coastal towns. Zanzibar was blockaded until its ruler agreed to pay an annual amount to the Portuguese.

These first conflicts were but a prelude to actual conquest. The Portuguese aim was to control the entire Indian Ocean trade. To facilitate this they seized key positions in the Persian Gulf, Red Sea, and along the coast of Oman and Muscat as well as east of India. Compared to these ventures the East African area was relatively unimportant. Two factors, however, decided the Portuguese to conquer the independent African towns. One was the belief in the riches that could be obtained by controlling the coastal and interior mines. The other factor was the need for way stations on the route to India. In 1505 Francisco d'Almeida with an expedition of over 1500 men was dispatched to secure the necessary bases. His major objectives were Sofala, Kilwa, and Mombasa. Sofala succumbed with little opposition.

Kilwa was taken and a part of the town was burned. A Portuguese garrison was left behind to construct a fort and make certain that the puppet rulers would not get out of hand. The fort was abandoned in 1512 when it became obvious that Kilwa was not going to provide the riches once imagined. D'Almeida also had difficulty in taking Mombasa, but eventually the town fell and was sacked by the Portuguese. In 1507 and again in 1509 Portuguese fleets attacked and looted coastal towns. By 1510 the Portuguese were dominant along the east coast, and to make this control more permanent they established a loose system of government under two captains. One was located at Mozambique and the other at Malindi. Each of these officials was responsible to the viceroy of India at Goa.

Portuguese activities in the early sixteenth century were primarily destructive. Concerned with gold, they so disrupted the interior trade with the Vakaranga that the volume fell drastically. By diverting the gold from the south they almost ruined Kilwa, which had depended upon its control of the gold trade. Coastal cities such as Mombasa traded with their hinterlands, but not in a regular, organized fashion. Caravan expeditions to exploit the interior were not attempted in large-scale fashion until the latter eighteenth century. Ivory, slaves, and other materials reached the coast after having passed through many hands. The Portuguese did not end this type of trade, but the destructiveness of their early raids impoverished many of the cities. There is evidence that some of the towns had been almost exclusively agricultural, depending upon foodstuffs as their major export. After the arrival of the Portuguese more of them were forced to rely on agriculture and such local products as pitch or timber.

Instead of penetrating the interior or opening new trade routes the Portuguese were content to overawe the lesser cities by establishing small garrisons in the most important towns. When really threatened the captain at Malindi would call for naval support from Goa. Lack of men combined with their increased knowledge of the interior were responsible for the Portuguese failure to explore East Africa. Before the middle of the sixteenth century the best trading route to India was discovered to be directly across the Indian Ocean, thus bypassing the East African towns. Always pressed for men, the viceroy of India could not afford large numbers of soldiers in East Africa. In the early seventeenth century the Mombasa garrison, the largest in East Africa, had less than 100 men. Increased knowledge of the hinterland also convinced the authorities that there were no riches to be obtained by sending military expeditions into the interior as had been done on the Gold Coast and in Angola and Mozambique.

The ruling aristocracies of the towns were left relatively intact by the Portuguese. Although the rulers had lost their Semitic racial characteristics, they cherished a portion of the cultural heritage of Islam and the bulk of the town population was Muslim. With the few men available the Portuguese could not control the activities of these "Arabs" and therefore there was a series of revolts in the sixteenth and seventeenth centuries. The missionaries, primarily Jesuits, Dominicans, and Augustinians, made few converts from either the African or Islamic sectors of the communities.

The first to challenge the Portuguese in the Indian Ocean area were the Ottoman Turks. By the middle of the sixteenth century they controlled the bulk of the Red Sea trade and had pushed their seapower beyond Aden. The primary direction of Turkish activities, however, was Europe, and they only raided south of Arabia. In 1586 Amir Ali Bey with a few galleys led a revolt of the northern coast against the Portuguese. In 1588 this type of Turkish-led rebellion was repeated once again, only on a larger scale. The dispatch of a large Portuguese fleet from Goa quieted most of the towns. A landing force took Mombasa and drove the Arabs and their Turkish supporters into the walled section of the town where the Portuguese commander left them to the tender mercies of the Zimba.

The point of origin of the mysterious Zimba was probably in the mid-Zambesi area. For some reason these Bantu agriculturists abandoned their older ways and became warlike, marauding cannibals. In the mid 1580s a few thousand of the Zimba moved north along the coast, killing everything that stood in their way. Kilwa fell to them in 1587 and it was reported that three quarters of the population perished. The Arabs and Turks of Mombasa who opposed the Portuguese also were killed by the Zimba. Before these cannibals were defeated the following year near Malindi they had depopulated much of the immediate hinterland of the coast.

Aside from the slaughter of thousands of Arabs and Africans the most important result of the events of the 1580s was the building of Fort Jesus at Mombasa. Fear of more direct

Turkish intervention was obviously the major factor behind the construction of the fort. The government was also reorganized, with the captain in charge of the northern towns moving from Malindi to Mombasa. The captain's power to influence economic and political affairs in other towns declined in the early years of the seventeenth century, however. The revival of Persia drove the Portuguese from the Persian Gulf in the 1620s. Dutch and British competitors in India and the East Indies had also undermined Portugal's position in the richest portion of their eastern empire. The captains in East Africa had always been able to depend upon punitive forces from Goa to overawe the Arab towns, and this coercive factor was all but eliminated by the middle of the seventeenth century.

At Mombasa, Yusuf bin Hasan, the ruling sheikh in the late 1620s, was a Christian who had spent eighteen years being educated at Goa. In 1631 after having renounced Christianity he led a revolt, captured Fort Jesus, and massacred the bulk of the Portuguese garrison. Other coastal towns did not support Yusuf fully, but they did refuse to pay the customary tribute to the Portuguese. Yusuf's troops within Fort Jesus withstood the assault of the small punitive force sent from Goa. For reasons that are unclear Yusuf abandoned Mombasa, leaving the town and fort in shambles. He and his followers, however, continued to prey upon Portuguese shipping until his death in 1637.

Despite their weakened position the Portuguese continued to rule Mombasa, Lamu, and Pate in the 1640s. In 1650, however, the imam of Muscat, Sultan ibn Saif, expelled the Portuguese from their positions in south Arabia. Soon ships of Oman had reasserted the imam's dominance over seaborne traffic near Muscat. This turn of events combined with continued dissatisfaction with Portuguese rule in East Africa introduced a new phase to coastal history. Representatives of the towns appealed to the imam for assistance against the Portuguese. The imam responded by sending expeditions to East Africa in 1652, 1660, 1667, and 1679. In 1670 Omani forces even took and looted Mozambique, Portugal's strongest outpost on the coast. By that date all the East African towns north of the Ruvuma River with the exception of Mombasa were free of Portuguese rule.

Although the government at Goa was too weak to recapture the lost prestige of Portugal, it could retaliate. In 1678 Viceroy Pedro d'Almeida captured Lamu and Pate and executed the leading men of the towns. In 1686 another Portuguese force took Pate and carried away its ruler and his advisers to be executed at Goa. In 1696 a major Omani expedition landed over 3,000 men at Mombasa. After a siege of almost two years Fort Jesus was captured. Following the fall of the fort the Portuguese made only one brief attempt to restore their rule at Mombasa. They took the fort in 1728 and held it for less than a year. After this Portugal was content to abandon all claims to the areas north of the Ruvuma River and concentrate upoń holding Mozambique, Quelimane, and Sofala in the south.

Restoration of Arab hegemony over the coast

Soon after the expulsion of the Portuguese the Omani rulers sent garrisons and governors to the most important coastal towns. The degree of authority exercised by the imams varied directly with the state of affairs in their south Arabian kingdom, and dynastic quarrels within Oman continuously interrupted their aims. Throughout most of the eighteenth century Pate, Pemba, Malindi, and Kilwa were independent of Oman political control. Zanzibar, which became very important at the close of the century, was the East African area most loyal to the Omani. Mombasa was the town most hostile to the centralizing aspirations of the imam.

The third governor of Mombasa appointed by the imam was Muhammed ibn Uthman al Mazrui. In 1741 the ruling dynasty of Oman was overthrown and a new ruler, Ahmed bin Said el Busaidi, seized power. Muhammed took advantage of this disturbance and declared Mombasa independent of Omani control. In 1746 Muhammed was assassinated by Busaidi agents. The murderers were executed and Ali ibn Uthman al Mazrui, Muhammed's son, retained control. This series of events ushered in a period of relative truce between the Mazrui rulers of Mombasa and the Busaidi imams of Oman. In the latter eighteenth century Mombasa's hegemony extended over the island of Pemba, whose grain helped balance the food deficiencies of the hinterland.

Indian Oceàn trade in the early 1700s was remarkably similar to that which had preceded the Portuguese occupation. Ivory, some gold, a few slaves, pitch, timber, and foodstuffs were the primary export products. These were carried by Persian, Omani, Turkish, and Indian ships to all sections of the western Indian Ocean. To obtain these goods the foreign

merchants brought coins, beads, Indian cloth, silk, and porce-
lain. The Portuguese controlled the gold trade of the Sofala
hinterland and also maintained some trading contact with the
northern cities. The new European powers of the Indian Ocean,
Britain, and France, had little contact with the east coast until
the latter eighteenth century. Both states were primarily concerned wih securing trading and political supremacy in India.
The best trading routes from Cape Town to India bypassed the
East African towns.

One change that was to have significant effects later was
the primacy placed on the slave trade by the French. By 1750
their two islands of Bourbon and Ile de France had been converted to tropical plantation agriculture. As with similar economic systems in the New World, this created a demand for
slave labor. There is no way of ascertaining the increase in the
number of slaves exported from East Africa in the last half of
the century. In 1776, however, Maurice, a trader from Ile de
France, received from the sultan of Kilwa a monopoly of slaves
exported to the number of 1,000 per year. By 1790 this figure
had been increased to almost 1,500 per year. Among other
statistics that indicate the increased importance of the East
African slave trade is that by 1800 there were an estimated
100,000 slaves on Ile de France.

In 1784 old Ahmed bin Said el Busaidi died at Muscat. In
the subsequent struggle for power a rival claimant to the
Busaidi dynasty in Oman briefly seized power at Lamu, Kilwa,
and Zanzibar. This event illustrated that if the imam wanted to
continue to reap the benefits of a prospering East Africa he
would have to establish better and firmer political control. Such
a direct incorporation of the East African towns was not seriously attempted until Sayyid Said bin Sultan became the sole
ruler of Oman in 1806. After killing his rival and assuring himself that his enemies in Oman were too weak to overthrow him,
he turned his attention to East Africa. Within twenty years
Sayyid Said had become master of the heretofore divided
towns, including Mombasa. The British, following the logic of
their antislaving activities, also became more active in East
Africa. The interaction between the British and Sayyid Said
became the dominant theme of the history of the coast in the
early nineteenth century.

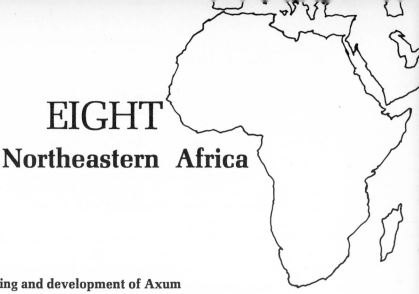

EIGHT
Northeastern Africa

The founding and development of Axum

The very early period of Ethiopian history is only
imperfectly known even though there are considerable artifacts belonging to this phase present in
Ethiopia, particularly in the lakes region. Bones, stone
implements, and pottery can be seen imbedded in the
sedimentary strata in some places. In a number of
areas there are also rock paintings which date to the
Stone Age. Few formal archeological investigations
have been attempted, however. Until more detailed
accounts of Stone Age sites are available any statements about pre-Semitic Ethopia must be regarded as
highly general and speculative. One fact does emerge
clearly. The pre-tenth-century B.C. inhabitants of the
northern part of Ethiopia were Cushites who were
pastoralists in the lowlands and who practiced sedentary agriculture in the cooler, more fertile highlands.
There are still enclaves of Cushitic speakers in
modern-day Ethiopia, the chief among these being the
Agaw people.

Across the Red Sea in the territory known to the
ancient world as Arabia Felix there were a number of
Semitic tribes, such as the Sabaeans and Minaeans.
They were accomplished agriculturists and traders
who had converted the plateaus of Yemen into a
highly productive land by constructing dams and
aqueducts which provided water for grain crops,
incense trees, and spices. The plains of Tigre, similar
to those of Yemen, held promise for similar agricultural development. In the period after 1000 B.C. a

series of Semitic invaders entered Ethiopia from Yemen. Few in number, some of the Semites established themselves in the Harar area and others in Azania. The most important groups, such as the Habashat and Aguezat, settled in northern Ethiopia. One ancient name for Ethiopia was Abyssinia, which was a corrupted form of Habashat. The interaction between these more culturally advanced Semites and the indigenous population in time produced the population and culture of the Axumite kingdom.

The new settlers brought with them a more complex political and cultural organization, a more sophisticated religion, advanced architectural practices, and written languages. At first the political system was not highly centralized, although the high priest acted as the governor of a restricted territory. Collectors of tribute also served as rulers of smaller subdivisions of such an area. The political and economic connections between the Ethiopian rulers and those of southern Arabia are not known, although it is possible in the earlier period that the Ethiopian rulers were vassal princes. The emergence of kingship came later and signified personal rule rather than collective responsibility. The late evolvement of kingship in Ethiopia was also paralleled by developments on the mainland of Yemen.

Arabian religious beliefs replaced the older forms of nature worship. The invaders built temples to their most important gods and as cities began to develop each had its own special diety. At Yeha, the most important of the pre-Axumite cities, it was Sin, the moon god, and at Axum it was the sun god. Ashtar, the greatest of the dieties, Medr, the earth god, and Mahram, the god of war, also had temples and priests in all Ethiopian areas touched by the Semitic invaders. These temples were constructed of stones carefully dressed to fit closely together with no mortar between them. Some of these buildings were quite large. The remains of one such temple at Yeha is over sixty feet long and almost fifty feet wide. Monumental stelae and altar carvings also attest to the artistic skill of the Semites. Offerings were made to the various gods either by individual devotees or on ceremonial occasions. Blood sacrifices were common, and in the period before Ethiopia's conversion to Christianity victories in war were celebrated by the sacrifice of prisoners.

Perhaps the most important contribution of the Yemenites was the introduction of a written language. Early writing for stone inscriptions were Yemen dialects expressed in the southern Arabian form which utilized only consonants. Some time in the early Christian era a new form of cursive notation was adopted, with signs to represent vowels. The language represented had also evolved from the Sabaean. It was called Ge'ez after one group of Semitic settlers, the Aguezat. The literary developments of medieval Ethiopia were dependent upon the adoption of this standard written language. Ge'ez orthography later was utilized for Amharic, the present dominant language of Ethiopia, and Ge'ez remains the liturgical language of the Ethiopian church.

Adulis, the port city of Axum, by the first century had become a major trading station. Spices, ivory, frankincense, tortoise shell, and grain were exported from Ethiopia. Roman and Greek sources mention the importance of the port as a collecting station for goods brought from the Mediterranean and also from the Indian Ocean areas. Many of the traders from the north, even those of Ptolemaic Egypt, were Greeks. Although they seemed to have had little influence on Ethiopian political development, these traders did for over three centuries establish Greek as the official language of trade and diplomacy. The prosperity of Adulis gave the Axumite kings the wealth to expand their sphere of influence into the interior and across the Red Sea to Yemen. From the first century B.C. through the third century A.D. Axun intermittently controlled the Arabian coastline opposite Ethiopia. These ventures are not well documented, and it appears that after King Aphila's invasion of Arabia in the third century A.D. Ethiopian political control there remained dormant for over a century.

Axumite conquests in the interior of Africa gradually became more important than their exploits across the Red Sea. A lengthy Greek inscription on a throne at Adulis dating probably to the late third century A.D. records the exploits of an unnamed Axumite ruler. He is represented as the conqueror of the peoples of Ge'ez, Adowa, and Semen. It also records that he sent armies deep into the mountains and northward to the borders of Egypt. Axumite forces probably were represented in the armies supporting Queen Zenobia of Meroë in her struggle against Egypt and Rome. The Axumite armies of King Ella-Amida were responsible in the fourth century for the overthrow of their great political and economic rival, Meroë. Ella-Amida appears to have been powerful enough to challenge Roman power by seizing their ships in the Red Sea. The strength and wealth of this king was but a prelude to the rule of his son Ezana, who represents the high point in the long history of Axum.

It was Ezana who instituted the most far-reaching cultural change in Ethiopian history — the acceptance of Christianity. This event has been so overlain with myth that it is difficult to winnow fact from fiction. The traditional account relates the rescue of two Syrian Christian youths, Frumentius and Aedisius, from a shipwreck during the latter years of the reign of Ella-Amida. After the death of the king the two Christians exercised an important influence over the queen mother and Frumentius became the tutor to young Ezana. Much later Frumentius returned to Ethiopia and convinced the mature Ezana to accept Christianity. It is conceivable that one reason for the king's conversion is that he saw in this a way to cement political and economic ties with the eastern Roman Empire. After the conversion of Ezana and the high court officials Frumentius was consecrated bishop of Ethiopia by Athanasius, patriarch of Alexandria. This act began the dependence of the Ethiopian church hierarchy upon Alexandria for the appointment of their bishop, or abuna, which was to last into the twentieth century.

The acceptance of Christianity had many ramifications. In time it gave to Ethiopia a sense of mission and a direction that made the kingdom unique in Africa. It immediately set the Axumite kingdom apart from its pagan neighbors, even their kinsmen in Arabia. The relaxation of Axum's control of the Yemen coast after Ezana is attributable in part to the cultural differences between the two Semitic groups. The acceptance of Christianity by the bulk of the peoples under Axumite control coincided with the great debates on theology which threatened to tear Christianity apart in the fourth and fifth centuries. From the beginning the rites and liturgy of the Ethiopian church were adaptations of the Alexandrine model. In the latter part of the fifth century many monks who believed in the one divine nature of Christ were forced to flee from Syria following the decisions of the Council of Chalcedon. Some of these Monophysite monks settled in Ethiopia and in time their theology prevailed over more conservative attitudes. They also introduced the eastern monastic system, which stressed isolation of the monks from the sinful world. From the Ethiopian monasteries established after the fifth century there flowed a constant stream of religious interpretation, literature, art, and architecture, which in the medieval period overshadowed the developments in the secular world. The monasteries also provided generations of men who could read and write whose services were sought by the kings.

Ezana also expanded the sphere of influence of Axum over the hinterland. His forces defeated the nomadic Beja tribesmen in the north and followed up his father's campaign in Nubia. Using the Takkaze (Atbara) River route, his armies invaded the Sudan, defeated the Nubian forces, burned and pillaged towns, and completed the downfall of Meroë. Such destruction did not imply direct political control but rather the end of an economic and political rival. In all probability Ezana also dominated the Yemen littoral, if not directly through governors, certainly by the potentiality of his power. Ezana's immediate successors maintained their domination of the interior and Red Sea trade routes. In the early sixth century in response to Yemenite persecution of Christians King Kaleb of Axum invaded the territory. For a brief time Axum embarked on the task of conquering southern Arabia. Later in the sixth century, however, Axumite troops rebelled and established a semi-independent kingdom of Yemen. Axum and its offspring kingdom in Yemen then united with Byzantium in its wars with Persia with disastrous effects. By the opening of the seventh century all of the Arabian peninsula was under Persian control. Persian ships operating from Yemenite ports cut deeply into Axum's overseas trade. Thus even before the Islamic conquests Axum's trading contact with the outside world was greatly restricted.

The expansion of Islam in the seventh century did not mean immediate conflict with Axum, perhaps because of the high opinion held by the prophet and his immediate successors of the culture as well as the military prowess of the Ethiopians. The isloation of Ethiopia from the outside world, however, became more pronounced. Muslim power was substituted for Persian in the Red Sea. In the course of their conquest the great Mareb dam in Yemen was destroyed, thus hastening the decline of that once very productive area. Muslim conquest of Egypt also cut off continuous Axum contact with the Mediterranean. Attacks by Beja pastoralists also helped to block Axum's northern outlets. The rulers of Axum, perhaps to end the economic monopoly of Islam, sanctioned in the seventh century raids against Muslim territory in Arabia. Finally early in the next century Muslim forces captured Massawa and the Dahlak

Islands and took and devastated Adulis. With the loss of Adulis the Ethiopians, who only a century before had been politically powerful and cosmopolitan, turned to maintaining their hold over the interior. Without major ports, surrounded by a dominant Islam, and threatened by hostile Beja pastoralists, they retreated physically and philosophically into a unique isolation. Partially protected by the terrain, Ethiopian rulers in the medieval period sought to maintain their independence and their culture against a succession of enemies. In this long period Ethiopia was all but cut off from the outside world.

Ethiopia — seventh through sixteenth centuries

The period following the destruction of Adulis witnessed a gradual retreat of the Ethiopians from the plateaus of Tigre to the more mountainous interior. It is an oversimplification, however, to picture this reorientation as a result of the confrontation between Islam and Christianity. It is true that certain coastal ports such as Suakin and Zeila fell to the Muslims and that Islam from the seventh to the thirteen centuries was spreading into the Sudan. However, the bulk of the new settlers, even in the fertile uplands of Ifat, were not primarily motivated by religious zeal. They were more concerned with the trade in ivory, gold, slaves, and rare spices obtainable from Ethiopia. There are indications that as late as the tenth century Ethiopian power was still dominant along certain portions of the coast and that Muslim merchants paid tribute to the emperor.

One reason there was little open confrontation between Islam and Ethiopia was that the major concern of the medieval rulers of Ethiopia had ceased to be coastal. The movement of the center of Ethiopian life from Axum to the interior presented new challenges to the Ethiopians. They were forced to defend themselves from the incursions of the short-lived Beja state which lay immediately north of the Ethiopian frontier. More pertinent to the fixing of primary interest in the interior were the campaigns of conquest and conversion of the non-Ethiopian populations of the highlands. Although little is known of the details, the period through the twelfth century was one of gradual Christianization of Gojjam, Lasta, Amhara, Begameder, and Shoa.

It is always dangerous to use terms that have been designed to describe phenomena in a different culture area.

Thus terms such as medieval, Dark Ages, and feudal, although convenient to use for Ethiopia, are suspect. The major reason for calling the epoch from the seventh through the twelfth centuries in Ethiopia the Dark Ages is European lack of knowledge of events there. By turning their attention to the interior the Ethiopian rulers minimized their contact with the outside world. Perhaps more to the point, a parochial, proselytizing Christian Europe was cut off from its previous Eastern contacts by Islamic control of the Mediterranean and the Red Sea. There appears to have been no degeneration in the culture of Ethiopia that would warrant calling this period dark or medieval. The remnants of Ethiopian art and architecture from this period show a continuous development within the context of a basically Christian society.

The veil of our ignorance of the details of Ethiopia's consolidation in the hinterland is lifted only briefly in this long period. One such time is toward the end of the tenth century when the new state was overrun by the Falasha, a segment of the Agaw people who had been converted to a form of Judaism. Toward the end of tenth century this group, led by a warrior-queen, spilled out of their territory near the bend of the Blue Nile into Ethiopian territory, driving the Ethiopian ruler and his army from one place to another, burning churches and monasteries, and destroying the ancient city of Axum. The leader of this movement is remembered today in Ethiopia as Queen Gidit (the prodigious one). The destruction of Axum turned the interests of Ethiopians more firmly toward their mountainous territories.

Little is known of the events following the Agaw invasions until the twelfth century. Then an Agaw commoner, Takla Haymanot, usurped the Ethiopian throne and established the Zagwe dynasty. Scraps of information concerning this ruling house reached Europe and were probably responsible for the legends of Prester John. The greatest of the Zagwe rulers was Lalibela (1190–1225). From direct reports and indirect evidence of the monuments left it is known that Ethiopia at this time was rich and prosperous. Lalibela sent two major diplomatic missions to Cairo, and his Egyptian contemporaries reported on the wealth of the emissaries as well as the strange animals brought as gifts by the diplomats. Lalibela is remembered today for the many great churches constructed during his reign. Most impressive were the eight built at his capital city of Roha. These are all monoliths, hewn directly from the rock. Although constructed with the aid of foreign workmen, they represent the culmination of the architectural style of ancient Axum. After seven and a half centuries they are still impressive monuments to an advanced Christian civilization.

Around the year 1270 the Zagwe dynasty gave way to Amharic rulers. This action has been labeled, in large degree mythical, the return of the Solomonic line. Ethiopian records are not clear on how this shift of power was accomplished. Some accounts tell of warfare between the Zagwe kings and Yekuno Amlak, the first prince of the new dynasty. Others state that the transition was peaceful, the Zagwe relinquishing the throne without a major struggle. However it was accomplished, this was one of the major events in Ethiopian history. To bolster their claims to the throne the new rulers surrounded themselves with an elaborate ritual and made the kingship, in theory, the divinely ordained cornerstone of the kingdom.

The *Kebra Nagast* (Glory of Kings), a lengthy document, parts of which had existed as early as the fourth century, was reworked and refined. Its primary function was to demonstrate the pure descent of Yekuno Amlak and his successors from King Solomon. The chronicle relates the story of Makeda, queen of Saba (sheba) and Tigre, who paid a ceremonial visit to Jerusalem. Later Makeda gave birth to Solomon's son, Ebna-Hakim (Menelik I). After he had reached maturity Ebna-Hakim traveled to Jerusalem to receive consecration from his father. In revenge for the treatment of his mother he and his followers stole the Ark of the Covenant from the temple and later deposited it at the capital city of Saba. From that time onward, according to the narrative, the laws of Israel were established throughout the kingdom. The *Kebra Nagast* also describes the military campaigns of Ebna-Hakim. Obviously the work can lay little claim to historical accuracy. It is, however, a most important document in understanding the development of Ethiopian institutions. All emperors after Yekuno Amlak took great pains to show that they fit into the line of rulers traceable through the *Kebra Nagast* to Solomon.

The kingdom ruled by Yekuno Amlak and his fourteenth-century successors was actually a collection of small states — Tigre, Shoa, Gojjam, and Begameder — ruled by a landed military aristocracy appointed by the emperor. This system, which continued until the twentieth century, has its closest European

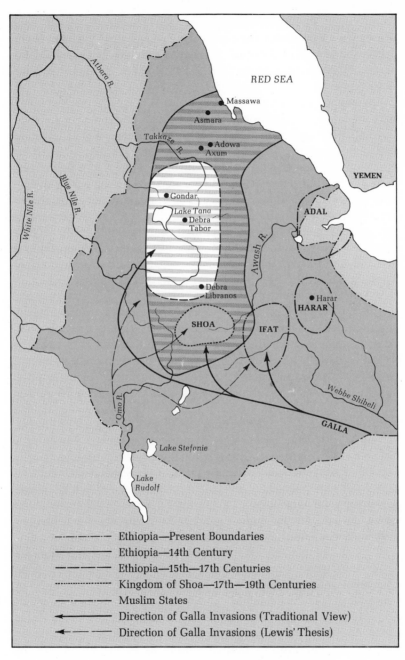

RED SEA

Massawa

Asmara

Takkaze R.

Adowa
Axum

YEMEN

Gondar

Lake Tana

Debra
Tabor

ADAL

Awash R.

Debra
Libranos

Harar

HARAR

SHOA

IFAT

Webbe Shibeli

Omo R.

GALLA

Lake Stefanie

Lake
Rudolf

Atbara R.

White Nile R.

Blue Nile R.

—·——·—— Ethiopia—Present Boundaries

—————— Ethiopia—14th Century

———————— Ethiopia—15th—17th Centuries

················ Kingdom of Shoa—17th—19th Centuries

—·—·—·— Muslim States

◄———— Direction of Galla Invasions (Traditional View)

◄—·—·— Direction of Galla Invasions (Lewis' Thesis)

Expansion and Contraction of Ethiopia

235

counterpart in the feudalism of the medieval world. The Ethiopian system, like the European, was basically divisive and depended for its unity upon the strength of the monarch. If the emperor was a tillak sew (strong man), then the empire functioned as a unity. If he was young or weak, then the aristocracy could act as almost independent rulers. The church, an ever-present factor in Ethiopian life, was also very active in politics. Powerful monasteries such as Debra Tabor and Debra Damo as well as the abuna (bishop) could by their support determine whether the kingdom was a unity or merely competitive segments. This factor more than distance from Alexandria explains why the position of abuna was left vacant many times for years.

The period of the fourteenth and fifteenth centuries was one of expansion of the kingdom and strengthening of the central government. In the fourteenth century the emperor became the official protector of the patriarchate of Alexandria. There was also a good relation with the Mameluk rulers of Egypt. It appears that they sent military advisers to Ethiopia and introduced Greek fire as an offensive weapon to the Ethiopian arsenal. Most of the physical expansion of Ethiopia was accompanied by a program of conversion of the heathen and attempts to extirpate heresy. This involved the Ethiopians in a series of wars with the Falashas and increasing conflict with the Muslim coastal states. These clashes with Afar, Adal, Danakil, and Somali sultanates became very serious after the 1470s. It was in the latter part of the fifteenth century that contacts between Ethiopia and Europe were reopened. Letters were exchanged between the emperor and Portugal, Spain, Venice, and the papacy. The expansion of Portugal into the Indian Ocean combined with the legends of Prester John led to the dispatch of the first European mission in 1493. From that date throughout the sixteenth and seventeenth centuries the Portuguese became a very important factor in Ethiopian history.

As noted earlier, the Muslim states were dominated by merchants who were more concerned with trade than with conquest. Indulgences, which violated the basic precepts of Islam, were practiced openly in all the Muslim states. A revolt against these vices and a debauched Islam was begun in Harar in the 1520s. The leader of this effort at purification was Imam Ahmed al Ghazi, better known simply as Gran. The sultan of Harar was killed and Gran and his followers began a campaign to purify all elements of life in the state. The stage was set for a confrontation between two expansive states, much of whose power was based upon a narrowly conceived religious belief. The war with Ethiopia initiated by Gran in 1527 was thus a holy war.

The Ethiopian emperor was Lebna-Dengel, who as a very young man had seen his armies triumphant everywhere against Islam. After the victory against Adal in 1516 he was so convinced of Ethiopian superiority that briefly he thought of conquering Mecca. Lebna-Dengel had been distant and superior with the first Portuguese ambassador who left Massawa in 1526 and he had not concluded any definite treaty with the Portuguese. The wars with Gran were disasters for Ethiopia. Much of Gran's army was composed of fierce, near-fanatical Somali converts. Lebna-Dengel was driven from one area of Ethiopia to another. Gran occupied Dawaro, Shoa, Amhara, Lasta, and Sidamo. Wherever his armies marched he left destruction in his wake. He sacked churches, monasteries, and destroyed centuries of literature and art work. Lebna-Dengel, his dignity gone, sent messengers to the Portuguese asking for help from another Christian country against the infidel. He died in 1540 before any reinforcements could reach Ethiopia.

In 1541 400 picked Portuguese troops under the twenty-six year old Don Christofe da Gama landed at Massawa in response to Ethiopian pleas for aid. Of this number over 100 soldiers were musketeers. Marching overland with Ethiopian reinforcements to join the new emperor, Galawdewos, da Gama's forces met Gran and defeated him twice. The imam was wounded and withdrew to Harar to reorganize his forces. Later his new army, based on 900 musketeers loaned by the Ottoman Turks, all but destroyed the Portuguese force. Da Gama was captured and later tortured and killed. Gran then made a major tactical error by sending back his Turkish troops and continuing the war. In October 1542 Galawdewos' army, reinforced by the Portuguese remnant, defeated the Muslims in the deciding battle of the long war since Gran was killed. Without their charismatic leader the Muslim attempt to dominate the highlands faded away, even though periodically throughout the rest of the century the conflict continued. Galawdewos was killed in one of these skirmishes in 1559 and his head was taken to Harar where it was publically displayed.

The fifteen-year struggle with Gran had deeply affected Ethiopia. Thousands of men had been lost and irreplaceable art treasures, books, and churches had been destroyed. Wherever Gran's armies had conquered they practiced forced conversion of the population to Islam. Thus many people only newly recruited for Christianity had either become Muslim or had reverted to animism. Ethiopia had been saved only with the aid of da Gama's small band of soldiers. The future of Ethiopia after the Gran interlude was to be tied in part to Portuguese ambitions in the Red Sea. More important than even this was the threat to the kingdom of a new series of invaders — the Galla.

The Somali and Galla

The Somali and Galla people of northeastern Africa are obviously related ethnically and linguistically. Both groups today are the results of mixtures of Cushite, Negro, and Semite. Their languages are variants of eastern Cushitic. The Galla, who settled in parts of the Ethiopian highlands, and the Somali, who live between the Juba and Shebelle rivers, practice sedentary agriculture. The great mass of both Galla and Somali people before the nineteenth century were pastoralists who followed regular patterns of movement with their herds of goats, sheep, and cattle. Both the Galla and Somali were broken into competitive clan or clan group units and one segment tended to view the others not as members of the same political or social nation but as competitors for grazing land and water. Except in rare instances neither the Galla nor Somali combined in any meaningful larger political unit. The aridity of much of the horn of Africa meant that the land could support only a limited number of people and livestock. When the population grew beyond certain limits people had to move away from their older grazing areas, pushing any indigenous people aside.

The outlines of Galla and Somali life in earlier periods can be partially reconstructed from the present mode of living of these people. However, little is known of their history before they became such an important part of the forces invading Ethiopia in the sixteenth and seventeenth centuries. Until quite recently it was believed that the Somali clan families originated in Arabia between the tenth and thirteenth centuries. According to this theory, the first area of settlement of the Somali was in the northern coastal areas. Here, presumably, they encountered Galla pastoralists already in control of the grazing lands of what is now northern Somalia. Overpopulation in a short time caused fragmentation of the Somali, which resulted in increased pressure upon the Galla. The Somali clan groups moved west and south, forcing some Galla to retreat before them but also bypassing large numbers of Galla. This process of settlement, fragmentation, and migration continued until different Somali groups had occupied the area between the Juba and Shebelle rivers and even further south to the borders of modern-day Kenya. In general, the displaced Galla retreated westward into Ethiopia where in the seventeenth century they posed the major threat to the stability of the Ethiopian throne.

The entire reconstruction of Somali and Galla origins and movements as outlined above has been challenged by Herbert Lewis. Utilizing primarily linguistic evidence, Lewis presents a strong case for a southern Ethiopian origin for both the Somali and Galla. His arguments on the basis of present evidence seem to be the most logical answer to Galla and Somali origin. There are twenty-four different languages of the eastern Cushitic group. Lewis utilized the maxim that probabilities of migrations are in inverse ratio to the number of reconstructed language movements. Twenty-one of the twenty-four languages, including Galla and Somali, are spoken today in southern Ethiopia. Thus it appears obvious that the Somali and Galla did not originate in northern Somalia or Arabia. Lewis also questions past use of oral tradition and the few scraps of history available. He finds no evidence that the Galla were in the horn of Africa prior to the sixteenth century. The conclusion is that the Somali, Galla, and other Cushitic groups originally lived in the Borana area of southern Ethiopia near Mount Wolabo and Lake Abaya.

Based on linguistic analysis the Somali and some other smaller Cushitic groups were the first to move from Ethiopia. This theory is based on the great divergence of Somali dialects from one another. The migration path of these people then was originally from south to north. As they encountered land more suited to herding than agriculture they adapted themselves. On the basis of the few historical records Lewis concludes that the Somali have been relatively stable in the northern and central areas for the past seven centuries. Little was noted of the Galla until the sixteenth century. From these later accounts Lewis concludes that the initial invasions of Ethiopia were from west to east and that this must have been their first great movement from the Borana area. This conclusion again is linguistically determined because of the slight differentiation of language among Galla groups.

Arabs and Persians were established in northern Somaliland in significant numbers as early as the eighth century. The port cities of Zeila, Berbera, Mogadishu, Brava, and Merca were all centers of Arab trading activity. From these cities the Islamic faith spread slowly into the interior. There is no way of knowing in any precise way how this was done and how long the process took. It is probable that its progression was similar to that in the Western Sudan, where the merchants and traders first introduced the new faith to the interior. Acceptance of Islam was a slow process because many Somali had only recently been converted in the sixteenth century. The largest segment of the Galla population remained unconverted even at that late date.

Knowledge of the Galla becomes more precise when they begin to play a dominant role in the history of Ethiopia. Early in the sixteenth century they began to infiltrate Ethiopian territory and also predominant Somali areas in the south. The struggles between Gran and the Ethiopians gave the Galla greater opportunities for expansion into the Ethiopian kingdom, for in this period the attention of the emperors was concentrated in the north. The major effort of the Galla was temporarily diverted by Galawdewos after 1545 in the direction of Harar, which they took and sacked. Soon, however, they returned to the eastern highlands. Within ten years the Galla had penetrated into eastern Amhara, Begameder, and Wollega. The Galla invasions combined with the Turkish threat to the north proved too much for Emperor Minas. By the time of his death in 1559 over one third of Ethiopia had been overrun by the Galla.

From this time until the late nineteenth century the Galla were an ever-present menace to the stability of Ethiopia. The great emperors of the seventeenth century were constantly on campaigns against them. A frontier of sorts was established in southern Shoa against the pagan Galla. To the southeast of Ethiopia proper the Galla who settled in Wollo become converted to Islam and joined with other more coastal Muslims in presenting a continuing problem. The Galla who had cut their way into Amhara and Begameder were gradually Christianized and utilized by numerous emperors of the seventeenth and eighteenth centuries as a prop for the throne against the factional activities of the nobility and church. The history of the Galla is inextricably interwoven with that of the kingdom of Ethiopia.

The rise of Gondar and the breakup of the empire

The kingdom bequeathed by Minas to his son Sarsa-Dengel (1563–1597) was devastated. There were no cities under his control and he was forced to move from one area to another until late in his reign. Ethiopia was surrounded by enemies. The Turks after defeating Egypt in 1517 had become the dominant power of the Red Sea. They controlled Yemen and after mid-century took Massawa and other strong points on the northeastern Ethiopian coast. The Turks were on the point of invading Tigre when Sarsa-Dengel became emperor. The threat of the Muslim state of Adal, although greatly reduced, was still present and the Falasha threatened in the northwest. More dangerous than all these were the previously discussed Galla invasions. To compound the difficulties there were a number of claimants to the throne of Ethiopia and the country itself was badly divided. Sarsa-Dengel in a series of brilliant campaigns ended the menace of Adal, leaving of it only Harar, which became an independent city. The Turkish forces combined with those of Tigre loyal to its Ethiopian governor were defeated in 1578. The emperor's armies checked the advance of the Galla, destroyed Falasha power in Semen, and campaigned against the Nilotes to the west. Foreshadowing the actions of later rulers, the emperor established a semipermanent capital at the castle of Guzara near Lake Tana. At the time of his death Ethiopia was well on its way to being restored to its previous power and grandeur.

The unity so bloodily won was almost lost in the struggle for power after Sarsa-Dengel's death. Not until 1608 with the accession of Susenyos, a grandson of Sarsa-Dengel, was order restored. Susenyos in his youth had been a captive of the Galla and had established friendly relations with segments of these still-pagan people. In all his campaigns, whether against dissidents in the kingdom or against the Falasha and Funj, he depended heavily upon Galla armies. From this date one can trace the assimilation of large numbers of Galla into the kingdom.

Susenyos' control of the kingdom was undermined not by

exterior enemies but by his conversion to Latin Christianity. To understand this one must briefly recount the activities of the Portuguese in Ethiopia after the death of da Gama. Most of the 150 survivors of da Gama's expedition settled around the town of Fremonat near Adowa. Many became important landholders and in time, except for their language and religion, they behaved little differently from other Ethiopians. The few Latin priests in Ethiopia throughout most of the sixteenth century were located at Fremonat. Even though a bishop, the Jesuit Andre de Oviedo, was sent from Goa in 1557, there were few attempts at converting the Ethiopian nobility. With the arrival of Pedro Paez, a middle-aged Jesuit, there was introduced a more active proselytizing. Living at the emperor's court, Paez became an active part of the literary and artistic rebirth of Ethiopia. He helped design churches, restore paintings and illuminated manuscripts, and was an indefatigable teacher of the young sons of the nobility. His first major convert was Za Dengel, who was briefly emperor in 1603. This conversion played an important role in the excommunication and later defeat of Za Dengel.

Susenyos, despite the example of his predecessor, early toyed with the idea of becoming a Latin Christian. In 1621 the emperor went to Paez for confession. This display of public favor combined with the conversion of many nobles had already divided the kingdom before the arrival in Ethiopia of a new bishop, Alfonso Mendes. With the support of the emperor Mendes attempted to substitute Latin Christianity for the traditional form. Mendes was too uncompromising and moved too fast, thus creating a religio-political division within the kingdom that led to civil war. Ethiopian tradition records that Susenyos and his Latin adherents won a major battle over the traditionalists. Over 8,000 men died, however, and Susenyos, rather than continue the war, abdicated in favor of his son Fasiladas in 1632.

The Jesuits had lost their gamble to convert Ethiopia to the Latin rite. In 1633 Fasiladas ordered all Jesuits sent to Axum. Those who remained in Ethiopia were later killed. Fasiladas considered all Europeans a threat to Ethiopian institutions and barred their entry into Ethiopia. To assure the observance of this order the emperor established better relations with the Muslim coastal cities. The Muslim rulers promised to prevent Europeans from leaving their territories for Ethiopia. Thus the reaction against Jesuit proselytizing resulted in the further retreat of Ethiopia from contact with the outside world. The isolation of Ethiopia from Europe was broken only briefly by a few visitors such as the Frenchman Poncet in 1698 and the Scotsman Bruce in 1769.

Gondar became the capital of Ethiopia under Fasiladas, who built a great palace there. Other nobles of the court settled there and for almost a century the Ethiopian emperors ruled in splendor from this location near Lake Tana. Yohannes (1667–1682) and Yasu the Great (1682–1706) increased the power and prestige of the kingship, built new palaces and churches, and kept the Galla and Muslims in check. The administration of Ethiopia was reformed with a revision of the civil code for administration. The Alexandrine church prospered in harmony with the emperors and the great nobles were overawed by the power of Yohannes and Yasu. In 1702 a palace revolution nevertheless overthrew Yasu. The reasons for this action are unclear but possibly were connected with the fears of the church that Yasu was being attracted by Latin Christianity. His overthrow came soon after the visit of Poncet and a representative of European Catholicism. Shortly after the abdication Yasu was murdered.

Yasu was the last great emperor of Ethiopia in the eighteenth century. The emperors who succeeded him became the victims of palace intrigues begun by rival claimants to the throne. The church itself became divided in its support of different factions. In the twenty years after Yasu's reign there were five different emperors, two of whom were murdered. In this atmosphere there developed at Gondar a Praetorian Guard type of operation. With the kingship growing weaker, the great nobles became more and more independent. By midcentury the real power within Ethiopia was wielded by Ras Michael Sehul, the strong man behind the emperors Yasu II, Isos, Yohannes II, and Takla Haymanot II. The Scottish adventurer James Bruce lived at Gondar during a part of the reign of Takla Haymanot II. His report of the mixture between civilization, Christianity, and barbarism in this period of a decaying Ethiopia was considered to be too farfetched for his European contemporaries to believe. Nevertheless, Bruce presented a generally accurate account of Ethiopian society tearing itself apart.

Ras Michael, who controlled Takla Haymanot II almost completely, was defeated and deposed by his enemies in 1771, and the emperor was killed by another powerful noble, Ras

Gusho, eight years later. The united kingdom was by then a myth. The emperors became nothing but figureheads to be dominated or deposed at the will of the nobility and the church. The best example of their helplessness is the career of Talka Giorgis, who was emperor five times between 1779 and 1800. The church was the only unifying factor in the divided polity. Ethiopia remained a fragmented, pale reflection of its former greatness until the bandit Ras Kassa seized the throne in the middle of the nineteenth century.

Arab activities in the Sudan

Despite the quick, overpowering success of Islam in northern Africa, Muslim influence in the Sudan until the thirteenth century was minimal. The area south from the second cataract of the Nile to the confluence of the Blue Nile was controlled by three Christian kingdoms. Immediately adjacent to Egypt was Nobatia; the middle state was Makuria, based on the major cities of Dongola and Napata; and in the extreme south was Alwa, with its capital at Soba on the Blue Nile. There are many reasons why powerful Islam allowed these states to exist. One was the nature of the terrain in the Sudan. Early Arab invaders found campaigning there difficult and costly. A second reason was the internecine strife that developed in Islam after the ninth century. Egypt was torn by a series of wars and a succession of different dynasties. Thus the treaty of peace with the Sudanese kingdoms fashioned by the most successful of the early Muslim invaders, Abdullah ibn Said, in the seventh century continued in force for over six centuries.

Although the treaty prevented major warfare between the Christian states and Egypt, it did not eliminate all friction. Arab pastoralists very soon violated the treaty and began to settle in northern Nobatia. This process was accelerated after the ninth century when non-Arab rulers in Egypt sought to rid their state of the troublesome Bedouin Arab. By the opening of the thirteenth century northern Nobatia was almost completely controlled by the wandering invaders. The Mameluk rulers of Egypt after 1250 claimed that the Christian states had broken the treaty by not paying the required annual tribute and sent a series of military expeditions up the Nile. Nobatia fell quickly and in 1276 Dongola was taken and sacked. The way was then opened for Arab settlement as far south as the confluence of

the Nile and Atbara rivers. The kingdom of Alwa in the far
south, blocked on all sides by Arab occupation, still retained
its independence until the first years of the sixteenth century.

Some of these Arab invaders of the Sudan were townsmen,
not pastoralists, and settled among the Nubians in the towns
and villages north of Dongola. In a short time a loosely inter-
preted Islam became the accepted way of life for the mixed
people resulting from the fusion between the Arabs and the
original population. Other Bedouin groups infiltrated the Beja,
and some moved southwestward to the grazing lands of the Nile
and further to Kordofan and Darfur. Some Arab groups reached
the Blue Nile and by the fifteenth century had almost enclosed
the Gezira region, the most fertile portion of the kingdom of
Alwa.

The Arabs of the Sudan were fragmented into a number
of separate and usually competing groups. The northern or
Jaliyin group of Arabs were those who usually abandoned pastoral pursuits for a sedentary life near the Nile. This group was
further subdivided into a number of competitive branches. The
Jaliyin lived among non-Arab people who were also divided
into tribes. This subdivision of the non-Arab Nubians probably
took place after the Arab invasions. The Beja to the east, however, remained for a long time separate from the Arabs. In the
south the Juhayna group of tribes remained pastoralists when
they settled in the Blue Nile basin in Kordofan and Darfur.
Their political and tribal divisions, reinforced by needs for pas-
ture and water, were generally more significant than those of
the sedentary northerners. In Darfur, Kordofan, and the area
of the later Funj kingdom there were also important non-Arab
segments in the population. The Zaghawa and Bedayyat were
of Libyan origin. The Fur and the Funj were predominantly
Nilotic or Negro. In the far south of modern-day Sudan were
found Nilotic tribes such as the Dinka, Shilluk, Anuak, and
Nuer.

The system of government common to the Sudan even
after the destruction of the Christian kingdom of Alwa and the
rise of the Funj was tribal. The tribal sheikh and his advisers
were the closest approach to centralized government in the
central and northern Sudan. The later Funj kings did little to
break down this decentralized system. They simply imposed
a common direction which most of the tribal leaders followed.
The various Arab groups of the Sudan were ostensibly Muslim,

but their religious devotion was minimal. One commentator has noted that the bulk of the population prior to the sixteenth century was neither Christian nor Muslim. Little effort was made until the establishment of the Funj empire to reform the tribal religious practices and to bring the Sudan in line with the mainstream of Islam philosophy which had been developed in North Africa and the Middle East.

The Funj empire

The origin of the people who first established the Funj state is not yet definitely established. A. J. Arkell, an expert on the Sudan, has suggested two possible theories. One connects them to the kingdom of Bornu while the other locates their homeland in Ethiopia. James Bruce, the eighteenth-century visitor to Ethiopia and the Sudan, was the first to suggest another explanation for the Funj. He reported that a war party of Nilotic Shilluk entered the central Sudan, established themselves on the Blue Nile, and eventually came to dominate their Arab neighbors. Of the three theories the one with least validity based on present evidence is the one linking the Funj to Bornu. A recent monograph by P. A. Holt, another Sudanese specialist, concludes that there is no overwhelming evidence in favor of either the Shilluk or Ethiopian origins of the Funj.

There do exist nineteenth-century versions of what is called the Funj Chronicle that have been accepted by many authors as describing the early relations between the Funj and the Arabs. By comparing these commentaries with other sources only a few generalizations seem valid. The Funj, whatever their point of origin, were black — either Nilotic or Negro. In the late fifteenth or early sixteenth century they established themselves at Sennar on the Blue Nile. David Reubeni, a Jewish traveler of the sixteenth century, confirms both these points. According to Bruce, the black invaders in the sixteenth century won a major battle over the southward-moving Arab pastoralists. After this a balance between the two peoples was struck. The Funj, if not Muslims before this victory, became at least occasional conformists by the close of the sixteenth century.

There are traditional stories relating the cooperation between the Arabs under their leader Abdullah Jamma and the Funj to destroy the Christian kingdom of Alwa. Whether the stories are correct in specific details is not presently known.

However, the capital city of Soba was taken by Muslims in the
sixteenth century and the inhabitants scattered throughout the
Sudan. Some time in this century the curious type of double
rule that characterized the Funj empire was established. In its
mature form the Arab sheikhs of Qarri became vizirs of the
empire and commanders of the army and were given the responsibility of administering conquered areas north of Qarri.
The Funj kings remained at Sennar and governed directly the
areas immediately adjacent to that town. The southern portion,
or that part under the king, was subject to a more centralized
government apparatus than the areas responsible to the sheikhs
of Qarri. Both rulers, however, maintained only loose control
over the petty rulers on the periphery of the kingdom. The
strength of the Funj rulers lay in their ability to convince by
argument or coercion the sheikhs of the various Arab groups
to cooperate with the central government.

The dual system of rule functioned well. The sheikhs of
Qarri in the sixteenth century advanced their influence north
of Dongola. The king at Sennar expanded the kingdom west to
the White Nile and east to the borders of Ethiopia. In these
latter areas the people were forced also to accept Islam. However, military conquest north of Dongola was blocked by the
military commanders (kushaf) of the Ottoman Empire. After
Ottoman rule in Egypt began to decline these commanders became independent but still retained enough power to prevent
the Funj conquest of their territory.

The Funj empire of the seventeenth and eighteenth centuries became very rich. Sennar was a city of more than 10,000
and the commercial hub of the Sudan. Products of central
Africa passed through Sennar on their way to Suakin and
Massawa. Goods in transit from Ethiopia and Egypt also reached
Sennar via a number of important caravan routes. All manner
of products were to be found in the markets of the cities. Gold,
ostrich feathers, hides, dates, horses, slaves, cattle, and ivory
were a few of the most important items traded either by barter
or by using cloth or Spanish and Turkish coins for exchange.
A commercial center almost as important as Sennar was Shendi,
located just north of Qarri on the Nile.

Although a portion of the population of the Sudan professed Islam before the rise of the Funj empire, it was the per-
functory-type Islam of the wandering Bedouin. Once the area
from Sennar to Dongola was brought under the settled rule of

an Islamic king missionaries and teachers from Egypt, North Africa, and the Hejaz came to the Sudan. The Funj rulers encouraged the establishment of schools and mosques in all parts of their kingdom. The Maliki code and Sufism were introduced to the Sudan during the height of Funj power. By the close of the eighteenth century the bulk of the Sudanese population had been introduced to the more sophisticated and rationalized Islam of North Africa and the Near East.

During the reign of King Badi Abu Shillukh (1723–1761) the Funj empire reached its greatest extent. Commercial rivalry brought on a major war with Ethiopia early in his reign. In 1738 the emperor Iyasu II dispatched a large army against the Funj which despoiled the eastern areas of the kingdom. One large segment of the army was sent to take Sennar. Although the town was abandoned by the Funj, this part of the Ethiopian army was soon cut to pieces. The Ethiopian detachment under the emperor's command then retired with a large amount of booty into Ethiopia but without humbling the Funj rulers. The Funj soon turned this costly war to their advantage by forcing the submission of eastern tribes up to the Ethiopian border. In 1747 Badi decided upon war to gain the area of Kordofan, which had previously been contested between the Funj rulers and the kingdom of Darfur. The most powerful of the Kordofan clans was the Mussabbaat, whose leaders were related to the sultans of Darfur. After initial defeats the Funj armies were rallied by General Abu Likaylik and the Mussabbaat-Fur forces were defeated. Kordofan became an integral part of the empire and remained so until its reconquest by the Fur in 1786. In gratitude for his services Badi made Abu Likaylik vizir of the kingdom, commander of the army, and sheikh of Kordofan.

After the conquest of Kordofan the Funj empire extended from Suakin in the east to Darfur in the west. However, King Badi in accomplishing his victories set in motion forces that soon destroyed his vast empire. As already noted, the Funj government was never as centralized as the great empires of the Western Sudan. Instead, it remained a loose federation of highly individualized tribal units whose leaders were never made subservient to a central bureaucratic regime. Badi unwisely upset the delicate balance of self-interest that had maintained the regime for 250 years. He attempted to interfere more directly in affairs previously left to the sheikhs, executed some members of important families, and attempted to create a loyal

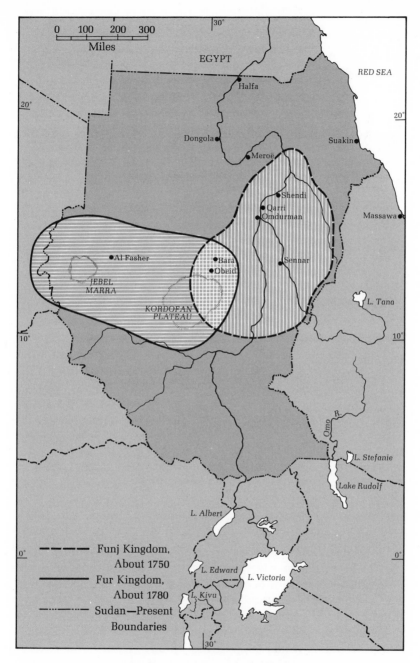

Kingdoms of the Funj and Fur

bureaucracy composed of Nubians. Dissident elements in the state appealed to Abu Likaylik, the powerful sheikh of Kordofan, to aid in the overthrow of the king. King Badi's son joined the conspirators. Faced with this coalition, the king voluntarily went into exile.

Actual power in the Funj state devolved upon Abu Likaylik and his successor-leaders of the Hamaj who were the vizirs. Kings were deposed at will and in the latter years of the Funj state the Hamaj were themselves divided. Various sections of the kingdom revolted against the Funj kings. The important Shukriya, Fazzara, and Halfaya tribes became almost completely independent and the Kordofan was reconquered by the Fur in 1786. By the opening of the nineteenth century the Funj rulers exercised almost no control over the Sudan north of Khartoum. In 1821 Ismail Pasha, the son of Muhammed Ali, the Ottoman governor general of Egypt, conquered the Sudan and ended the long, colorful, if obscure, history of the Funj empire.

The Fur sultanate

The Fur were the dominant people in the extreme western portion of what is today the Sudan. Like the Funj, the Fur were a composite people. They were the result of intermarriage between the lighter-hued Nubians, Negro invaders from the south, and the Arabs from the north and west. The origin of the Negroid element in the Fur population is even more in question than in the case of the Funj. By the seventeenth century there were discernible a number of branches among the Fur, the most important of which was the Kunjara, the people responsible for the establishment of the powerful Fur sultanate which was contemporaneous with the Funj empire.

The first great Fur ruler was Sulayman Solonj (about 1650), who established order in the territory immediately adjacent to Jebel Marra. He then extended his control over areas that had never before been considered subservient to the Fur. One conquered area that was not absorbed directly into the sultanate was Kordofan. According to tradition, Kordofan was given to Sulayman's brother Mussabba with the understanding that his dynasty would support the sultans of Fur in their wars. This arrangement seems to have been well observed and Kordofan was a type of client state for the Fur until its conquest by the Funj in the early eighteenth century. The Funj empire after the reign of King Badi Abu Shillukh was not able to retain Kordofan. It was briefly independent before the Fur sultans reconquered it in 1786. During the reign of Sultan Abd al Rahman at the close of the eighteenth century the Fur controlled territory almost to the junction of the two Niles in the east and west along the caravan routes deep into what is today Chad.

The Fur sultans were committed to spreading Islam throughout the lands under their control. By the close of the eighteenth century only southern Kordofan remained unconverted. The sultans built mosques and supported religious teachers. Laws relating to marriage and inheritance were Islamic, and their enforcement was left to the religious authorities. Education was in the hands of religious teachers, many of whom were able to carry out their instruction because of the generosity of the sultan and the great nobles of the kingdom. Advanced students who traveled to al-Azhar University in Egypt were allotted a separate section known as the Darfur cloister.

The government of the Fur in the eighteenth century was more centralized than that of the Funj. The sultan was in theory absolute. At his capital city of Tayra and later al-Fasher he had developed a working bureaucracy. Aided by the vizir and council of state, the sultan made the basic decisions concerning government, foreign affairs, and taxation. The sultanate was divided into four large administrative sections, each under a viceroy appointed by the sultan. The four segments were further subdivided into districts and subdistricts, each with an appointed official. The tribal sheikhs, unless they were appointed to a high position, were made subservient to the central government. This relatively efficient and flexible system stayed in effect until the conquest of Darfur by the Turco-Egyptian forces in the nineteenth century.

The wealth of the state was due to the important caravan routes that crossed the sultanate. From Wadai and Bornu in the west, from southern Kordofan, and from the Bahr-el-Ghazal came ivory and slaves. These and such trade items as gum arabic, ostrich feathers, and honey were carried to the east and the north. Perhaps the main route of trade was the Forty Days Road which connected al-Fasher to Egypt. Merchants brought back to Darfur cloth, gold, silks, and manufactured goods. The sultan's wealth was primarily derived from his investments in such trading activities and from the ten percent tax levied on all merchandise.

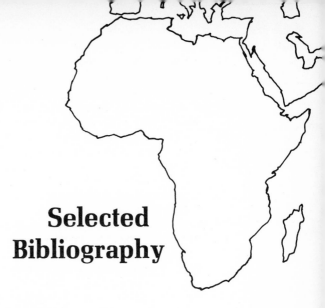

Selected
Bibliography

Chapter One
THE DEVELOPMENT OF EARLY SOCIETY

No attempt has been made to construct an exhaustive bibliography of materials dealing with Africa. The following list represents those books and articles that the author has found useful and that are not too advanced for students at this level of college work. The bulk of the works cited are available in most libraries. Many have been published in inexpensive paperback editions. A number of books, particularly general histories, have application to several topic areas covered in this textbook, although each work is cited only once under the most appropriate chapter heading. The books most helpful for students who wish to do reading corollary with the text have been briefly annotated.

Ardrey, Robert. *African Genesis.* New York: Dell Books, 1967. The author is a professional dramatist and amateur anthropologist who was acquainted with Dart, Broom, Oakley, and Le Gros Clark. He tends to overstress certain aspects of the new theories on early man, although the excitement which he can engender in the subject makes this book a good place to begin further reading into prehistory.

Arkell, A. J. *Early Khartoum.* London: Oxford University Press, 1949.

Arkell, A. J. *A History of the Sudan.* London: Oxford University Press, 1955.

Barker, H. G. "Comments on the Thesis That There Was a Major Center of Plant Domestication Near the Headwaters of the River Niger," *Journal of African History,* III, 1962.

Barrow, R. H. *The Romans*. London: Penguin Books, 1949.

Breasted, James. *A History of Egypt*. New York: Charles Scribner's Sons, 1959. Although there has been much new material discovered since this work was published, Breasted's history remains one of the better surveys of Egypt.

Clark, Grahame. *World Prehistory*. Cambridge: Cambridge University Press, 1961.

Clark, J. Desmond. "Prehistoric Origins of African Culture," *Journal of African History*, V, 1964.

Clark, J. Desmond. "The Spread of Food Production in Sub-Saharan Africa," *Journal of African History*, III, 1962.

Cole, Sonia. *The Prehistory of East Africa*. New York: Mentor Books, 1965. This paperback does an excellent job of presenting the extremely complex subject of East African prehistory in an understandable though detailed manner.

Coon, Carleton S. *The Origin of Races*. New York: Alfred A. Knopf, Inc., 1962.

Davidson, Basil. *Africa: History of a Continent*. New York: The Macmillan Company, 1966. This book is primarily a work of art. The text is sparse and is used primarily to introduce its many pictures and line drawings. The colored photographs of African scenes and art are among the best yet printed.

Davidson, Basil. *The African Past*. Boston: Little, Brown & Company, 1964. There is perhaps no better single book that captures the mystery and glory of African history. Davidson is a journalist turned historian and therefore the book is better written than most histories.

de Blij, Harm J. *A Geography of Subsaharan Africa*. Chicago: Rand McNally & Company, 1964. Although not historical in nature, this is one of the best geographic surveys of Africa. Divided into regional studies, it introduces the student to the realities of African physical and human geography.

Dunham, Dows. "Notes on the History of Kush, 850 B.C.–A.D. 350," *American Journal of Archaeology*, L, 1946.

Fage, J. D. *An Atlas of African History*. London: E. Arnold, 1958. Beautifully done, this Atlas is too expensive for most students to own. The colored maps and well-written text makes it a reference work that should be consulted.

Fage, J. D. *An Introduction to the History of West Africa*. Cambridge: Cambridge University Press, 1955. At one time this was the standard book for students beginning the study of West Africa. Some of it has now become dated because of the monographic work completed after its publication. Its simple text, many maps and dates, and its over-all organization make it still a very useful book.

Fairservis, Walter A. *The Ancient Kingdoms of the Nile and the*

Doomed Monuments of Nubia. New York: Mentor Books, 1962. A companion volume to that on East African prehistory written by Sonia Cole. It is particularly good in detailing the development of Egyptian authority and culture in Nubia and Kush.

Fordham, Paul. *The Geography of African Affairs.* Baltimore, Md.: Penguin Books, Inc., 1965.

Frank, Tenney (ed.). *An Economic Survey of Ancient Rome,* 4 vols. Paterson, N. J.: Pagent Books, 1959.

Gailey, Harry A., Jr. *The History of Africa in Maps.* Chicago: Denoyer-Geppert Company, 1967. This atlas was designed to provide students with an inexpensive African atlas. Each of its forty-six maps dealing with such diverse topics as climate, prehistory, migrations, and European intervention is accompanied by a short explanatory text.

Greenberg, J. H. *Essays in Linguistics.* Chicago: University of Chicago Press, 1963.

Greenberg, J. H. *Studies in African Linguistic Classifications.* New Haven, Conn.: Compass Publishing Company, 1955.

Guthrie, Malcolm. "Bantu Origins," *Journal of African Languages,* I, 1962.

Guthrie, Malcolm. "Some Developments in the Pre-History of the Bantu Languages," *Journal of African History,* III, 1962.

Harden, Donald. *The Phoenicians.* New York: Frederick A. Praeger, Inc., 1962.

Harden, Donald. "The Phoenicians on the West Coast of Africa," *Antiquity,* September 1948.

Herodotus (Selincourt, trans.). *The Histories.* Baltimore, Md.: Penguin Books, Inc., 1954.

Jones, A. M. "Indonesians in Africa — An Ancient Colonial Era?" Paper presented at the Third Conference of African History and Archaeology, University of London, July 3–7, 1961.

Kees, H. *Ancient Egypt: A Cultural Topography.* Chicago: University of Chicago Press, 1961.

Leakey, L. S. B. "New Finds on Olduvai Gorge," *Nature,* February 25, 1961.

Le Gros Clark, Sir Wilfrid E. *The Fossil Evidence for Human Evolution.* Chicago: University of Chicago Press, 1964.

Le Gros Clark, Sir Wilfrid E. *A History of the Primates.* Chicago: University of Chicago Press, 1957.

Le Gros Clark, Sir Wilfrid E. *Man Apes or Ape Men.* New York: Holt, Rinehart and Winston, Inc., 1967. This is an extremely well-written book by one of the world's foremost anthropologists which focuses upon the Australopithecines.

Lewis, N., and M. Reinhold. *Roman Civilization,* 2 vols. New York: Harper & Row, Publishers, Inc., 1966.

Mercer, S. A. B. *The Religion of Ancient Egypt.* London: Luzac, 1949.

Miracle, Marvin P. "Interpretations of Evidence on the Introduction of Maize into West Africa," *Africa,* XXXIII, 1963.

Morgan, W. B. "The Forest and Agriculture in West Africa," *Journal of African History,* III, 1962.

Murdoch, G. P. *Africa, Its People and Their Culture History.* New York: McGraw-Hill Book Company, Inc., 1959. When this book was first published it created a storm in academic circles primarily because of the author's bold assertions concerning the migration of food crops in Africa. It is still required reading for anyone who wants to understand the relation between food and African development.

Oakley, Kenneth P. *Man the Tool-Maker.* London: British Museum, 1956.

Oliver, Roland (ed.). *The Dawn of African History.* London: Oxford University Press, 1963. This is a collection of essays by African experts. Each of the short articles is written to introduce students to the various problems, theories, and attitudes related to a specific area of ancient Africa.

Oliver, Roland, and J. D. Fage. *A Short History of Africa.* Baltimore, Md.: Penguin Books, Inc., 1962. This book remains one of the most thought provoking of all the general works on Africa. Its style is lucid, its organization good, and its theorizing places it far above the average work on Africa. The authors thoroughly analyze the Sudanic state as it seems to have been diffused from Meroë to various parts of Africa.

Palmer, H. Richmond. *The Carthaginian Voyage to West Africa.* Bathurst, West Africa: Gambia Government Printers, 1931.

Pedler, F. J. *Economic Geography of West Africa.* London: Longmans, Green & Company, Inc., 1955.

Porteres, R. "Berceaux agricoles primaires sur le continent Africain," *Journal of African History,* III, 1962.

Rostovtzev, M. *The Social and Economic History of the Roman Empire.* London: Clarendon Press, 1957.

Rotberg, Robert I. *A Political History of Tropical Africa.* New York: Harcourt, Brace & World, Inc., 1965. Coverage of sub-Saharan Africa is not uniform. In some places this history is too detailed for beginning students while other areas are barely mentioned. Nevertheless, it is a mine of information on certain parts of Africa and should be used as a reference work for these areas. The bibliography is excellent.

Schoff, Wilfred (trans.). *The Periplus of Hanno.* Philadelphia: The Commercial Museum, 1913.

Smith, W. S. *The Art and Architecture of Ancient Egypt.* Baltimore, Md.: Penguin Books, Inc., 1958.

Stamp, J. Dudley. *Africa: A Study in Tropical Development.* New York: John Wiley & Sons, Inc., 1953.

Warmington, B. H. *Carthage*. Baltimore, Md.: Penguin Books, Inc., 1960.

Warmington, B. H. *The North African Provinces*. Cambridge: Cambridge University Press, 1954.

Weidner, Donald L. *A History of Africa South of the Sahara*. New York: Random House, Inc., Vintage Books, 1962.

Wilson, J. A. *The Burden of Egypt*. Chicago: University of Chicago Press, 1951.

Wrigley, Christopher C. "Linguistic Clues to African History," *Journal of African History*, III, 1962.

Wrigley, Christopher C. "Speculations on the Economic Prehistory of Africa," *Journal of African History*, I, 1960.

Chapter Two

ISLAM AND THE WESTERN SUDAN IN 1800

Bovill, E. W. "The Camel and the Garamantes," *Antiquity*, XXX, 1956.

Bovill, E. W. *The Golden Trade of the Moors*. London: Oxford University Press, 1958. Originally published as *Caravans of the Old Sahara* in 1933, this revised version is the best survey of the interrelations between North Africa and the Western Sudan from Carthaginian times through the period of the great empires of Mali and Songhai.

Davidson, Basil. *The Lost Cities of Africa*. Boston: Little, Brown & Company, 1959. This book could be more appropriately named *Lost Cultures*, since Davidson is concerned with introducing the reader to a variety of brief descriptions of some of the most important African cultures.

Fage, J. D. "Reflections on the Early History of the Mossi-Dagombu Group of States," in J. Vansina, R. Mauny, and L. V. Thomas (eds.), *The Historian in Tropical Africa*. London: Oxford University Press, 1964.

Greenberg, Joseph. "The Negro Kingdoms of the Sudan," *Transactions of the New York Academy of Sciences*, XI, 1949.

Hirschberg, H. Z. "The Problem of Judaized Berbers," *Journal of African History*, IV, 1963.

Hozben, S. J. *The Muhammadan Emirates of Nigeria*. London: Oxford University Press, 1930.

Hunwick, J. O. "Ahmad Baba and the Moroccan Invasion of Songhay," *Journal of the Historical Society of Nigeria*, II, 1962.

Ibn Abd al-Hakam (Charles Torrey, trans.). *The History of the Conquest of Egypt, North Africa and Spain*. New Haven, Conn.: Yale University Press, 1922.

Ibn Battuta (H. A. R. Gibb, trans.). *Travels in Asia and Africa, 1325–1354*. Cambridge: Cambridge University Press, 1953. Ibn Battuta was one of the great Islamic travelers and geographers of the fourteenth century. His impressions of the Mali state still form a large portion of our knowledge of the political, social, and economic structures of the Western Sudan. The Gibb translation is good and the book is quite readable. However, it should be read only after the student has read Bovill's work and the appropriate section of Davidson's *Lost Cities*.

Ibn Khaldun (Paul Casanova, trans.). *Histoire des Berberes et des dynasties musulmanes de l'Afrique septentrionale*, 4 vols. Paris: P. Guethner, 1925–1956.

Levtzion, N. "The Thirteenth and Fourteenth Century Kings of Mali," *Journal of African History*, IV, 1963. Many of the best recent studies of Africa appear as articles in various journals. This article is particularly good for establishing dating for various kings and discussion of the internal stresses within the Malian empire.

Mauny, Raymond. "Le Judaisme, les Juifs et l'Afrique occidentale," *Bulletin de l'Institut Français d'Afrique Noire*, XI, 1949.

Mauny, Raymond. "Une Route prehistorique à travers le Sahara occidental," *Bulletin de l'Institut Français d'Afrique Noire*, IX, 1947.

Mauny, Raymond, and Paul Thomassey. "Campagne de fouilles à Koumbi Saleh," *Bulletin de l'Institut Français d'Afrique Noire*, XIII, 1951.

McCall, D. F. "The Traditions of the Founding of Sijilmassa and Ghana," *Transactions of the Historical Society of Ghana*, V, 1951.

Palmer, H. Richmond. *Sudanese Memoirs*. Lagos, Nigeria: Government Printers, 1928.

Shinnie, P. L. "Old Kanuri Capitals," *Journal of African History*, III, 1962.

Skinner, Elliott P. "The Mossi and Traditional Sudanese History," *Journal of Negro History*, XLIII, 1958.

Smith, M. G. "The Beginnings of Hausa Society," in J. Vansina, Mauny, and Thomas (eds.), *The Historian in Tropical Africa*. London: Oxford University Press, 1964.

Thomas, Benjamin E. *Trade Routes of Algeria and the Sahara*. Berkeley, Calif.: University of California Press, 1964.

Trimingham, J. Spencer. *Islam in West Africa*. London: Oxford University Press, 1959. This is a good survey of Islam and its historical development within the many different West African cultures. The book is particularly good in introducing the student to the changes that were wrought in traditional Islamic beliefs by their close association with animist religions.

Wilks, Ivor. *The Northern Factor in Ashanti History*. Legon, Ghana: Institute of African Studies, 1961.

Chapter Three

FOREST STATES OF THE GUINEA COAST

Adloff, Richard. *West Africa, the French Speaking Nations*. New York: Holt, Rinehart and Winston, Inc., 1964.

Akinjogbin, I. A. *Dahomey and its Neighbours*. Cambridge: Cambridge University Press, 1967. This is an excellent, although detailed, work by a Nigerian historian which describes the rise of Dahomey. Akinjogbin pursues the thesis that the development of Dahomey did not depend upon the slave trade but was due to other forces inherent within the political structure of the state.

Argyle, W. J. *The Fon of Dahomey*. London: Clarendon Press, 1966.

Bradbury, R. E., and P. C. Lloyd. *The Benin Kingdom*. London: International African Institute, 1959.

Crowder, Michael. *A Short History of Nigeria*. New York: Frederick A. Praeger, Inc., 1966. This extremely literate work should be required beginning reading for any student interested in doing further work in Nigerian history. Crowder, like Davidson, is a journalist turned historian. The book is capably researched, well written, and covers in a general, easily understood fashion the major developments in an extremely complex part of West Africa. It is far better than the histories of Nigeria written by the colonial historians Nivens and Burns.

Dalzel, Archibald. *The History of Dahomey, An Island Kingdom of Africa*. London: Frank Cass, 1966.

Egharevba, Jacob. *History of Benin Kingdom*. Cambridge: Cambridge University Press, 1960.

Fage, J. D. *Ghana, A Historical Interpretation*. Madison, Wisc.: University of Wisconsin Press, 1959. This is a short, well-written, easily read book which as the title implies is interpretive rather than a detailed discourse on the chronological development of Ghana.

Flint, John E. *Nigeria and Ghana*. Englewood Cliffs, N.J.: Prentice-Hall, Inc., Spectrum Books, 1966. Flint, who is better known for his research in Nigeria at a later period, has produced here a very basic work of approximately secondary school level. However, the author does touch upon the major themes in the history of both regions and the book could serve as an introduction to more specialized reading.

Forde, Daryll. *Efik Traders of Old Calabar*. London: International African Institute, 1956.

Forde, Daryll. *The Yoruba-Speaking Peoples of South-Western Nigeria*. London: International African Institute, 1951.

Forde, Daryll, and G. K. Jones. *The Ibo and Ibibio-Speaking Peoples of South-Eastern Nigeria.* London: International African Institute, 1950.

Fuller, Francis C. *A Vanished Dynasty: Ashanti.* London: J. Murray, 1921.

Fyfe, Christopher. *A History of Sierra Leone.* London: Oxford University Press, 1962. This book is large and overly detailed for the ordinary beginning student. It is recommended only because its thoroughness makes it the reference book for anyone concerned with the history of the region adjacent to Freetown.

Gamble, David P. *The Wolof of the Senegambia.* London: International African Institute, 1957.

Gray, John. *A History of the Gambia.* London: Oxford University Press, 1940. Sir John Gray wrote this while serving in the judiciary of the Gambia. It is the best source for European activities in the Senegambia. Gray's treatment of the indigenous populations is not equally thorough. The book should be used as a reference work in the same way suggested for Fyfe's *History of Sierra Leone.*

Hodgkin, Thomas. *Nigerian Perspectives.* London: Oxford University Press, 1960. This work relates the development of Nigeria by presenting excerpts from various explorers' accounts and descriptions. Thus it presents a flavor of immediacy which is often lacking in straight historical narrative. Hodgkin's introduction is excellent.

Johnson, Samuel. *History of the Yorubas.* Lagos, Nigeria: C. M. S. Bookshops, 1960.

Meyerowitz, Eva L. R. *Akan Traditions of Origin.* London: Faber and Faber, 1952.

Newbury, C. W. *The Western Slave Coast and Its Rulers.* Oxford: Clarendon Press, 1961.

Priestley, Margaret, and Ivor Wilks. "The Ashanti Kings in the 18th Century," *Journal of African History,* I, 1960.

Talbot, P. A. *Peoples of Southern Nigeria,* 4 vols. London: Oxford University Press, 1926.

Ward, W. E. F. *A History of Ghana.* London: George Allen & Unwin, 1958. Although older than many, this narrative history remains one of the best-written accounts of the history of the Gold Coast, particularly for European activities there.

Wilks, Ivor. "The Rise of the Akwamu Empire, 1650–1710," *Transactions of the Historical Society of Ghana,* III, 1957.

Wolfson, Freida. *The Pageant of Ghana.* London: Oxford University Press, 1960. Although not as successful, this book is part of the same series as *Nigerian Perspectives.* The format of the work is slightly different from Hodgkin's, but the aim of the book is the same. This is a good work to use in conjunction with a good narrative history of the Gold Coast.

Chapter Four

EUROPEANS IN WEST AFRICA

Adanson, M. *Voyage to the Senegal, the Isle of Goree and the Gambia in the year 1750.* London: J. Nourse, 1759.

Akinjogbin, I. A. "Archibald Dalzel: Slave Trader and Historian of Dahomey," *Journal of African History,* VII, 1966.

Barbot, J. "A Description of the Coasts of Northern and Southern Guinea," in Awansham Churchill, *A Collection of Voyages and Travels.* London: 1732.

Blake, J. W. *Europeans in West Africa, 1450–1560,* 2 vols. London: Longmans, Green & Company, 1942.

Coupland, Reginald. *The British Anti-Slavery Movement.* London: T. Butterworth, 1933. Coupland was one of the great chronologers of the history of the British Empire and this is one of his best works. Written in a highly erudite fashion, it traces in some detail the development of the strong Evangelical opposition to the slave trade and the result of their nationwide endeavors.

Coupland, Reginald. *Wilberforce.* Oxford: Clarendon Press, 1923. This biography should be read in conjunction with Coupland's longer work on the antislavery movement. The student will then have a good foundation for understanding British Evangelicalism in the eighteenth and early nineteenth centuries.

Cultru, Prosper. *Histoire du Sénégal du XV Siècle à 1870.* Paris: E. Larose, 1910.

Davidson, Basil. *Black Mother.* Boston: Little, Brown & Company, 1961. This is another of Davidson's contributions to African history. Although not as detailed as the Daniel Mannix and Malcolm Cowley book, *Black Cargoes,* it is probably a better work for introducing students to the full range of European slave-trading activities.

Davis, K. G. *The Royal African Company.* London: Longmans, Green & Company, 1957. This is one of the most thorough studies undertaken of British chartered companies. It presents a good synopsis of British involvement in West Africa prior to the creation of the company. The major portion of the book is devoted to the problems of keeping the company solvent in a period of warfare between Britain and France and at a time when the bulk of the British slave trade was passing to independent merchants.

Gailey, Harry A., Jr. *A History of The Gambia.* London: Routledge & Kegan Paul, 1964. This work focuses on the history of The Gambia after 1889. However, the early chapters are valuable for the early period, since they are not as detailed or as complex as the same material in John Gray, *A History of the Gambia.*

Hakluyt, Richard. *Principal Navigations of the English Nation, IV.* London: Hakluyt Society, 1927.

Hakluyt Society. *The Voyages of Cadamosto and other Documents on Western Africa in the Second Half of the 15th Century.* London: Hakluyt Society, 1937.

Hallet, Robin. "The European Approach to the Interior of Africa in the 18th Century," *Journal of African History,* IV, 1963.

Jobson, Richard. *The Golden Trade.* London: Penguin Press, 1932. This is one of the classics of early writings concerning western Africa. Jobson was a factor of a British company in the early seventeenth century. His observations of African societies on the Gambia River and their relations with European traders is presented with great insight. The book has the advantage of being free from great amounts of detail and archaic phraseology which mar many books written at the same period.

Kup, Peter. *A History of Sierra Leone, 1400–1789.* Cambridge: Cambridge University Press, 1961.

Lloyd, Christopher. *The Navy and the Slave Trade.* London: Longmans, Green & Company, 1949.

Mannix, Daniel P. and Cowley, Malcolm, *Black Cargoes.* New York: Vintage Press, 1968.

Martin, E. C. *The British West African Settlements, 1750–1821.* London: Longmans, Green & Company, 1927.

Polanyi, Karl. "Sortings and the 'Ounce Trade' in the West African Slave Trade," *Journal of African History,* III, 1961. The very important element of just how Europeans conducted the slave trade and what systems of currency were used has been largely neglected by historians. This article by the late Karl Polanyi is the best single work on the highly complex aspect of the methodology of the trade.

Rodney, Walter. "African Slavery and Other Forms of Social Oppression on the Upper Guinea Coast in the Context of the Atlantic Slave Trade," *Journal of African History,* VII, 1966.

Rodney, Walter. "Portuguese Attempts at Monopoly on the Upper Guinea Coast, 1580–1650," *Journal of African History,* VI, 1965.

Verger, Pierre. *Bahia and the West African Trade.* Ibadan, Nigeria: Ibadan University Press, 1964. This small book is one of the few works in English that focuses on the important trade in slaves between Brazil and West Africa. It is particularly important as a second step for students who have already read Davidson or Mannix and Cowley on general aspects of the slave trade and want to pursue the subject further into more specialized fields.

Wyndham, H. A. *The Atlantic and Slavery.* London: Oxford University Press, 1935.

Chapter Five
CENTRAL AFRICA

Abraham, D. P. "Maramuca: An Exercise in the Combined Use of

Portuguese Records and Oral Tradition," *Journal of African History*, II, 1961.

Birmingham, David. *The Portuguese Conquest of Angola*. London: Oxford University Press, 1965. Birmingham's book is recommended for students to read in conjunction with Diffie's and Duffy's more general works on Portuguese expansion. The book is one of a series issued by the London Institute of Race Relations in paperback. It is short, easily read, and ideal as corollary reading with this text.

Childs, Gladwyn M. "The Kingdom of Wambu (Huambo): A Tentative Chronology," *Journal of African History*, I, 1964. The history of the Ovimbundu people of Angola has been neglected by non-Portuguese writers. This article taken in conjunction with appropriate sections of J. Vansina, *Kingdoms of the Savannah*, helps to fill the void. The article is quite detailed and presumes some previous knowledge of the general history of Angola.

Childs, Gladwyn M. "The Peoples of Angola in the Seventeenth Century According to Cadornega," *Journal of African History*, I, 1960.

Clark, J. D. *The Prehistory of Southern Africa*. London: Harmondsworth, 1959.

Cunnison, Ian. "Kazembe and the Portuguese," *Journal of African History*, II, 1961.

Cunnison, Ian. *The Luapula Peoples of Northern Rhodesia*. Manchester, England: Rhodes-Livingstone Institute, 1959.

Diffie, Bailey. *Prelude to Empire*. Lincoln, Nebr.: University of Nebraska Press, 1960. Diffie has little to say about Portuguese expansion in Africa. He is concerned with tracing the social, political, and economic beginnings of the Portuguese kingdom in the medieval period and sets the foundation for the later Portuguese empire.

Duffy, James. *Portugal in Africa*. Baltimore, Md.: Penguin Books, Inc., 1963. This is a survey of the Portuguese imperial experience, with a primary focus upon the nineteenth and twentieth centuries. Nevertheless, the first portion of the book discusses in very general terms the establishment of Portugal's African empire.

Fagan, Brian. "The Greefswald Sequence: Bambandyanola and Mapungubwe," *Journal of African History*, V, 1964.

Fagan, Brian. "Pre-European Ironworking in Central Africa with Special Reference to Northern Rhodesia," *Journal of African History*, II, 1961.

Oliver, Roland. "The Problem of Bantu Expansion," *Journal of African History*, VII, 1966. No comment has previously been made on the linguistic reconstructions of Guthrie and Greenberg, since they are quite complex. Oliver in this article attempts a reconciliation of the competitive theories of these two men as they relate to the migration of the Bantu. He does a fine job of relating the complex elements of that migration as a compromise between the experts.

Phillipson, D. W. "The Early Iron Age in Zambia — Regional Variants of Some Tentative Conclusions," *Journal of African History*, IX, 1968.

Vansina, Jan. "The Foundation of the Kingdom of Kasanje," *Journal of African History*, IV, 1963. This article and the four others listed below should be read as adjuncts to Vansina's *Kingdoms of the Savannah*. One could find no better way of becoming familiar with the early history of the Congo basin.

Vansina, Jan. *Kingdoms of the Savannah*. Madison, Wisc.: University of Wisconsin Press, 1966. This book is a major contribution to African historiography. Vansina is one of the world's foremost oral historians, and he has utilized this skill to its fullest extent in writing of the fifteenth- and sixteenth-century kingdoms of the Congo and northern Angola. The subject matter treated is quite complex and therefore the book might prove difficult for students who have not read considerably in more general works.

Vansina, Jan. "Long-Distance Trade-Routes in Central Africa," *Journal of African History*, III, 1962.

Vansina, Jan. "More on the Invasions of Kongo and Angola by the Jaga and Lunda," *Journal of African History*, VII, 1966.

Vansina, Jan. "Notes sur l'Origine du Royaume de Kongo," *Journal of African History*, IV, 1963.

Vansina, Jan. "Recording the Oral History of the Bakuba, Part I and Part II," *Journal of African History*, I, 1960.

Wills, A. J. *The History of Central Africa*. London: Oxford University Press, 1964. The focus of this book is on the nineteenth and twentieth centuries. Nevertheless, the Introduction and first two chapters present a very lucid introduction to the movement of the Luba, Lunda, Maravi, Shona, and other Bantu groups in Central Africa.

Chapter Six

SOUTH AFRICA

Barnard, Anne. *South Africa a Century Ago, 1797–1801*. London: Smith & Company, 1908.

Bjerre, Jan. *Kalahari*. New York: Hill & Wang, Inc., 1960.

Bond, John. *They Were South Africans*. London: Oxford University Press, 1956.

Bryant, A. T. "The Zulu State and Family Organization," *Bantu Studies*, No. 2, 1923.

Crawford, J. R. "The Monk's Kop Ossuary," *Journal of African History*, VIII, 1967.

De Kiewiet, C. W. *A History of South Africa*. London: Oxford University Press, 1966.

Gibbs, Henry. *Background to Bitterness*. New York: Philosophical Library, Inc., 1954. This small, very general book concentrates almost entirely on the role of the white South Africans. The Hottentot and Bantu populations are scarcely mentioned. However, its simple format makes it an adequate introductory work for the white history of the Cape.

Hepple, Alex. *South Africa*. New York: Frederick A. Praeger, Inc., 1966.

Hofmeyer, J. H. *South Africa*. London: Oxford University Press, 1931.

Hunt, D. R. "An Account of the Ba Pedi," *Bantu Studies*, No. 5, 1931.

Jacques, A. A. "Terms of Kinship and Corresponding Patterns of Behavior among the Thonga," *Bantu Studies*, No. 3, 1929.

Junod, H. P. *Bantu Heritage*. Johannesburg: Hortors, Ltd., 1938.

Macmillan, William M. *Boer, Bantu and Briton*. Oxford: Clarendon Press, 1963. This classic work is focused primarily on nineteenth-century relations among the constituent population groups of South Africa. It does treat in some detail the background to friction and is particularly good for the development of government policy.

Marais, J. S. *The Cape Coloured People, 1652–1937*. Johannesburg: Witwatersrand University Press, 1962.

Marquard, Leo. *The Peoples and Policies of South Africa*. London: Oxford University Press, 1962.

Marquard, Leo. *The Story of South Africa*. New York: Roy Publishers, n.d. This is a readable, well-written, although extremely general book that covers the entire period of South African history. Only the first part of the book is applicable for the period under survey in this text.

Mentzel, O. F. *Life at the Cape in Mid-18th Century*. Cape Town, Union of South Africa: Darter Bros., 1920.

Moodie, Donald. *The Record or A Series of Official Papers Relative to the Condition and Treatment of the Native Tribes of South Africa*. Cape Town, Union of South Africa: A. A. Balkema, 1960.

Morris, William. *The Washing of the Spears*. New York: Simon and Schuster, Inc., 1965. The author is primarily concerned with the coming of the Zulu War of 1879. Nevertheless, he devotes three long sections of the book to the early development of the southern Bantu and the rise of the Zulu nation. The book is well enough written that the reader is not aware of the mass of detailed information which is being presented.

Raven-Hart, R. *Before Van Riebeeck*. Cape Town, Union of South Africa: C. Struik, 1967.

Rose, J. H., A. P. Newton, and E. A. Benians. *The Cambridge History of the British Empire*, Vol. VIII, South Africa. Cambridge: Cambridge University Press, 1929.

Roux, Edward. *Time Longer Than Rope*. Madison, Wisc.: University of Wisconsin Press, 1966. This book also concentrates upon the nineteenth and twentieth centuries, but its short first section discusses in very readable form the early contacts between Boer and Bantu.

Schapera, I. (ed.). *The Bantu Speaking Tribes of South Africa.* London: Routledge and Kegan Paul, 1953.

Schapera, I. *The Khoisan Peoples of South Africa.* London: Routledge and Kegan Paul, 1930.

Schapera, I., and B. Farmington (eds.). *Early Cape Hottentots in the Writings of Dapper, Ten Rhyne and Grevenbroeck.* Cape Town, Union of South Africa: Van Riebeeck Society, 1933.

Soga, J. H. *The Southeastern Bantu.* Johannesburg: University of Witwatersrand, 1930.

Theal, George McCall. *History and Ethnography of Africa South of the Zambesi before 1795,* 3 vols. London: Swan Sonnenscheim & Company, 1910.

Theal, George McCall. *History of South Africa, 1795–1872,* 5 vols. London: George Allen & Unwin, 1908–1910.

Theal, George McCall. *The Portuguese in South Africa.* London: Fisher & Unwin, 1896.

Thomas, Elizabeth M. *The Harmless People.* New York: Alfred A. Knopf, Inc., 1959.

Vedder, Heinrich. *South West Africa in Early Times.* London: Frank Cass, 1966.

Walker, Eric A. *A History of Southern Africa.* London: Longmans, Green & Company, 1957. Walker's monumental work is probably the best introductory history of southern Africa, although Walker is primarily concerned with the development of white society. It is very detailed, well organized, and well written.

Chapter Seven

EAST AFRICA

Abrahams, R. G. *The Political Organization of the Unyamwezi.* Cambridge: Cambridge University Press, 1967.

Axelson, Eric. *Portuguese in South-East Africa, 1600–1700.* Johannesburg: Witwatersrand University Press, 1960. This is one of the best general works on the very early European contacts with the eastern coast of Africa.

Chittick, Neville. "The 'Shirazi' Colonization of East Africa," *Journal of African History,* VI, 1965.

Coupland, Reginald. *East Africa and Its Invaders.* London: Oxford University Press, 1938. Although written over thirty years ago before the bulk of the new research data was available, Coupland's book remains one of the best introductions to preninenteenth-century East Africa.

Ehret, Christopher. "Cattle-keeping and Milking in Eastern and Southern African History: The Linguistic Evidence," *Journal of African History,* VIII, 1967.

Fallers, Lloyd A. *Bantu Bureaucracy*. Chicago: University of Chicago Press, 1965.

Fallers, Margaret Chave. *The Eastern Lacustrine Bantu*. London: International African Institute, 1960.

Freeman-Grenville, G. S. P. "East African Coin Finds and Their Historical Significance," *Journal of African History*, I, 1960.

Freeman-Grenville, G. S. P. *The Medieval History of the Tanganyika Coast*. London: Oxford University Press, 1962.

Gray, John. *Early Portuguese Missionaries in East Africa*. London: The Macmillan Company, 1958.

Ingham, Kenneth. *A History of East Africa*. New York: Frederick A. Praeger, Inc., 1967. This is a good introductory text, although its focus is upon a later period. The first thirty-five pages give a good survey of the era before 1828.

Kenyatta, Jomo. *Facing Mt. Kenya*. New York: Random House, Inc., Vintage Books, 1962. A personal memoir of the Kikuyu couched in anthropological terms. Although focused upon the twentieth century, it is a good introduction to the life and customs of the Kikuyu.

Kirk, William. "The North-East Monsoon and Some Aspects of African History," *Journal of African History*, III, 1962.

Kirkman, James C. *Men and Monuments on the East African Coast*. New York: Frederick A. Praeger, Inc., 1966.

Louis, William Roger. *Ruanda-Urundi, 1884–1919*. Oxford: Clarendon Press, 1963.

Marsh, Z. A., and G. K. Kingsnorth. *History of East Africa*. Cambridge: Cambridge University Press, 1963. This book is normally too simplistic in its approach to African History. However, the first few pages are devoted to a short, systematic discussion of various historical developments along the Zenj coast before the nineteenth century.

Middleton, John, and Greet Kershaw. *The Central Tribes of the North-Eastern Bantu*. London: International African Institute, 1965.

Munro, J. Forbes. "Migrations of the Bantu-speaking Peoples of the Eastern Kenya Highlands: A Reappraisal," *Journal of African History*, VIII, 1967.

Oliver, Roland, and Gervase Mathew. *History of East Africa*, Vol. I. London: Oxford University Press, 1963. This is a collection of excellent essays on various aspects of the early history of East Africa by a number of specialists. It is particularly good for students who wish more detailed, authoritative treatment of the movement of peoples, Islamic influences, and the Portuguese invasions.

Saberwal, Satish. "Historical Notes on the Embu of Central Kenya," *Journal of African History*, VIII, 1967.

Taylor, Brian K. *The Western Lacustrine Bantu.* London: International African Institute, 1962.

Chapter Eight

NORTHEASTERN AFRICA

Arkell, A. J. "Fung Origins," *Sudan Notes and Records,* XV, 1932.

Arkell, A. J. *A History of the Sudan to 1821.* London: Oxford University Press, 1955. This is an excellent work, although it may be too detailed for beginning students. For them it might be best to read El Mandi's less complex work, and use Arkell's as a reference.

Arkell, A. J. "More about Fung Origins," *Sudan Notes and Records,* XXVII, 1946.

Blundell, H. W. (ed.). *Royal Chronicle of Abyssinia, 1769–1840.* Cambridge: Cambridge University Press, 1922.

Bruce, James. *Travels To Discover the Source of the Nile.* Edinburgh: Edinburgh University Press, 1964.

Cheesman, R. E. *Lake Tana and the Blue Nile.* London: The Macmillan Company, 1936.

Crawford, O. G. S. *The Fung Kingdom of Sennar.* Glouchester, England: John Bellows, 1951.

Doresse, Jean. *Ethiopia.* London: Elek Books, 1959.

El Mahdi, Mandour. *A Short History of the Sudan.* London: Oxford University Press, 1965. In this small paperback the author presents an extremely readable simplified account of the history of the Funj and Fur kingdoms.

Greenfield, Richard T. *Ethiopia — A New Political History.* New York: Frederick A. Praeger, Inc., 1965.

Holt, Peter M. "Funj Origins: A Critique of New Evidence," *Journal of African History,* IV, 1963.

Huntingford, G. W. B. (ed.). *The Glorious Victories of Amda Seyon.* Oxford: Clarendon Press, 1965.

Jesman, Czeslaw. *The Ethiopian Paradox.* London: Oxford University Press, 1963. This easily available paperback is a part of a series issued by the Institute of Race Relations in London. Its organization borders on the chaotic, and the author, an Ethiopian, is far from objective on the more modern period. Nevertheless, the sections dealing with the land, people, and early history are well done and should be read by a beginning student interested in Ethiopia.

Jones, A. H. M., and E. Monroe. *A History of Ethiopia.* London: Oxford University Press, 1955. Beginning students can consider this as the basic textbook for early Ethiopian history. For more advanced students it should be read in conjunction with more detailed studies of the Gurage, Agaw, Galla, and Falasha.

Leslau, Wolf. *Falasha Anthology.* New Haven, Conn.: Yale University Press, 1963.

Lewis, I. M. "The Somali Conquest of the Horn of Africa," *Journal of African History,* I, 1960.

MacMichael, Harold A. (trans. & ed.). *A History of the Arabs in the Sudan and of the Tribes Inhabiting Darfur,* 2 vols. Cambridge: Cambridge University Press, 1922.

MacMichael, Harold A. *The Sudan.* London: Ernest Benn, 1954.

Matthew, David. *Ethiopia: The Study of a Polity, 1540–1935.* London: Eyre & Spottiswoode, 1947. This book is recommended primarily because of the insights the author gives into the social and religious life of Ethiopia while at the same time focusing upon political change. It contains some good illustrations and a fairly complete list of the kings of Ethiopia.

Pankhurst, E. S. *Ethiopia: A Cultural History.* Essex, England: Lalibela House, Woodford Green, 1955.

Pankhurst, Richard. *An Introduction to the Economic History of Ethiopia from Early Times to 1800.* Essex, England: Lalibela House, Woodford Green, 1961.

Pankhurst, Richard. *Travellers in Ethiopia.* London: Oxford University Press, 1965. In this book the author has collected and annotated many travelers' accounts of Ethiopia beginning with the *Periphus* and extending through the nineteenth century. It includes selections from the writings of Portuguese visitors as well as sections from James Bruce's *Travels.* The work thus gives the reader the flavor of both the scenes being observed and the attitudes of foreign travelers in different centuries.

Shack, W. A. *The Gurage: A People of the Ensete Culture.* London: International African Institute, 1966.

Simoons, Frederick J. "Some Questions on the Economic Pre-History of Ethiopia," *Journal of African History,* VI, 1965.

Trimingham, J. *Islam in Ethiopia.* London: Oxford University Press, 1952. This work contains an excellent summary of the expansion of Islam in northeastern Africa as well as an analysis of the long and complex struggle between Islam and Christianity in Ethiopia. The book also contains a number of excellent maps.

Ullendorff, Edward. *The Ethiopians: An Introduction to Country and People.* London: Oxford University Press, 1965. The title of this general work is somewhat misleading, since it is confined largely to the history of the Amhara-Tigre people. With this qualification it is a more than adequate introduction to that segment of Ethiopian history.

Index